ALIAS ASSUMED

OTHER TITLES IN THE SMART POP SERIES

ALIAS ASSUMED

SEX, LIES AND SD-6

EDITED BY

KEVIN WEISMAN

WITH GLENN YEFFETH

BENBELLA BOOKS, INC.
Dallas, Texas

Introduction © 2005 by Kevin Weisman

"Pieces of Sydney" © 2005 by Joyce Millman

"Viewing the Past in *Alias*" © 2005 by J. Mira Seo, Ph.D.

"Daddy Knows Best" © 2005 by Catharine Tunnacliffe

"Sydney and Me" © 2005 by Candace Havens

"The Science of *Alias*" © 2005 by David Harris

"Torturers Wanted" © 2005 by Sally D. Stabb, Ph.D.

"Geek Chic" © 2005 by Tracy S. Morris

"*Alias* and the Real Deal" © 2005 by Robert Stokes

"Why Sydney Has No Social Life" © 2005 by Jody Lynn Nye

"Psychological Profile: Subject J. J. Abrams" © 2005 by Misty K. Hook, Ph.D.

"The Night that *Alias* Reinvented Itself" © 2005 by Paul Levinson, Ph.D.

"A Spy in the House of Love" © 2005 by Erin Dailey

"The Great and Powerful Me" © 2005 by Amy Berner

"The *Alias* Guide to Parenting" © 2005 by Britta Coleman

"Alias Alice" © 2005 by Mary Lavoie

"Classical Mythology, Prime-time Television" © 2005 by Lee Fratantuono, Ph.D.

"Over Suds" © 2005 by Julie E. Czerneda

"You've Come a Long Way, Baby" © 2005 by Susan M. Garrett

"Only Ourselves to Blame" © 2005 by Leah Wilson

"They Scanned Our Brain Waves from Orbit..." © 2005 by Roxanne Longstreet Conrad

"The Sixth Stage" © 2005 by Adam-Troy Castro

All Additional Materials © 2005 Kevin Weisman

BenBella Books, Inc., 6440 N. Central Expressway, Suite 617, Dallas, TX 75206
www.benbellabooks.com
Send feedback to feedback@benbellabooks.com

Publisher: Glenn Yeffeth
Editor: Shanna Caughey
Associate Editor: Leah Wilson
Director of Marketing/PR: Laura Watkins

Printed in the United States of America
10 9 8 7 6 5 4 3 2 1

Library of Congress Cataloging-in-Publication Data

Alias assumed : sex, lies, and SD-6 / edited by Kevin Weisman.
    p. cm.
    ISBN 1-932100-46-6
    1. Alias (Television program) I. Weisman, Kevin.
PN1992.77.A482A44 2005
791.45'72—dc22

2005008236

Cover design by Todd Bushman
Cover photo by Laura Yeffeth
Text design and composition by John Reinhardt Book Design

Distributed by Independent Publishers Group
To order call (800) 888-4741
www.ipgbook.com

For special sales contact Laura Watkins at laura@benbellabooks.com

CONTENTS

KEVIN WEISMAN

INTRODUCTION

HELLO EVERYONE. Kevin Weisman here, a.k.a. Marshall J. Flinkman. When I was first asked to write this introduction, I have to admit I was surprised that so many articles on our little show had been amassed. As I started to read the pieces, I was taken aback by the depth of *Alias* knowledge that these writers have. Which brings me to the nature of the *Alias* fan (or fanatic, as is often the case . . .). You all are a learned, supportive, caring bunch. I marvel at how often I am stopped in the street for everything from a simple hug to technical support questions to new and often twisted theories on Rambaldi and The Prophecy. The *Alias* fan(atic) often knows more about the show than I do (and definitely more than Victor Garber does; trust me, he would be first to admit that). So, before I go any further, I want to thank you—the *Alias* fan—for sending the constant love our way, for caring about the characters like you do and for keeping us on the air with your fervent devotion!

Alias has been an amazing ride. We just wrapped our fourth year of the show and will be back for a fifth. As an actor, it's truly a unique experience to play one character for this long (eighty-eight episodes). Now, I've worked on other series, made films and done plays for months at a time, but I've never had the luxury of inhabiting the same character for four years. And the fact that it's the loveable techno-geek Marshall J. Flinkman makes it even more special.

When I first auditioned for the role, the description of the character was "an ex-hippie, late forties, fat, balding with a ponytail, wearing a Mötley Crüe t-shirt." I, of course, have none of those characteristics (though I might have an old Van Halen shirt somewhere . . .), but J. J. Abrams and I had worked together on *Felicity* and he wanted me to come in and read. My initial take on the character was one of much more confidence and flair. After hiring me, J. J. suggested we get together for rehearsal. Marshall only appeared in one scene in the pilot, but it proved to be a crucial rehearsal, as it would establish who Marshall was for potentially quite a long time. After much exploration and discussion, Marshall was born. And it's been beyond a pleasure.

The day-to-day work on the show is also a fantastic experience. The actors are all first-rate. From the regulars to the guest stars, J. J. and company have a very discerning eye when it comes to talent. Coming from the theater, I was impressed and excited to be working with theater veterans Ron, Victor and Carl. (In fact, about twelve years ago when I was broke and studying theater in New York, I ushered a show called *Three Hotels* which starred Ron Rifkin. I only ushered because most theaters in New York had a deal at the time that if you ushered a show, you could then stay and see it for free. Also, it should be noted that the show was written by esteemed playwright John Robin Baitz, who ended up writing a brilliant episode in season four, "In Dreams..." 4-19.) Everyone has been tremendous to work with. Hats off to Ron, Victor, Carl, Bradley, Merrin, David, Lena, Mia, Michael and, of course, Jennifer. Ms. Garner is the leader of our ship. She provides an energy on the set that is contagious—professional, truthful and, most of all, kind.

I think one of the reasons *Alias* works so well is because of the emotional depth in the relationships amongst the characters. Yes, espionage, stunts and sexiness abound, and, I mean, I have to admit, I'm a sucker for the continuous "mythology" story arcs, but without the ever-blossoming relationships, this show would not be what it's become. Speaking on behalf of the actors, we would get bored if these layered relationships didn't exist. Even Marshall has specific connections with each character, from his camaraderie with Weiss to his friendship with Sydney to his love for his wife and the cutest television kid around, Mitchell (who is actually my wife's nephew, Aiden David). I have to say, the writers have done an excellent job over these four years keeping it fresh for us, the actors. The characters, situations and relationships are always evolving while maintaining certain aspects, particularly personality traits, that audiences have grown accustomed to and are comforted by.

J. J. told me right away that I was to be the only actor who had free rein to improvise on the show. A lot of the little "Marshall moments" were created on the spot, and many others lie abandoned on the cutting room floor. As an actor, I like to keep each take fresh and loose, and speak like a real person would in the situation the character is in. Watching television over the years, I was often frustrated when I would watch actors on certain shows. The actors all seemed to be acting in a certain "way," creating characters that were infallible, good-looking robots. So, when I first got this job, I vowed to myself that I would commit to creating a three-dimensional being, complete with vulnerabilities and inconsistent speech patterns, i.e., someone who could actually stop themselves mid-sentence and begin another thought *as humans often do.* One of the greatest compliments I ever got was from legendary actress Faye Dunaway, who guested on our show in season one. She stopped me on the set and proclaimed, "I did a Marshall today...I spoke and stopped myself mid-thought and continued onto another thought. . . ." Just the fact that Ms. Dunaway recognized what I was attempting to do with this character meant a lot to me.

Everyone truly puts their best foot forward each day on the set of *Alias.* From the visual effects supervisor to our beloved Craft Service queen (props to Judy!), everyone takes their job seriously. I will not lie to you, it is truly exhausting work at times, with twelve- to fourteen-hour days, often without an end in sight. But I also think everyone knows it is worth it because this is one of those shows that will live on through DVDs and a cultish "lore" in television history. We've never been a top-ten show in the ratings, but I always took pride in that, to be honest. It simply means that a smaller, more devoted group watches the show. I value this core audience, and I always enjoy meeting *Alias* fans because they are a smart, appreciative group. You have to expend energy and be invested in the world of *Alias* to fully appreciate it. If you do take that time, you are truly rewarded. So if you ever see me on the street or in your local coffeehouse, please do not hesitate to say hi.

This book really explores the issues of *Alias,* from the plausibility of Marshall's gadgets to what it would be like to live your life as Sydney Bristow to the reaction of a real CIA agent. It's a real treat for the *Alias* fan.

I hope you enjoy this book as much as I did.

All the best,
Kevin

JOYCE MILLMAN

PIECES OF SYDNEY
ESPIONAGE, FEMALE IDENTITY AND THE SECRET SELF IN *ALIAS*

Ah, yes—the ladies of Alias. Beautiful, sexy, dangerous and...well, slightly psychotic. I have to say—certainly not like the characters on America's beloved show Friends. *These women have serious issues. For all their characters' problems—backstabbings, mother issues, being way too in touch with their inner bad girls—I've never met a sweeter and more professional group of actors. (And yes, my friends are all pretty jealous that I get to work with such a bevy of beauties....)*

DIMPLED GRAD STUDENT by day, spy chick in a sprayed-on rubber dress by night—that was the original premise of *Alias* when it premiered on ABC in 2001. And while Sydney Bristow is no longer in college, she remains the sweetest, most uncorrupted CIA operative in TV history.

Sydney is unflinching under pressure, a butt-kicking spiritual sister to Buffy, Trinity and the Bride. But beneath her supercool exterior, Sydney often seems as waifishly tossed by hard luck and tragedy as the heroines of such classics as *Jane Eyre* or *A Little Princess*. Sydney grew up without a mother (she died in a car crash when Syd was a girl, or so she was told) and was raised by her emotionally repressed father Jack, who was away on business a lot. While at college, Sydney was (osten-

5

sibly) recruited by a Black Ops division of the CIA, given a cover job at a bank and sworn to secrecy. When she told her fiancé what she really did for a living, he was murdered. Syd soon found out that she wasn't really working for the CIA; she was working for the bad guys, in an outfit named SD-6. And her dad was also working for SD-6, except he was a CIA mole. And her mother wasn't killed in a car crash, she was a KGB agent.

There's more. After Sydney switched allegiances to the CIA, she fell in love with her CIA handler, Michael Vaughn. Their happiness was tainted by the discovery that Vaughn's father, also a CIA agent, had been killed by—yes—Syd's mother. Oh, and then there was that plotline where Sydney "died" in a fire but was actually spirited away by "the Covenant" and rendered an amnesiac zombie assassin for two years. And when she woke up, she found out that Vaughn was married to someone else.

Despite, or because of, the show's dizzying cliff-hanger structure, it is impossible not to root for Sydney Bristow. Her bright, shining desire to do the right thing is never dimmed by the sleaze around her. And because of that you want her to find the truth and stability that eludes her. Sydney is Good. In fact, she'd be a tad too good—she'd be boring, even—if not for the fact that she regularly gets to don a disguise, go undercover and pretend to be bad.

The main theme of *Alias* is fractured identity, as illustrated by the double (sometimes triple) lives led by Sydney and her fellow spies. They lead fractured inner lives as well: contradictory behavior is the rule, not the exception, on the show. "Bad" characters have done good deeds—SD-6 mastermind Arvin Sloane founded a humanitarian organization to fight world hunger and cure disease. And "good" characters have done bad deeds—Sydney's earnest CIA colleague Marcus Dixon pursued vigilante justice after his wife was murdered. On *Alias*, as in life, the trick is to identify and hold on to your true self, and to be able to return to that self even after you've followed unfamiliar urges down blind alleys.

One of the ways *Alias* creator J. J. Abrams and his writers reinforce the fractured identity theme is by depicting Sydney and other female characters as good girl/bad girl split personalities. Indeed, the giddy brilliance of *Alias* is how knowingly it taps into fantasies of "dangerous" female sexuality and power. Sydney's CIA missions, for example, are stylish erotic scenarios straight out of romance novels, where the heroine is imperiled but never succumbs to victimhood, and where she engages in darkly thrilling sexual situations while remaining fundamentally virtuous. Sydney is in disguise on her missions, playing a role. Over the course of the show, she has been a leather-clad punkette, a whip-cracking dominatrix, a slinky chanteuse and all manner of club hoppers, mistresses, bohemians, bimbos, go-go dancers, Eurotrash social climbers and take-charge executives. And let's not forget her two lost years (shown in flashback during season three) as a ruthless blonde assassin.

As a spy, Sydney is able to be the bad girl in carefully controlled situations—she is protecting her country and saving innocent lives. When she's impersonating someone else, Sydney gets to be violent, powerful, lusty, dominant. She gets to play slut for a day or avenging angel. Yet, despite her constantly shifting aliases, Sydney is never a stranger to us, or to herself. She remains sweet, good Syd.

But sweet and sour are inextricably linked. And in her war with the enemy spy cabal, Sydney's fiercest, most personal battles have always been fought against other women, like malevolent, foxy K-Directorate agent Anna Espinosa and, notably, Sydney's mother Irina Derevko and the Covenant spy Lauren Reed. And these last two women are even more obviously divided than Sydney into good girl/bad girl extremes. Indeed, Sydney's struggles with her female nemeses could be seen as a metaphor for her own struggle to keep her "inappropriate" bad girl side in check. Like the wicked queen's looking glass in *Snow White*, *Alias* is forever reflecting its identity-conflicted female characters' fears, desires and secret selves.

SYDNEY BRISTOW AND IRINA DEREVKO: MY MOTHER, MY SELF

Alias is a journey of self-knowledge for Sydney. It's a fairy tale, really: a lonely girl from a broken home discovers that she is, in fact, special. When the show began, Sydney was naïve enough to believe that she could fit her magical talent for espionage into the sort of perfect marriage she thought her parents had. After her fiancé was killed as a result of her naïveté, Sydney fell into a depression. Still coddled in the lie of her mother's "tragic death," Sydney built up the idea of Laura Bristow as a domestic saint. She never seemed to question from whom she had inherited her spy skills. They must have come from Dad.

Late in the first season of *Alias*, Sydney discovered the truth about her mother. And in the season two opener, Sydney finally came face-to-face with the prodigal mom, alias Laura Bristow, alias "The Man," alias Irina

Derevko. Played by Lena Olin with a wild gleam in her eye, Irina was all stone-cold cunning and sexy, sinewy allure, even while imprisoned in a glass cell by the CIA. The caution with which Irina was handled while in federal custody recalled the nervous care taken with Hannibal Lecter in *The Silence of the Lambs*. Unlike Dr. Lecter, though, Irina didn't need to touch her victims to do damage. Irina's piercing intelligence and serene yet intense emotionalism were her weapons. Irina zeroed in on Sydney's—and Jack's—vulnerabilities.

Despite Irina's perfidiousness, Jack can't resist her. In season two, Jack had her released into his custody (she was implanted with a CIA tracking chip as an extra precaution) because he needed her expertise in the field. And Irina dove into the mission with an incandescent energy that was frankly sexual. It was no surprise that Jack fell into a steamy clinch with his ex-wife (after he lovingly dug the chip out of her shoulder with a knife). Though she dupes him again and again, Jack can't let go of the fantasy he married —Laura Bristow, the good wife. Nor can he let go of the seductive, treacherous reality of Irina Derevko. No wonder Jack looks so pained all the time. He suffers from the bitter frustration, and the exquisite sexual tension, of loving a good girl/bad girl.

As for Irina's relationship with Sydney, like any good mother, she knows just where to kiss to make it better, and, like any bad mother, she knows just which buttons to push to keep Sydney under her control—and often did both in the same gesture. Behind bars, she tried to convince Sydney that whatever Irina had done (like shooting her in the arm to cause a diversion when they first met in a Taipei torture chamber), she had done to protect Sydney from a larger evil. In the episode "Trust Me" (2-2), Sydney resisted Irina's maternal advances, telling her, "You are not my mother. My mother was Laura Bristow. Laura Bristow died in a car accident twenty-one years ago. You are a traitor and a prisoner of the United States government." But Sydney eventually found herself falling under the convincingly penitent Irina's emotional sway, especially when Irina gave her the motherly advice she craved. ("You're so willing to take risks for your country. Why aren't you willing to do the same for your own happiness?" Irina told Syd, urging her to act on her attraction to Vaughn.)

Irina is the key to the show's long-running plotline (and possible red herring), the prophecy of Milo Rambaldi, a (fictional) fifteenth-century seer over whose prescient inventions and formulae the CIA and Covenant are engaged in spy-vs.-spy intrigue. Irina is the mother of Rambaldi's prophesied "Chosen Woman," who is supposed to bring about world-altering events; that woman is believed to be Sydney, as depicted in a centuries-old sketch. Irina is also the mother of the woman whom Rambaldi named as the Chosen Woman's enemy, "The Passenger"—Sydney's half-sister, Nadia. Over the course of the series, Irina has enigmatically helped both the good guys and the bad guys to get their hands on Rambaldi artifacts. And in season three, we were shown the essential piece of the Rambaldi puzzle needed to set his apocalyptic prophecy in motion; it was a box inscribed with the word *irina*, ancient Greek for "peace." Mother as both creator and destroyer—Irina Derevko is the ultimate good girl/bad girl, the archetypical Madonna/whore. And the implications for Sydney are troubling. Clearly, she inherited her mother's intelligence and fearlessness. But did she also inherit Irina's amorality and appetite for violence?

When we last saw her in season two, Irina was rappelling down the face of a skyscraper, blasting out windows with a machine gun, like Bruce Willis in *Die Hard*. Radiant with the excitement of the chase, Irina escaped from Sydney and the CIA and remains in hiding as of this writing. (Lena Olin left the show after season two, and the producers could not lure her back for season three.) She is still an enigma in her absence, which is fitting, given the psychological construct of the show. A woman becomes her own person when she fully separates from her mother. But when Mom is as overpowering a figure as Irina Derevko, it isn't enough to separate. Sydney must vanquish Irina, either symbolically or otherwise, to be free, and Irina remains a potent presence in her daughter's psyche. It's the shadow of Irina that makes Sydney work so hard at being the good spy, the good girl. She is determined to prove that she is not her mother's daughter.

FRANCIE CALFO: FRIEND TO THE END

For the first season and a half of *Alias*, Sydney and her roommate Francie Calfo were the sort of supportive, unconditionally accepting girlfriends we've seen celebrated in everything from *Sex and the City* to chick lit. Syd and Francie engaged in all the precious clichés of female bonding—eating ice cream out of the carton after a bad day, crying on each other's shoulders about boy troubles. But their relationship was also a subtle parody of this Hallmark-card type of idealized female friendship: Sydney, of course, couldn't share everything with Francie. She couldn't reveal the truth about her job, or the circumstances of her fiancé's murder. She had to listen sympathetically to Francie whining about her two-timing boyfriend and her struggling restaurant business while she, *Sydney*, was covertly engaged in matters of life and death. How unfair!

But grown-up good girls like Syd don't want to admit this guilty little secret: sometimes, when your self-absorbed friend is droning on and on about her latest crisis and you're making sounds of commiseration, deep down inside *you just don't care!* So it was a lucky break for Sydney in season two when the real Francie was shot dead by the Covenant and replaced with a genetically engineered double, who had orders to destroy Syd. This story line made Francie a chilling—and amusingly literal—embodiment of a good girl/bad girl; it also made the show's parody of friendship more overt and more perverse. Sydney didn't know that Bad Francie was an imposter who faked affection and sneered at her behind her back. But we knew.

With the Francie doppelganger plot, *Alias* slyly acknowledged the "bad" impulse which lurks under the surface of female friendships—the *Mean Girls* urge to torment other girls, not to be nurturing or selflessly available to your friends. The second season of *Alias* ended with the roommates unleashing their inner bad girls in a house-trashing fight to the death. Sydney prevailed, of course, and without guilt—after all, she wasn't actually pumping bullets into the real Francie, she was killing off Francie's evil fake twin. But, metaphorically, Good Sydney was enjoying the forbidden pleasure of being the worst best friend ever.

NADIA SANTOS: MY SISTER'S KEEPER

In the tense home stretch of season three, we were suddenly introduced to Nadia Santos, the half-sister Sydney never knew she had. A spy with Argentina's intelligence agency, Nadia was (we were told) the product of an extramarital affair between Irina and Arvin Sloane. Nadia was born while Irina was in a Soviet prison, and placed in an orphanage. As a child, she had no contact with Sloane, whom we are told had been searching for her for years. Nadia is a totemic figure in the Rambaldi mythology. As The Passenger, whose fate is bound up with that of Sydney, Nadia's DNA has somehow been encoded with Rambaldi's consciousness. She is a conduit to Rambaldi, and Sloane, clearly suffering from a God complex, has obtained a serum that will reveal the message locked inside Nadia's head.

In the episode "Blood Ties" (3-20), Jack cautioned Sydney about getting emotionally involved with this mysterious girl. Still hurting over

Irina's latest disappearance, Syd assured him that she had no delusions of sisterly closeness:

> After Mom died I used to have these daydreams. I would imagine her leading my Girl Scout troop or taking me shopping for new school clothes. I thought, if only she'd lived, she would have been my best friend. When I learned the truth about her, and I saw Irina for who she truly was, I was devastated. I won't make the same mistake twice.

But Sydney's face dissolved into tenderness when she first saw the helpless, catatonic Nadia in the Chechen labor camp where Irina (we presume) had hidden her. We realized how desperately Sydney wanted this connection. For an only child like Syd, it must have seemed like a wish granted to learn that she had a sister, an ally, someone who could validate her resentment over being abandoned by Irina. But maybe, at the same time, Nadia could provide the crucial information that would help Sydney understand and forgive Irina. Growing up without a mother, Sydney had felt as if part of her was missing. Nadia represented the possibility of completion.

Nadia, though, had her own missing piece—her father. In the episode "Legacy" (3-21), Sloane stole her away from CIA protection and was finally able to inject her with the green goo that would bring forth Rambaldi's consciousness. Strapped to a chair while her father loomed over her with a syringe, Nadia made a tough little speech that, in its sense of loss and bitterness, echoed Sydney's "I won't make the same mistake twice" assurance to Jack:

> Every Sunday at the orphanage in San Telmo, they made us dress up in our finest clothes. They would have us stand in line for hours waiting to be chosen by families. I wouldn't do it. I'd make myself filthy and always frown. I didn't want to be chosen because I knew...I knew that somewhere my dad was still looking for me and one day he'd come to take me away from that place. If I had known it was you I was waiting for, I would have cleaned up.

Despite seeming to loathe her father, the opaque Nadia chose to escape from Sydney and join Sloane on a quest for the Rambaldi holy grail. As of this writing (awaiting season four), Nadia has not provided Sydney with the validation for which she had hoped. Their relationship is charged with mutual curiosity and suspicion. They are not very much alike: Nadia is dark while Sydney is fair. She is stoic while Sydney is expressive. Although she is younger than Sydney, she seems older, more womanly, with a hint of Irina's almost feral sensuality. Yet, when Nadia was coolly kung-fu-fighting her way out of the Chechen labor camp alongside Sydney, the sisterly resemblance became clear: they both resembled Irina in the heat of battle. Nadia *is* Sydney—or rather, she's Good Sydney's shadow self, her photonegative image. She is Sydney as her mother's daughter, the Bad (or, at least, Ambiguous) Sydney who might have been, if Syd had grown up without the melancholy yet steadying presence of Jack Bristow.

After an initial period of suspicion at the beginning of the series, Sydney had come to trust her father as a colleague and a protector. Father and daughter had been betrayed and wounded by Irina together, and their love has become deeper and more complex through the run of the show. Jack was the one constant in Sydney's life. No matter how many times she rebelled against his advice regarding Irina, or dismissed him as being consumed by the desire for revenge, she remained Daddy's girl. He was her dad. He was good. Therefore, she was good. But, is Jack Bristow really good? Sydney knows that Jack was once involved in a CIA program called Project Christmas, which was supposed to turn American children into a generation of sleeper superagents. She knows that Jack subjected her to the program after Irina's disappearance. Wasn't his use of her similar to the way Sloane violated Nadia in order to further his own agenda?

Sloane and Nadia's father-daughter bond—captured in the grotesque tableau of Sloane injecting Nadia with the powerful Rambaldi hallucinogen—is an unwholesome version of the bond between Jack and Sydney. It represents the fears about her own dad that Good Sydney does not want to face: that Jack is not a loving father, that he betrayed her trust and abused her, that he is even more false and hurtful than Irina. In her genetic mirror Nadia, Sydney sees what she fears she would become if Jack proved to be a fraud. If she has a Bad Daddy and a Bad Mommy, what does that make Sydney?

LAUREN REED: SEE YOU NEXT TUESDAY

The good girl/bad girl theme came to a spectacular climax in season three with the introduction of Lauren Reed, whom Michael Vaughn married during the time that Sydney was presumed to be dead. A pallid blonde with a prim British accent, Lauren was the daughter of a U.S. senator and worked as the NSC's liaison to Vaughn and Sydney's CIA section.

At first, Lauren was presented to us entirely through Sydney's perspective. Imagine waking up with two years of your life unaccounted for and then finding out your true love has married someone else. Understandably, Lauren never had a chance with the show's fans. She was seen as the woman who stole Syd's guy, however inadvertently. (Lauren Reed hatelistings, the opposite of fan clubs, began popping up on the Internet right after her first appearance on the show.) The thing was, Sydney (and viewers) had no immediate reason to hate Lauren, other than that she was with Vaughn and that Vaughn went all wussy in her passively manipulative presence. Lauren certainly played the poor insecure rebound-bride to the hilt, putting on the injured-doe eyes whenever she caught Syd and Vaughn exchanging longing glances. Predictably, Good Sydney felt guilty over her visceral dislike for Lauren, and how much she envied her. If Lauren Reed's presence was a litmus test for what women are willing to forgive in each other, then we all failed miserably.

For the first part of season three, Sydney (and by extension, the Lauren-haters in the audience) had to endure repeated scoldings from Vaughn, who put on his "I am disappointed in you" face and accused her of being unfair to his wife. But then *Alias* did an amazing thing: it proved that Sydney's (and our own) gut instincts about Lauren had been right all along. In a juicily thrilling plot twist, Lauren was revealed to be a Covenant mole who had lured Vaughn into her marriage trap. We saw her pull the trigger as a deadly sniper; we saw her secretly working to sabotage a plane on which her husband and Sydney were passengers. As far as good girl/bad girls go, two-faced Lauren was the queen.

The vindicating moment for Lauren haters occurred midway through the third season, in the episode "Crossings." In a short but significant scene, Lauren approached Sydney at the office with a symbolic olive branch, asking if they could give each other another chance to be friends. To show her good faith, Lauren invited Sydney to dinner with her on some future Tuesday—Michael's weekly hockey night. Sydney accepted, there were some awkward pleasantries, and then Lauren looked at Sydney and smiled like the Cheshire Cat. "See you next Tuesday," she said crisply, the camera holding her in close-up an extra beat for emphasis. You could almost hear the thud of knowing viewers falling off their chairs. In decades-old high-school-girl vernacular, "See you next Tuesday" is code for the word that starts with the letters "c-u," means female genitalia and is used to insult a woman when "bitch" just isn't strong enough. That line was the show's canny (and a little surreal) acknowledgment of what Lauren haters had been thinking about Ms. Reed for weeks.

As the extent of Lauren's duplicity was unveiled, she evolved—fascinatingly—into Sydney's near-double. Her plumped lips became even more noticeably plumped and Sydney-like. She started wearing her hair pulled back, straight and sleek, like Sydney's. It was revealed that her mother was an enemy spy, just like Irina. And, of course, Lauren had replaced Sydney in Michael's bed. In the episode "Conscious" (3-9), Sydney had a hallucination while undergoing an experimental brain procedure to try to regain her lost memories: she was pursuing Lauren through a maze of stairwells and corridors, and when she finally caught her, Lauren turned and Sydney was looking at herself.

The more evil Lauren's behavior, the more over-the-top entertaining she became. At her most villainous, Lauren was made up and photographed like one of Hitchcock's bad blondes (think Tippi Hedren in *Marnie* or Kim Novak in *Vertigo*). Her hair got lighter; she was costumed in sexy black; she was accompanied by lush, noirish background music. In a memorable scene, she got so turned on after murdering one of her targets that she hauled her partner in crime, the eely little Covenant agent Sark, off to bed for a wild tryst. Lauren was Sydney's funhouse-mirror image, representing Bad Sydney's dangerous spy-girl impulses, her anger and aggression, her espionage-fueled libido, in the extreme. In an admirably warped stroke of irony, Lauren betrayed Vaughn in the same ways Irina had betrayed Jack. In effect, Lauren was the personification of Sydney's murkiest fear—the fear of turning into her mother.

In the chilling psychodrama that ended season three, Lauren and Sydney "became" each other. Wearing a false Sydney face, Lauren set off bombs in the CIA offices and shot Michael. Later, wearing a false Lauren face and a voice alterer, Sydney seductively interrogated a captive Sark. It was the perfect climax to the Sydney/Lauren story line, suggesting that the two women made up halves of a whole, bringing the show's good girl/bad girl subtext to the fore.

At the end of the third season finale, Lauren was about to shoot the unarmed Sydney when Vaughn arrived to save the woman he loved. He shot his wife, then shot her again. And again. The poor guy was entitled. Staggering from her wounds, Lauren managed to draw one last parallel between herself and Sydney, sneering, "We're both pawns in the same game!" When Lauren finally fell backwards and disappeared down a gaping, open mine shaft, it was reminiscent of the scene in Hitchcock's *Psycho* in which Norman Bates locks Marion Crane's body in the trunk of her car and pushes it into a swamp. We watch the car sink down, down, down, until it's swallowed under the muck. Lauren Reed was similarly dispatched to the depths of the unconscious (both Sydney's and our own), where bad girls live. But, knowing *Alias*, she'll probably be back.

Joyce Millman's essays about television have appeared in the New York Times, *the* Boston Phoenix *and Salon.com, among other publications. She was a founding staff member of Salon.com, and also coedited that magazine's "Mothers Who Think" section. She has contributed to the BenBella anthology* What Would Sipowicz Do? *and the Random House anthology* Mothers Who Think: Tales of Real-Life Parenthood. *In 1989 and 1991, she was a finalist for the Pulitzer Prize in criticism for columns written while she was television critic for the* San Francisco Examiner. *A native of Massachusetts, Millman now lives in San Mateo, California, with her husband and son.*

J. MIRA SEO, Ph.D.

VIEWING THE PAST IN *ALIAS*
ANTIQUITY, DIVINITY AND PROPHECY

*I've always been interested in mythology, legend and storytelling. In
Alias, all of these roads point toward our dear old friend Rambaldi, the
source of most of my character's many long-winded musings. Could
Rambaldi really have prophesized Sydney as the purveyor of doom?
Could his creations really amount to one end? If so, what is it— salvation, destruction, what??? I have to admit, I'm a fan of all this crazy
shit. It's what makes Alias cool, dammit! Read on. . . .*

DOES *ALIAS*, a television series endowed with all the prerequisite
gadgets of its spy thriller genre, have any contact with the world of
the past? How can ancient concepts of prophecy help the contemporary viewer understand or even anticipate the remarkable plot twists
of the series?

This essay will analyze the construction of Rambaldi and the narrative function of his prophecy against the background of ancient Greek
oracles. Prophecy as a mode of communication between mortals and the
gods in the ancient world can provide a model for interpreting the show's
representations of divinity and the past. But here the conventions of ancient literature and contemporary television overlap: a prophecy isn't
always all it's cracked up to be. In ancient Greek and Roman literature,
prophecies require human interpretation, and this interpretation may
be misguided or plain wrong. In an action-suspense series like *Alias*,

spectacular reversals are the rule, not the exception. The more infallible a given seems to be, especially when delivered by a quasi-divinity and confirmed by the Lab, the more likely it is that a surprise is lurking.

In the ancient Mediterranean, Apollo's oracle at Delphi was widely recognized among Greeks and other peoples as the most reliable contact point with the gods. Archaeological evidence reveals a sacred enclosure as early as the eighth century B.C.E., and it is mentioned in Homer and numerous other texts as the most famous oracle in the Mediterranean world. Prophecy at Delphi usually came as a response to a question posed by a visitor, and was delivered by the famous Pythia or priestess, then rendered into hexameter verse by a specialized priest. Despite Delphi's excellent reputation, its prophecies were notoriously ambiguous. According to the fifth-century Greek historian Herodotus, the Lydian king Croesus once tested all the most famous oracles of the Mediterranean by asking them what he was doing at the time of the request (he was inexplicably boiling a cut-up tortoise and a lamb in a bronze cauldron with a bronze lid). After Delphi's Pythia responded correctly, he then asked the oracle whether he should attack the kingdom of the Persians. The oracle responded, "If you attack the Persians, you will destroy a great kingdom." Trusting the prophecy, Croesus engaged the Persians in battle and suffered a crushing defeat. The Lydian kingdom was destroyed and Croesus himself enslaved by the victorious Persians. Evidently, the interpretation required by these enigmatic prophecies served to preserve the oracle's reputation; if the outcome was not what the questioner expected, failure could always be attributed to the interpretation.

But how did the oracle become so trusted in the first place? The Homeric Hymn to Apollo gives the official origins of the oracle and the religious sanctuary to the god at Delphi. Aeschylus' *Eumenides* also explains how Apollo came to settle at Delphi. Inside the temple, and still visible in the ruins today, a large rounded stone, called the Omphalos, was an important part of the sacred precinct. Omphalos means "navel" in Greek, and according to Greek mythology, Delphi's Omphalos was the navel or birthplace of the world. This venerable artifact clearly enhances the oracle's divinity. Though the site represents the origins of the world, the story of Apollo's cult at Delphi focuses on what happened afterwards, a history of inheritance and competing claims that eventually concludes with Apollo claiming the cult site after killing a monstrous beast, the Python. The Python symbolizes the old, chaotic, earthborn generation of gods that the Olympians must overcome to bring the world into a new order.

Antiquity did possess a special significance for the Greeks, but their mythology more often represents history as a progress toward increased sophistication and civilization. Though Hesiod's *Theogony* presents the generations of man as a decline from Gold to Clay, this decline corresponds to technological advances that contribute to the development of human civilization. The distance humanity travels from idyllic or brutish (depending on one's perspective) primitivism represents a kind of technical progress, just as the myth of Eden juxtaposes a fall from God's presence and the acquisition of knowledge. Still, antiquity represents a time more in harmony with the supernatural powers that control our existence. Before plowing, sailing and television surrounded us with their myriad distractions, as the Greeks would have it, we were closer to the divine. Therefore the oracle gains authority and power by permitting humans to go back in time and contact these primal forces in a physical location that reminds us of the world's birth.

In *Alias*, we might expect that the past has very little to offer the CIA and other global organizations that seek to control the world through technology. Even the Alliance, the original enemy of the first season and a half, was so futuristic that it disdained physical resources like oil and water, preferring to deal in a digital commodity: information ("Q&A," 1-17). The series initially introduced Rambaldi as a kind of Leonardo da Vinci figure, a fifteenth-century inventor with remarkable technological insight. Engaged in reconstructing the incomplete Rambaldi equation, Marshall gave a spectacular account of Rambaldi's improbable ingenuity:

> I've designed a program to extrapolate the rest, but these permutations are, like, vast. It seems to be written in some kind of pre-Galilean algebra, which, you know, kinda makes you think these guys were, you know [gesture of inhaling], you know, back in the... [cut to an expressionless Dixon]. It should be about eight hours.

Rambaldi's inventions are so advanced that all the greatest world superpowers have been engaged in their pursuit for years.

The artifacts that Sydney recovered through the first three seasons seemed to justify Rambaldi's supernatural powers: an artificial heart built in the fifteenth century that still beats in a living person's chest, plans for a cellular phone-type communications device and, most spectacularly, page 47 of Rambaldi's manuscript, which revealed a drawing of Sydney and a prophecy about the world-destroying power that she will engender. The extraordinary value of these artifacts resides not only in the fact that they have potential that exceeds even the resources of the most modern technology, but also in that they were created by the fifteenth-century architect of Pope Alexander VI. These inventions are simultaneously futuristic and (from the show's perspective at least) ancient, thus creating a paradox that seems to imbue them with a supernatural origin. They contain the venerable authority of the past, but their impossibility suggests that they might also represent something more.

The very creakiness of Rambaldi's inventions adds to their mystery and fetishistic value. Whenever Sydney recovers an artifact, she must preserve and package it with the delicate touch of an art restorer, usually performed under highly unfavorable conditions like hostile gunfire in a Siberian ice cave. The fragility of the articles, such as the partially rusted music box that plays an encoded tune ("Cipher," 2-3), emphasizes Rambaldi's distance from the present. In contrast to the CIA, whose weaponry and communications systems are always state of the art and apparently—considering how liberally they are produced, used and discarded—infinitely replaceable, Rambaldi's moldering drawings on parchment and handblown glass vials of mysterious fluid represent a miracle of preservation. The organic materials (wood, leather, paper) from which Rambaldi fashioned his objects embody the intervening centuries' unlimited potential for decay. When a flashback showed Rambaldi himself at work in his laboratory ("Time Will Tell," 1-8), we saw a shadowy figure in fifteenth-century dress moving among lambic fires and alchemical globes. The immediate cut to Sydney with a Rambaldi acolyte in Positano dramatically contrasted the two worlds as impossibly distant, connected only by the familial tradition of the Italian clockmaker. Similarly, the Rambaldi device Sloane and Sark set to attack the Vatican embassy in Mexico City was a rickety wooden construction held together with copper wires that shuddered violently as an LED timer counted down to detonation ("Firebomb," 2-16). (Sark characteristically sloped off to observe at a safe distance.) The image of this ramshackle device was followed by Marshall's incredulous explanation that the machine generated focused microwaves capable of combusting organic material from within. This juxtaposition of ancient and modern exemplifies the presentation of Rambaldi's power. Though we expect the CIA and especially organizations of evildoers like the Alliance or the Covenant to have the latest technology—this fetishization of technology has been an integral part of the spy thriller genre since the character Q in Bond—Rambaldi's position in the past sets him apart from Marshall or any of the other scientists shown in the show; contemporary scientists work within the possible, whereas Rambaldi is performing miracles.

With the introduction of the prophecy narrative, the series begins its consistent representation of Rambaldi as more than just an inventor. As the protagonists struggle to understand how Rambaldi could have created such implausible objects, they encounter others who accept Rambaldi as a semi-divinity. This conflict between rational, post-Enlightenment skepticism and religious, messianic faith illustrates the power of Rambaldi in the most enigmatic light possible. Even those who pursue the power that his works provide express disbelief. As Sark said to Sloane after the demonstration of one Rambaldi device, "When we agreed to combine our resources, you promised you would show me incredible things. But a suitcase neutron bomb designed in the sixteenth century—is that even a theoretical possibility?" ("Firebomb"). But this incredulity only serves to enhance Rambaldi's supernatural stature; by constantly making physical proof the means by which Rambaldi's power is confirmed, the series replicates familiar patterns from religious narratives, such as Doubting Thomas and Croesus' test of the oracles. Doubt and faith are both important parts of religious narratives that confirm a divinity's power. A divinity gains its power from the uneasy balance between irrational faith and manifest proofs in whatever terms the society requires. *Alias* represents technology as a force that can omnipotently monitor (the Echelon satellite system) and manipulate (especially through nuclear threat) the world around it. Marshall and his Op Tech presentations are more than humorous leavening for the series; his centrality indicates the status of technology as a kind of divine power, to which Rambaldi represents a challenge on its own terms.

Sloane's pursuit of Rambaldi represents the faith part of the equation. Though other organizations may seek Rambaldi's artifacts solely for their instrumental use, Sloane describes his lifelong quest for Rambaldi's secrets as a religious mission. Though he tends regrettably toward Eurotrash villain glasses and oversized suits, Sloane believes no less fanatically than Rambaldi's robed acolytes of the past. In his search, he has encountered other individuals embodying a politically correct array of religious traditions (including David Carradine's enigmatic Nepali monk, delightfully and referentially skilled in martial arts). The variety of their affiliations demonstrates the global, universal range of Rambaldi's following, much as the exotic international deposits of his artifacts reveals Rambaldi's extensive reach. Rambaldi unites peoples of every nation, and his influence is not limited either by time or geography. The most explicit statements of Sloane's faith in Rambaldi came after he had recovered Nadia, his daughter with Irina Derevko. In an unusual example of father-daughter communication, she begged him not to administer more of the Rambaldi fluid and finally asked why he was torturing her ("Legacy," 3-21). Sloane replied portentously, "When Abraham was asked to offer his only child, Isaac, up to God, he didn't hesitate. And he took in his hand the fire and the knife, and it was only then that the angel came. But Abraham had to be willing to make this unbearable choice."

NADIA: I understand.
SLOANE: You do?
NADIA: You're a man of faith.

Sloane used an example from the Judeo-Christian tradition to illustrate his devotion to his "god," Rambaldi. Nadia's agreement, however, played on his desire to be exonerated as a faithful disciple, and she immediately exploited his surprise at her supposed acquiescence by attempting an escape.

Sloane's faith did nonetheless gain a surprising convert at the end of season three. After Nadia survived his brutal treatment and produced a nearly complete Rambaldi equation, she was rescued by Sydney and taken into CIA custody. Sloane infiltrated the CIA safe house and gained confirmation from Nadia of Rambaldi's vision. Like Christian saints such as Teresa of Avila, or the divinely inspired Pythia, Nadia experienced visions while under the influence of the Rambaldi fluid. Though Marshall had already explained how Nadia's automatic writing was probably induced by protein strands in the fluid that triggered noncognitive muscle memory encoded in Nadia's DNA, Sloane suggested a different kind of interpretation when he asked how it made her feel. At first, she rejected his quest for Rambaldi, retorting, "Your beliefs are your own." Sloane replied, "I understand your skepticism. But tell me this: when you were under the influence of the Rambaldi fluid, what you experienced, what you saw, was it not transcendent? Was it not divine?" ("Resurrection," 3-22). Sloane took Nadia's silence as agreement, and left instructions for how to reach him if she chose to escape CIA custody. Though she should have little reason to trust him, at the end of the episode Nadia joined Sloane with the true coordinates of Rambaldi's Sphere of Life.

They escaped together, united in a father-daughter mission—an ironic contrast to Sydney's horrified confrontation with her father in Wittenberg. Though left in suspense for months until the beginning of the fourth season, we eventually learned that Sydney's trust in her father had again been shattered by the revelation that he ordered her mother's execution. Despite the brevity of their exchange in Wittenberg, we were immediately aware that yet again, her father had let her down. Through Nadia's voluntary return, Sloane gained the ultimate confirmation of his faith: he obtained the most precious Rambaldi artifact of all, Rambaldi's consciousness incarnate in his daughter, and as a bonus, the paternal relationship that Sydney had always denied him. His ability to win a convert, especially one whom he had already abducted and tortured in the name of his beliefs, seemed to validate his faith. Like Abraham, Sloane had his child and his faith restored in a single action.

If Sloane enacts a personal narrative of faith, Sydney and her colleagues at the CIA cling desperately to alternative systems of values. Though Sydney has found herself in innumerable improbable and death-defying situations episode after episode, Rambaldi's prophecy seems to test her credulity. When first shown her picture on page 47, Sydney herself could only implausibly protest, "Thousands of women have looked like this in the last 500 years." ("The Prophecy," 1-16). Turning to her friends, Francie and Will, Sydney attempted to assimilate this revelation to a commonsense perspective. Mentioning a "dream" she had about a fortune-teller, she took an informal poll.

SYDNEY: Prophecy. Does that sound good or bad to you?
WILL: Bad. Definitely bad.
FRANCIE: Oh yeah. Totally.

As ever, Sydney's friends remained obliviously outside her work concerns. Rambaldi clearly does not function as part of normal reality. Vaughn and her father, Jack, remain steadfast in their skepticism of Rambaldi, particularly in any aspect of his works that refer to Sydney, but their conviction comes from an equally profound and competing faith. While Sloane may express a fanatical devotion to Rambaldi, Vaughn and Jack consistently claim emotional attachment to Sydney as their prime motivation. When Sydney asked Vaughn if he was ever tempted to believe in Rambaldi's prophecy, he denied it without hesitation. Sydney asked why, and his answer was simple, "Because I believe in you" ("Q&A").

Jack and Vaughn are prepared to use any resources at their disposal to save Sydney from the predations of Rambaldi fanatics. Their support was vital when *Alias* met *The X-Files* as a division of the FBI, the Department of Special Research (DSR), entered with a team of Rambaldi specialists. Led by Carson Evans, a scientist with unlimited support from Congress and other governmental bodies that superseded the CIA's authority, the DSR represented another type of Rambaldi fanatic. Unlike the shadowy mystical figures attached to the original Rambaldi cult, these individuals combined the government's civil authority with its scientific resources; if personal faith requires acceptance of the irrational, the DSR applies a different kind of paradigm. They seemed to act rationally, taking the previous Rambaldi incidents as evidence of his accuracy. When the prophecy emerged, they assumed that, based on their previous experience with Rambaldi, this prediction must also be true—but they subjected Sydney to medical and scientific tests to confirm it. Nonetheless, their autocratic behavior and secrecy when performing these tests resembled the Spanish Inquisition: they withheld the prophecy from Sydney and the Agency until they took her into custody. Like secret initiates, only they knew what they were looking for, and they used their own arcane medical techniques to torture a helpless victim. In a confrontation with Dr. Evans, Assistant Director Devlin protested against their barbaric methods. After a montage of Sydney in dark red gown surrounded by doctors in masks, Devlin exploded, "This is a five hundred-year-old text, and based on that text we are treating Agent Bristow like a lab rat.... [Juxtaposition with unpleasant-looking spinal tap]...We should investigate, yes, but not persecute!" ("The Prophecy"). Even in the world of rationality and science, government scientists are part of the Rambaldi cult, and their supposedly empirical methods seem to sit uncomfortably with their mystical secrecy. The DSR has its own cult of Rambaldi, and its armies of doctors and scientists are the high priests.

This combination of empiricism and fanaticism proves irresistible to the weak-willed. As Steven Haladki, the Uriah Heep-like sycophant, put it, "Look! We've decoded forty-seven distinct verifiable Rambaldi predictions. The guy hasn't been wrong once!...What if Bristow does pose a threat?" ("Q&A"). The DSR gained its own convert in Haladki, who essentially betrayed the CIA and Devlin by agreeing with Dr. Evans in a confrontation between the two agencies. Though Haladki was eventually exposed as a double agent for The Man, his ultimate, fanatical appeal to Jack to join his master's cause contained a wild-eyed profession of devotion that remained consistent with his earlier behavior ("Almost Thirty Years," 1-22). This hieratic priesthood posed a greater threat to Sydney because it operated within her institutional universe. But its members' dogmatic belief in empirical evidence was turned against them when Vaughn decided to play by their rules. His two attempts to exonerate Sydney hinged on interpretation. Though Rambaldi's prophecy was written in his own hand, the DSR may have mistranslated the coded text using a key engineered from partial evidence. Like prophecies in the ancient world, human interpretation may reverse a seemingly dire prediction. After Vaughn and Sydney recovered the original code key (appropriately enough from the Vatican, clearly a model for the DSR) and delivered it to the FBI, Sydney was suddenly taken into custody. As Vaughn explained to the bewildered Sydney, "Those medical tests you took. They were looking to match three specific physical anomalies Rambaldi mentioned: DNA sequencing, platelet levels and the size of your heart. You match all three" ("The Prophecy"). The DSR accepted Rambaldi's description because his use of precise physical data corresponded to their own empirical methods. Carson Evans then revealed the translation of the prophecy: "This woman here depicted will possess unseen marks. Signs that she will be the one to bring forth all my works. Bind them with fury. A burning anger. Unless prevented, at vulgar cost, this woman will render the greatest power unto utter desolation." Though they operate within a rationalist paradigm, the words of Rambaldi, accurately decoded and confirmed by medical evidence, represent a dogma to these high priests of Rambaldi.

Speech patterns reveal the enigmatic and therefore vulnerable nature of the prophecy. The DSR may have had empirical evidence confirming Sydney's status as The Chosen One, but they still could not interpret exactly what it meant, as became obvious every time Vaughn repeated the words of the prophecy. The strangely halting syntax of the prophecy as related by Evans lent itself to a variety of equally Shatner-esque rephrasings and repunctuations that may or may not be significant to its meaning. Vaughn obtained the full text of the prophecy and read it aloud over and over again until Weiss warned him that he would go insane. Eventually, Vaughn burst out, "What's 'vulgar cost'? 'This woman without pretense will have had her effect. Never having seen the beauty of my sky behind Mt. Subasio, perhaps a single glance would have quelled her fire.'" ("Q&A"). Vaughn struggled with the occasionally nonsensical language of the prophecy, and yet, through these words, he discovered how to turn the DSR's literalism against it. In an urgent encounter with

Jack, Vaughn explained that if Sydney could somehow be sent to Mt. Subasio, Rambaldi's birthplace, this would nullify the prophecy's significance. Vaughn took the DSR's dogmatic belief to its logical conclusion: "If the FBI is taking this prophecy so literally, then every phrase must have equal weight, right?" ("Q&A"). By extracting Sydney and sending her to Italy, Vaughn and Jack exploited the DSR's extreme empiricism to save Sydney from indefinite and potentially permanent incarceration.

But why did Sydney have to free-climb up the sheer rock face of Mt. Subasio at the beginning of the following episode ("Masquerade," 1-18)? Couldn't she have parachuted to the top, or used any of the infinite gadgets at the CIA's disposal? Did Devlin approve transport but no other equipment? In a show where Sydney cannot even speak privately to her father without turning on a bug-killer hidden in a lipstick, is it plausible that she couldn't have hang glided to the top of the mountain? Explicitly denying Sydney technical assistance at this point made an ideological point: Sydney painfully climbed alone, relying on force of will and only the most primitive equipment to assert her independence against a secretive cabal of scientist-priests who regard text and data as more important than individual humanity. It's pretty hokey, but it provides a clue to the uneasy conflict at the heart of the series.

If, as this scene suggests, we must ultimately believe in the individual and the personal as the true guiding principle of humanity, how consistently does this principle apply throughout the series? Rambaldi and the different responses to him provide an obvious foil to this ethical position. Both Sloane and the DSR display religious elements: Sloane professes a personal faith while the DSR embodies the dangerous power of fanatical institutions like the Spanish Inquisition. Jack, Vaughn and Sydney counter these religious attitudes with their own brand of secular faith: personal loyalty. Their resistance to Rambaldi's prophecy follows possibilities established in ancient Greece; prophecies are always subject to human interpretation, as Vaughn and Jack turned to their advantage, and Croesus learned to his downfall. This victory of human interpretation over divine powers seems consistent with *Alias'* emphasis on individual agency. Sydney consistently places personal feelings above institutional and even supernatural directives; her concern for others shows that she is a Good Person, and therefore more capable of making correct moral choices than collective government agencies or organizations. Ultimately, our sympathies with the protagonist coerce a validation of her secular individualism against fanatical religious forces.

This blandly humanistic ideal is undermined, however, by the fact that Sydney's individualism inhabits a world in which technology is so pervasive that even the ancient semi-divinity Rambaldi must be cast as a prophet of gadgets and weapons. Though Rambaldi possesses some conventional qualities of a divinity—venerability, seeming omniscience and omnipotence—the show's use of his position in the past represents a complete reversal of traditional views of historical progress. Rambaldi seems supernatural only because he worked in the fifteenth century—a time that should be less technologically advanced than our own. *Alias* radically revises the concept of antiquity to reflect the inescapable influence of technology. Every television universe presents forces that correspond to its own established conditions: military hardware fails in the occult world of *Buffy the Vampire Slayer*, just as *Alias'* supernatural forces must be technological.

Though the show attempts to domesticate technological power in Marshall's comedic moments, every episode hinges on the creations that save Sydney's life and accomplish her missions. Technology remains the true divine force in the world of *Alias*, and the Rambaldi plotlines provide an explicit fetishization of it. In *Alias*, Rambaldi's supernatural power must be expressed in terms of technology if it is to have any validity at all. The mystical trappings and ancient religious elements confirm technology's divine status rather than challenge it. To this extent, the show's attempt to valorize individual choice and agency through Sydney's resistance to Rambaldi fanaticism seems unsuccessful. Even if she succeeds in defeating the primitive religious devotion of Rambaldi's followers, his construction as a technological divinity reveals a machine-centered universe in which human agency will always be limited.

J. Mira Seo received her Ph.D. in 2004 from Princeton University and is currently a visiting assistant professor at Swarthmore College. Her research centers on literary and ethical characterization in Latin literature.

DADDY KNOWS BEST

I've always felt that Alias really works well because of its emotional core. Cliff-hangers, beautiful women, exotic locales—all necessary and crucial elements of a good spy series. But without the relationships, chock full of guilt, love, subtext and raw emotion, Alias would not be what it is. That said, no relationship is more heart-wrenching than Syd and Jack's. Yes, each week their father-daughter moments happen while they're saving the world (or at least part of it), but in the end their relationship itself is real, a bond that every parent and child can relate to (even Marshall and his beloved television child, Mitchell!).

ALIAS IS A FAMILY SHOW. By that I do not mean that it should expect an endorsement from the American Family Association anytime soon, nor that its scenes of violence, set to a pounding soundtrack, are appropriate for all ages. What it does mean is that family and family relationships lie at the heart of the show, something which makes *Alias* almost unique in the TV landscape.

As *Alias* has progressed, family has supplied the majority of the drama. New characters were introduced, but the writers kept it in the family. Sydney Bristow had to contend with Irina, the mother she thought was dead; she also grappled with her new half-sister, Nadia. Jack Bristow had to deal with his long-lost sister-in-law, Katya, in addition to confronting Irina. Michael Vaughn was still haunted by the death of his father, a murder that connects him to Irina and possibly to Nadia, while his wife, Lauren, was revealed to have been leading a double life. Dixon was lucky enough to enjoy a stable family life free from the kinds of betrayals that characterize other characters' marriages, but this proved too good to be true. And even more minor characters like Marshall struggled with family issues—in his case, becoming a parent.

Not to be left out, the villains also had their own parents to contend with: Sloane had long hinted at a paternal connection to Sydney, and continues to act as though he's related to her. Season three featured a double patricide, as Lauren agreed to blow her own dad's head off, part of an emotional quid pro quo with her lover, Sark, whose father she had killed. (I'm guessing some Freudian therapist has just bought his second yacht thanks to series creator J. J. Abrams' violent Oedipal longings.)

But before this family tree multiplied uncontrollably, the central relationship of *Alias* was between Jack and Sydney, and it remains the series' most crucial. It's also intensely problematical, and not just because of the heightened circumstances in which the two superspies find themselves on a weekly basis. Covert missions aside, what makes the relationship between Syd and Jack so thrilling is the fact that *Alias* overlays a father-daughter relationship onto two familiar romantic paradigms: the unconsummated relationship and the love triangle.

The Syd-Jack relationship has the classic hallmarks of the odd-couple, on-again-off-again romance so common to long-running TV shows. This is such a familiar trope, it's hardly worth giving examples (Sam and Diane on *Cheers* is the classic; Mulder and Scully on *The X-Files* is another). More often than not, the characters are forced to work together, they appear to have opposite natures, and their relationship is characterized by moments of closeness followed by sudden and unpredictable periods of cooling off.

This perfectly describes the relationship between Jack and Sydney in season one. Father and daughter not only shared a workplace, but were intensely dependent on each other to stay alive as they negotiated between their SD-6 missions and their work for the CIA. Sydney is more emotional, impulsive and volatile; Jack experienced, steady and cool to a fault. They were strongly drawn toward a deeper intimacy with each other, but something always happened to push them apart again: usually this involved Syd finding out something about Jack, such as the fact he knew her fiancé, Danny, was going to be killed, or her mistaken belief that he was working for the KGB and was responsible for her mother's death.

And even when there was no plot complication to come between them, Jack's hardwiring to rebuff intimacy prevented them from furthering their relationship: in "A Broken Heart" (1-4), Sydney makes a dinner date with her father only to have him break it with a transparently false excuse. This prompted a tearful breakdown in front of Vaughn, and the scene between Sydney and her handler exposed the depth of Syd's need for intimacy with her father, which appeared as intense and uncontrollable as in any romantic relationship.

It's interesting to note how often that dynamic is repeated on *Alias*: Jack rebuffs Sydney, who goes reeling into Vaughn's (figurative) embrace. After two seasons of distance, father and daughter finally got it together in season three, when Vaughn was married and therefore unavailable. In the season three opener, "The Two," Jack and Sydney told each other "I love you" for the first time, immediately after Sydney brokenly admitted that Vaughn had married another woman. During season three, Jack and Sydney built on that admission of love, and their intimacy—if only measured in the number of hugs they shared—grew. However, it couldn't last, and season three ended as Sydney discovered documents which indicated Jack was responsible for Irina's death. In the beginning of season four, Syd could barely stand to be around Jack—she despised him, and flatly told him so in "Authorized Personnel Only, Part 1" (4-1)—which meant the way was cleared for a freshly widowed Vaughn to reenter the picture. While the relationship between Syd and Jack is never overtly sexualized, the characters are essentially placed in the classic romantic love triangle. Jack is continuously competing with various males—usually Vaughn, but also Sloane—for Sydney's love.

Our introduction to Jack in the pilot episode, "Truth Be Told," established him as the sharp end of a very pointed love triangle, as hopeful fiancé Danny called him for permission to ask for Sydney's hand in marriage. Jack cut him down to size in astonishingly few words: he suggested Danny didn't know Sydney at all, and stated that he would "not be used as part of a charming little anecdote you tell your friends at cocktail parties so they can see what a quaint, old-fashioned guy Danny really is." (He also called the engagement "a scenario," which speaks volumes about what kind of guy Jack really is.) But the scene did much more than establish Jack as having all the warmth of a canister of liquid nitrogen; it also set up Jack's jealousy over the men in his daughter's life. He didn't deny Danny access to his daughter, but it was clear he wasn't happy about it, either.

After Danny was killed, Michael Vaughn replaced him as Syd's hopeful suitor and, as a result, a new love triangle was born. Vaughn was Sydney's handler, but Jack is her father, and the two men clashed over what they believed was best for her. In their first meeting in "Color-Blind" (1-7), the clashing was all too literal, as Jack slammed Vaughn against the wall. Later in the same scene, he called the younger man unwise, told him his strategy was ill-thought-out and said that Daddy knew best when it came to his daughter's motivations and wishes. With scientific precision, Jack picked up on the attraction between Sydney and Vaughn and poked at it relentlessly, making it clear that he knew Vaughn was his main competition when it came to Sydney. When Vaughn asked what Jack's problem was, he replied, "You pulled my file last week, that's my problem, Mr. Vaughn. Now, did curiosity get the better of you, or were you trying to impress my daughter?" It was an echo of his conversation with Danny; what Jack was most annoyed about was being used in what he saw as a scheme to score points with Syd. Most of the first season was a silent competition between Jack and Vaughn, as both of them attempted to prove who loved Sydney best.

The rivalry between the men—and the underlying notion that each of them has a better idea of what's best for Sydney—came to a passionate head in "Mea Culpa" (1-9), when Sydney was suspected to be a mole by SD-6. Jack was convinced that Sloane had engineered a situation to test Syd's loyalty; Vaughn wanted to pull her out of there if there was even a chance her life was in danger. "How could you be willing to risk something like this?" Vaughn demanded. While it seemed that Jack was coldly indifferent to Syd's life, it turned out he was right—in this case, he really did know what was best for Sydney.

Some of Jack's calls with regard to Vaughn were more dubious, however. In season three, after intercepting one too many longing glances between his daughter and the married Vaughn, Jack collared him and demanded that Vaughn push Sydney away. "I know it's hard, but this isn't about you...and I will not allow my daughter to become your mistress," Jack said in "Remnants" (3-10). While Jack's knowledge of game theory and his uncanny ability to read people comes in handy in the field, his daughter's sexual relationships—even adulterous ones—are really none of his concern.

While Jack sounds a lot like a Victorian paterfamilias eaten up by sexual jealousy, what he's really jealous of is the easy intimacy that Syd shares with her friends and Vaughn. He felt intensely threatened when Irina reappeared in season two, and not just because she had burned him in the past; he was terrified of having to share Syd with her mother. It was another love triangle, this time between two effectively divorced parents and their beloved child. (Though nothing in *Alias* is straightforward—Irina's scenes with Sydney are far more akin to a long seduction than a getting-to-know you encounter between a mother and daughter.)

The other major love triangle in the show occurs between Sloane, Jack and Sydney, and the connections between these characters grew more convoluted over time as Sloane went rogue and it was revealed he and Irina once had an affair. Starting in the very first season, there were heavy hints that Sloane could be Sydney's biological father; initially, Sloane was speaking metaphorically about how he "believe[d] in her as if she were [his] own daughter" ("Color-Blind") and how he "always thought of [her] as [his] daughter, even from the beginning" ("Mea Culpa"). In a scene in which Sydney was making nice with Sloane while Jack eavesdropped, Sloane told Syd that, "Seeing the kind of woman you've become, knowing that I had something to do with it—that's as rewarding as if I had a child of my own." Jack, with uncharacteristic profanity, muttered, "Bastard."

By season three, Sloane was open about his belief with Dr. Barnett when he said, "I never tried to prove it, one way or the other. But the strength that Sydney finds within, I like to believe that comes from me" ("Blowback," 3-14). Whether Sydney sprung from the loins of Sloane, Jack Bristow or someone else entirely was largely irrelevant—what was more important was that Sydney was again in a situation where two men were vying for her affection. What made the situation unique was that they weren't competing as rivals in love, but as parents.

And that's a big part of what makes *Alias* compelling. The screenwriters have come up with a novel way to solve TV's most enduring problem: how to endlessly stoke the fires of sexual tension between two characters without it getting silly or tedious for the viewer.

In terms of this problem, screenwriters are in a bind: spin out the tension too long and things get boring—the relationship between Mulder and Scully in *The X-Files* is a good example of an unconsummated relationship that made audiences want to heave a brick at their TVs. After a while, the plot devices and excuses designed to keep the lovers apart just get ridiculous. But the fact remains that most viewers are secret puritans: allow characters to give in to hot bunny lust and you can more or less kiss your ratings good-bye. Which makes Jack and Sydney more or less the perfect couple: resisting temptation is the only thing that makes narrative sense. (Well, unless they're subject to mind-altering drugs that make them forget who they are, which, in the improbable world of *Alias*, is likely to be next year's end of season cliff-hanger.) But the drive toward greater intimacy between Jack and Sydney is a hugely powerful force in the script; the fact is, their relationship can deepen and grow without the sexual issue ever needing to come up.

Where genuine sexual tension does crop up is between Vaughn and Sydney, and the writers do a reasonably competent job of throwing plot curveballs at the pair to believably keep them from acting out their relationship on a sexual level. (The device of skipping ahead two years between seasons two and three and having Vaughn suddenly married to Lauren was one of TV's more extreme examples of a plot twist designed to tamp down on the lust between two characters.) While Vaughn presents a marked contrast to Jack—he's younger and more emotionally accessible, for starters—the introduction of Lauren and the slow revelation of her duplicity exactly mirrored Jack's relationship with Irina some thirty years earlier. Watching Sydney and Vaughn develop as a couple in season four, it is hard to avoid the conclusion that, presuming the two survive the season's cliff-hanger car crash, Sydney will be marrying her father.

Again, though, the fact that a major love triangle in the show is between a man, a woman and her father actually solves the traditional love triangle, which involves forcing the woman to choose at some point. *Alias* manages to have its cake and eat it, too—the fact is Sydney doesn't really have to choose. Her father will always have an edge over Vaughn, by virtue of their familial bond, while at the same time, Vaughn will always have an edge over Jack, because he can offer her romantic love and sex, along with a closeness that Jack will always struggle to provide. Several episodes into season four, Sydney appeared to have found an equilibrium between her father and her new relationship with Vaughn, but whether the show will suffer without the energy provided by their emotional tug-of-war remains a question.

Like no other show on television, family bonds and relationships are crucial to *Alias*—almost to the point of absurdity, since no character related to Sydney (mother, father, aunt, half-sister) can be introduced without it being revealed that he or she is somehow into espionage. But this emphasis on blood ties—the most primal of all—is what makes the show unique, particularly in the action-adventure genre. Generally, when it comes to superheroes (which is essentially what Sydney is), the loss of a beloved parent or parents is part of the hero's creation myth. (Again, there are so many example of this, it's almost silly to start enumerating them, but there are Superman and Batman, to name the most obvious.) While this initially appeared to be the case with Sydney—she started off thinking she lost her mother in an accident when she was aged six—it proved not to be true, and her mother returned to play an important part in the series.

Usually, as a TV series progresses, the family members around a character—particularly in a drama or an action-adventure—are killed or otherwise fall away. *The X-Files* whittled away at the families of both Mulder and Scully, and in the world of *Buffy the Vampire Slayer*, a show that also featured a strong female heroine and a Byzantine mythology, Buffy went from living in an intact family to losing her father to divorce, then her mother to a brain aneurysm and finally her Watcher (the guiding force in her life) to England.

Alias, by contrast, features a blossoming of the family tree. Sydney started off with a dead mother and a distant father, but by the end of season three had a living mother, a closer relationship with Jack, a weird paternal relationship with Sloane, an occasionally helpful (and occasionally deadly) Auntie Katya and a new half-sister in the picture. (By contrast, characters who were closest to her in the pilot episode but were unrelated by blood proved expendable, such as Danny, Francie and Will.) Although the relationships Sydney has with these family members are often tempestuous, confusing and/or unhealthy, she's almost always better off because they're a part of her world. However bizarre and edgy the rest of the show gets, the message *Alias* sends is a traditional, almost conservative one: family looks out for one another, and blood ties almost always win out over friendship. It's rare that a TV show privileges family over romantic love; in *Alias*, love doesn't conquer all—though family might. More often than not, Jack is better at calling a situation and figuring out Syd's best interests, as in "Mea Culpa" and elsewhere. And it's interesting that, while Vaughn broke faith with Syd to marry Lauren in the interregnum between seasons two and three—a betrayal that was still haunting Syd in season four's "Nocturne"—Jack never doubted that Syd was alive, and was willing to be imprisoned in pursuit of that truth.

TV shows like *Alias* are about escapist entertainment, but if they're to be successful at all, they have to provide an element of fantasy fulfillment. There's no denying the fantasy element takes the form of Sydney's jet-setting from country to country, breaking into top-secret locations and saving the world roughly once a week. But the fantasy also works on an emotional level, particularly in terms of the relationship between Syd and Jack.

A significant number of people would like a closer relationship with their father, so there's an element of wish-fulfillment fantasy present in Jack Bristow, who kills, maims and puts his own life in jeopardy to save his adored child on a regular basis. Many parents say they'd kill for their kids, but Jack literally does so, and unhesitatingly puts his own life in jeopardy for Syd over and over. He even killed the mother of his child when he learned Irina had decided to eliminate Syd, an act that speaks to something deeply primal, a kind of reverse-gender reen-actment of the Greek myth of Agamemnon. (Agamemnon was killed by his wife in revenge for sacrificing their daughter Iphigenia for a good wind to sail to Troy.) It seems almost counterintuitive, given that Jack submitted Sydney for experimental indoctrination when she was in grade school to mold her into a superspy in his own image, but in many ways, Jack should be considered an ideal parent: protective, steadfast, single-minded.

Jack Bristow, because he's Sydney's father, can also act as the accept-able face of the female rescue fantasy without undermining Syd as a strong, independent woman. Again, the father-daughter relationship is the twist that keeps the male-saves-female dynamic fresh: parents are supposed to protect their children, so when Jack swoops in at the last possible moment to untie Sydney from the figurative train tracks, the action seems natural and right rather than infuriating. (The classic structure of an *Alias* episode involves Jack saving Sydney, then Sydney saving Vaughn.) For all *Alias'* improbability—and sometimes it features the most ludicrously baroque plots on television—there's something gripping and utterly believable about this father-daughter archetype.

Catharine Tunnacliffe grew up in Ottawa, was educated at Cambridge University in England and currently resides in Toronto, Canada. She is a freelance film and culture critic for various publications, and is heard regularly on CBC radio. She is also the associate publisher of the alternative newspaper Eye Weekly.

CANDACE HAVENS

SYDNEY AND ME

Yes, it would be fun and exciting (for most women) to be sexy, svelte superspy Sydney Bristow. But I have to say, while Jennifer Garner may make it look easy, she puts in an incredible amount of time. For the first three years of filming, she was up every work day at four A.M. to work out, adhered to a strict diet, was on set twelve to fourteen hours and then, as Joe Jackson said, would "get up and do it all again." Heck, I'm sour when I have to be at work at seven A.M. and they've run out of sugar-free Red Bulls at Craft Service! (Hey... Marshall has to look good too!) Different methods to the madness, I guess...

WOULDN'T IT BE GREAT if we could all live our lives like our favorite superspy? Imagine the adventure, the men and, best of all, the clothes.

I want to be Sydney Bristow. Really. I want to look like her. I want to fight like her. I even want to live dangerously like she does and travel the world as a secret agent. I want her body and her linguistic talents. And I definitely want her cool spy call signs: Freelancer and Mountaineer.

I know there are other women in the world who want the same thing I do. Who wouldn't? Sydney is one of the most beautiful women in the world, and she kicks ass.

But I'm a special case, because, well, I'm me. So I sat down and took a serious look at Sydney's life, dissecting and studying exactly what it takes to be a superspy who can wear Prada heels and kick butt at the same time.

Unfortunately, there are a few problems with my plan to infiltrate and take over Sydney Bristow's life. Not the least of which is that I would have to grow about nine inches and lose a "few" pounds.

I decided to settle on second best. I would incorporate Sydney into my own life. I would learn to be more like her and use what I learned to enhance my own little world.

Of course this transformation isn't without its trials and tribulations.

The most immediate crisis is I don't have the danger gene: that ability to walk into an office building, pretend like I know what I'm doing, plant a bomb and then jump out a window with a parachute.

I'm afraid of heights and bombs, and really, who isn't scared of parachutes?

Sydney isn't afraid of anything. Remember when she was tied to that chair and had the crap beat out of her? And then that nasty man yanked out her tooth? At the first sign of those pliers I would have screamed, "I'll tell you everything!"

Sydney didn't. She flipped the chair over and put the guy out.

When the people she loves are in trouble, her biggest fear is not being able to save them in time. But she will do whatever it takes to get the job done. When my family is in trouble I do step up, but God help them if I'm ever put in a position where I have to take a bullet to save them.

I'm also frightened of guns, but Sydney's not. She can take apart and put together any weapon; then she mows down the bad guys like an army of thirty.

Yes, Sydney has the danger gene in spades. I often wonder, what with all the secrets surrounding her parentage and birth, if perhaps she wasn't genetically engineered to seek out dangerous situations. (I was genetically engineered to eat chocolate cake, so I know about these things.)

As with most great things in life, there's a definite downside to being Sydney. She gets hurt a lot; she's survived being stabbed, shot and beaten over and over. And Sydney's lifestyle also endangers her friends and family.

Her boyfriends, beginning with fiancé Danny Hecht, usually end up dead. I bet Noah Hicks had no idea his association with Sydney would be detrimental to his health.

I haven't ever caused a man's death, but I'm pretty sure I had something to do with one of my seventh-grade boyfriends discovering he was gay soon after we started dating. (It was a horrible kissing fiasco. Please, don't ask.)

Sydney's latest conquest, her handler Michael Vaughn, has almost died several times because he knows Sydney. Oh, and who could forget her friend Francie. I know that woman is in heaven wishing she had never met the spy.

Will Tippin, another of Sydney's buds, is in a federal witness protection program, where he's gone from being a top-notch journalist to a construction worker who has to carry a gun in his duffel bag. All because he had the nerve to get close to her.

I can't say that knowing me has ever been detrimental for my friends and family. Except, perhaps, when I'm behind the wheel. I do like speed—something I have in common with Ms. Bristow. Have you ever seen her drive? She'd give those NASCAR guys a run for their money.

I don't think my husband would appreciate my putting his or our children's lives in danger. He's fussy about those kinds of things. But I have incorporated Syd's love for speed into my daily life. Sometimes I just rev the engine a bit and think about weaving through the miles of traffic ahead of me.

Another problem with my assimilating Sydney's life into mine is her incredible athletic ability. I, um, sit at a computer and type stories all day. So, I'm a little less than svelte. In fact, if I spent the next ten years working out six hours a day, I still wouldn't come close to her sleek body frame.

I've actually heard women say, "I want Sydney Bristow's arms." And I don't think they were talking about a transplant. Sydney takes good care of herself.

She eats what she wants, and pizza and beer are often on the menu. But she runs just for fun. (I don't get that at all.) She also studies Krav Maga martial arts and does Pilates. Now I don't know about you, but I've tried Pilates. It hurts.

The combination of self-defense and street fighting has served Sydney well. More often than not, she dispels her aggressors with relative ease. Of course, all that kicking, twisting and jumping keeps her in terrific shape.

I tried to jump once. It didn't go well. But I would like to think that if I were attacked I could kick the guy in the balls. Really, really hard. This is a technique Syd uses often, and I feel confident I could do the same.

I have incorporated the pizza, beer and Chinese food she dines on into my life, and that has been very successful. Mission accomplished.

The exercise routine? Not so much. I tried to do a roundhouse kick the other day just to see if I could, and I now walk with a limp. Let's pray it's not permanent.

Another small trouble spot in my plan to take over for Sydney is the memory thing. Go ahead; ask me what I had for lunch today. I have no idea. Thoughts come in, thoughts go out. Very seldom do they stick around in my head for any length of time. Memory isn't one of my gifts.

Sydney has a memory like a laptop. Seriously. She can remember faces, even when the other person is in disguise. She can spot a target from a mission three years ago and recall the details associated with that person.

Okay, so she had a bit of trouble remembering going undercover as Julia Thorne, but that wasn't her fault. There was some big-time brain altering going on with that situation.

For the most part, Sydney remembers all of the people she's ever worked with and everyone she's killed. (And trust me, there's been a lot of them on both counts.) She speaks thirteen languages and can commit the layout of a building to memory with a mere glance. And she can work all those wild and crazy gadgets that her buddy Marshall invents for her. She never forgets which way to point the poison dart pen or how long it takes the watch bomb to work.

She also never forgets when someone has done her wrong. Just ask Arvin Sloane or Julian Sark. When it comes to those two, Sydney's darker side comes out. She's tried to kill them more than once, usually leaving the scene with a vicious last word. When everyone else gave Sloane the benefit of the doubt after he started running Omnifam, Sydney made sure he knew that she didn't forgive so easily. And back when Sark joined Sloane at SD-6, Sydney threatened that if he squealed about her secret life, it would be the end of his.

Now, some people will tell you that I, too, can turn into scary Sydney. It's another of her traits I've taken to heart. Just ask my oldest son, who ate the last chocolate truffle, or the car salesman who suggested I might want to consult my husband before making such a large purchase. Yes, I have a dark side. Syd has taught me well.

Okay, now here we get to the really tricky part: being a brave and courageous spy. Those two traits are sort of tied to Sydney's danger gene, but she almost always goes beyond the call of duty.

I marvel at Sydney's bravery in every sense of the word. She's the first to run back for a fallen comrade or to walk into a building charged with explosives to save a loved one.

She has, on countless missions, put herself in danger in order to save her coworkers, friends and family members. And in true Sydney style she has protected people she doesn't even like.

I'm trying to be courageous, but it hasn't worked well. The scariest thing I've had to do on a regular basis is drive in Dallas traffic. People who think Texas is a friendly state have never driven at five P.M. on Central Expressway in bumper-to-bumper with a host of BMWs, Mercedes and Jaguars. I've tried to pretend I'm Sydney and use my techniques for dealing with danger, but usually I just end up with indigestion from the stress and need a nap when I get home.

By watching several seasons of *Alias*, I've discovered the most important part of being a superspy is knowing how to keep a secret.

In this respect, I am the worst. Keeping mum about exciting news is almost painful for me, but I'm trying. I know to be a good secret agent you have to keep your mouth closed.

Sydney was able to keep her double life a secret for years. Her closest friends thought she worked for a company that sent her around the world on boring bank deals. She would get beat up in Russia, crash a car, kill a double agent and still be home for dinner with the gang, never mentioning that she had a tough day.

But Syd comes by her secret-keeping honestly. When her fiancé died because she told him what she did for a living, Sydney decided to keep mum, no matter what. And who could blame her?

Although in hindsight, Francie, who ended up dead on the kitchen floor of her restaurant, might have found the information that one of her best friends was a secret agent useful. Perhaps when she saw her genetic double, Allison Doren, she would have had the forethought to run the other way.

Here's the thing: if someone tells me it's a big secret and begs me to keep it, I can do it. But if someone else holds a gun to my head and says, "Tell me that secret," I'm going to spill.

I have been covertly practicing secret-keeping. My husband still doesn't know about the new boots, slacks and shirt I bought (in an effort to look more like a secret agent, of course). When I came home I hid the purchases in my office. He asked what I had been doing all morning, and I deftly changed the subject with, "Look at this picture of Jessica Simpson. Do you think her boobs are real?"

I know. I'm good.

One of the best things I've learned from Sydney is that very art of diversion, especially when one's safety, sanity or secrets are at risk.

Syd's best diversion tactics are her breasts. If she wants to keep some security guard/receptionist/scientist from noticing she's stealing the key card, she simply zips down or loosens a few buttons on her blouse and smiles. It works every time. Well, every time it's a man.

I'm not ashamed to admit I use this diversion tactic all the time. When asking for a raise, I've been known to wear my black jacket that is cut down to "there." And when my husband is particularly cranky or inquisitive about my spending habits I whip out the push-up bra, unbutton the top three buttons, and all is well in the world.

But Sydney's the one who taught me the smile. Flash those pearly whites with a little cleavage and you can turn a man to mush.

One other thing Sydney and I have in common is our penchant for being attracted to gorgeous, if somewhat dangerous, men. Those beautiful guys with a dark side. Even her deliciously sweet handler Vaughn was able to torture and later kill his almost-ex-wife when push came to shove. And though I doubt she would ever admit it, I think Sydney had a wonderful time working with the evil Sark.

I, too, enjoy a hunk who could whisk me off at a moment's notice to the far reaches of the world. If either man showed up on my doorstep, I'd be gone faster than you could say, "Honey, I'm leaving town with a gorgeous hunk of a man." But I'm afraid I'd have to leave all the spy stuff up to him. As much as I like dangerous men, I don't enjoy my life being in peril. I'd prefer to wait in the Learjet with the champagne and strawberries while he traverses down dark, rat-infested tunnels in search of the latest Rambaldi artifact.

The truth is I probably wouldn't make a very good secret agent. Obvious characteristics aside, I don't have Sydney's superhuman talents for getting the bad guys. And quite honestly, we all know there's only one Sydney Bristow.

That is, until her genetic double comes to town.

And perhaps the genetic double will be "slightly" curvier, have a Southern drawl and be able to bend men's minds into thinking she looks like Sydney.

I better go practice that roundhouse kick again.

Candace "Candy" Havens is one of the nation's leading syndicated entertainment columnists for FYI Television. She has interviewed hundreds of celebrities and covers everything Hollywood for publications around the world. She is the author of Joss Whedon: The Genius Behind Buffy *and can be heard weekday mornings on 96.3 KSCS, which broadcasts in the Dallas/Fort Worth area. Havens' first fiction novel,* Charmed and Dangerous *(Berkley), will be released in September 2005.*

DAVID HARRIS

THE SCIENCE OF *ALIAS*

*I am usually asked two questions in interviews and by fans of the
show. 1) Are you as technically savvy as Marshall? And, 2) Do your
gadgets really work? Well, here are the most sought after answers
of the year, people! Yes, I am technically proficient when it comes to
my Mac computers and my surround-sound screening room system at
home. But, no—I have no idea how to build a bobsled that goes from
zero to sixty in 2.3 seconds. And sorry to disappoint you, but most of
the "gadgets" on Alias are nonworking "props" that usually rely on
our kick-ass visual effects and post-production team to provide the
true magic. I call these guys "the Marshalls behind the Marshall."*

ANY GOOD TELEVISION DRAMA is driven by its characters, but
the universe in which they live has a huge impact on the show as
well. More than most current programs, *Alias* is dependent on science and technology for its plot elements, surprises, gimmicks and even
characters.

Basing a series on such scientific subject matter requires extra care to
retain authenticity. One of the outstanding features of *Alias* is that even
though there is much that is outlandish and unrealistic about it, so many
of Marshall's inventions and so many of the major plot devices are based
in actual research, even if the specific applications wouldn't really work.
Basing these inventions and devices, even partially, on cutting-edge science gives the show a plausibility that it wouldn't otherwise have.

There is so much science and technology in the series that it would take an entire book just to analyze where the ideas and inspirations come from. So for now I'm going to examine nine interesting examples of science in the first three seasons of *Alias*. For each, I'm going to rate the Plausibility Factor, or how well the example reflects real-world research and scientific thinking, and the Realism Factor, or how feasible it is that the "science" in question would actually work. We'll see where the world of *Alias* aligns with our reality and where the ideas belong in an alternate one where SD-6 and the Covenant are the good guys.

#1: DOUBLE, DOUBLE, TOIL AND TROUBLE
Plausibility Factor: 5 out of 10
Realism Factor: 1 out of 10

CONTEXT
In one of the most harrowing scenes in season two, CIA agent Emma Wallace was blown up by her lover and fellow agent Jim Lennox. Wallace was forced to sing "Pop Goes the Weasel" in a public square in Berlin with C4 explosive strapped to her body while Lennox waited with a detonator in a telephone booth nearby.

We later discovered that Lennox was not the CIA agent Wallace had fallen in love with but his double, a person created to appear identical to the real Lennox using the "Helix" technology that Wallace was investigating at the time of her murder. The name "Helix" clearly refers to the double-helix structure of DNA molecules that contains a person's genetic code.

Later in the season we also found out that Francie was shot and replaced by Allison Doren.

The terminology gets confusing here when we talk about two identical people, so I'm going to call the person who is copied the "original" and the person who is the copy the "imposter."

The basic premise of the Helix technology is that the DNA of one person is replaced by that of another. This allegedly creates an impostor indistinguishable from the original person. But how possible is such a process?

PLAUSIBILITY
The heart of the concept of doubling as described in *Alias* is the idea that DNA can be transferred from one person into another. This idea,

truly science fictional not very long ago, is now an area of active scientific research.

The idea of replacing one person's DNA with another's takes us into the world of gene therapy and cloning. Some animals have been successfully cloned (so as to have identical DNA), but those processes begin with an unfertilized egg, not a grown creature. Dolly the sheep was the first cloned mammal. Since then, clones have been made of mice, pigs, rabbits, cats, cows, goats and a guar. No human has been cloned, despite one discredited religious group's claims, and to even attempt it is almost universally regarded as unethical. So let's leave the issue of cloning aside for the moment and concentrate on a process that might, in principle, be used to double a person. The distinction here is that doubling is designed to be done to a grown human, rather than at a pre-embryonic stage.

Even though cloning humans with the purpose of creating an identical person is considered highly unethical, scientists have much experience with the transfer of genes between organisms. Some highly promising therapeutic applications are being developed, and the techniques are usually called gene therapy. Significant progress has been made toward gene therapies for diseases, such as cystic fibrosis, which are caused by the mutation of a single gene.

There are many genetic diseases that could be cured by gene therapy if defective DNA could be replaced by healthy DNA. However, this presents a very serious challenge. DNA is contained in nearly every cell of the body, and to completely cure a disease, every relevant cell would need to be corrected.

Altering DNA involves using biochemical reactions that cut apart the long DNA molecules and insert new amino acid sequences in place of the old ones. Gene therapy can be attempted *ex vivo* (where cells are modified outside the body and then re-transplanted) or *in vivo* (where the cells are modified in place in the body). Either way, this replacement can't be done by hand because our control of atoms and molecules is not as precise as it would need to be. Also, there are simply too many cells (about 10 to 100 trillion) to even contemplate anything that isn't totally automated.

But scientists do know something that can enter cells and change them without requiring any other intervention: viruses. In fact, this is what viruses do naturally—they insert some of their genetic code into cells so that the host cells can reproduce the virus and spread it further.

In an attempt to use nature's own creations for their benefit, scientists are exploring ways to have viruses carry the corrective genetic information. They then release the corrective virus into the body and let it do its job naturally. The body, however, fights any viral infection and will do its best to eradicate the virus. (Gene therapy is much more complex than I can describe here, so I'm just giving you a taste of one form of the process.)

However, if you were to decide the risks were worthwhile, there are ways to proceed. The two main classes of viruses that are considered contenders for gene therapy are adenoviruses and retroviruses. Adenoviruses carry the DNA to be transplanted as part of their own genetic code. The downside is that when cells have had their DNA replaced this way, they do not pass on the correct DNA when the cells divide and grow. So an adenovirus strategy would require continued treatments, and cells could multiply too quickly for the virus to ever catch them all.

Retroviruses work slightly differently. They carry segments of RNA, a type of molecule the primary function of which is to build molecules such as DNA. The RNA is able to "transcribe" some genetic code right into the chromosomes of cells, and so any changes they make are permanent and will be passed on every time the cell divides. (Remember that I am seriously oversimplifying all of this. You'd also need different viruses to control other parts of the process, for example.) HIV is an example of a retrovirus.

A major downside of using retroviruses is that they can cause DNA segments to be inserted in the wrong place. And once you start putting DNA in the wrong place, you can mess up the basic genetic controls of cells; one of the common side effects of this is cancer. Some trials of gene therapy using retroviruses have been canceled after some patients developed leukemia.

Gene therapy has not yet had revolutionary success. Although some trials have looked promising, many have been canceled after the patient developed cancer or other diseases. Still, gene therapy approaches offer hope for treating debilitating genetic diseases that so far have no other cure in sight.

So, while this is a very new and undeveloped area of science, *Alias'* doubling idea is linked to ongoing scientific research—even if the actual work being done is a very long way away from actual doubling. —PLAUSIBILITY FACTOR: 5

REALISM

This discussion of retroviruses and DNA replacement does avoid many practical issues. To get away with doubling Jim Lennox, the imposter (originally Dr. Enzo Markovic) would need to do much more than assume his physical form. For a start, replacing DNA does not mean that the original and the imposter will have identical behavior. The imposter would need to learn everything from the way the original walks to his vocal mannerisms. And yet, in the world of *Alias*, agents are extremely skilled at such mimicry, so we'll give those problems a pass for the time being.

A second issue is that even having identical DNA does not guarantee that two people will have identical appearances. Even though identical twins, who have identical DNA, may appear indistinguishable at first glance, they are always different in some physical characteristics, including their fingerprints.

Although people's bodies are strongly influenced by their genetic codes, environmental factors have an important impact. Twins may come from identical cells, but even as they develop to embryos there are already subtle differences. By the time the twins reach adulthood, those differences have multiplied. Sometimes only an intimate associate will be able to tell them apart, or, at other times, the identical twins are easily differentiated, especially if they are mirror twins, a rare occurrence in which characteristics on one twin's left side are replicated on the other twin's right side.

But, even if we were to put aside these two issues, would the doubling work for Jim Lennox? If the gene therapy used retroviruses, there is a substantial risk that he could have cancer developing in his body (although the impostor was shot by Sydney before he would have found out). If the therapy was an adenovirus therapy, it would require ongoing treatments to convert newly born cells to the desired genetic code. *Alias* at least tries to mitigate some of the other common gene therapy difficulties by introducing the need for doubles to inject Provacillium regularly. This drug presumably counters any toxicity of the virus and reduces the body's natural immune and inflammatory responses.

To get even this far, we have had to suspend substantial disbelief. Gene therapy won't change the number of cells or their structure immediately, so it is unlikely that any substantial change in appearance would occur in the short term even if gene therapy didn't kill the impostor. A tall, heavy person could never be doubled into a short, lean person, for example. The original and impostor would need to be extremely similar from the beginning to have any chance of the process working.

So our verdict for doubling? Not a chance of it working. Although some of the steps required to double Jim Lennox and Francie are being researched, it is for the purposes of medical treatments, not international espionage. —REALISM FACTOR: 1

#2: DETECTING LIES
Plausibility Factor: 3 out of 10
Realism Factor: 9 out of 10

CONTEXT

Lie detection is a staple of police and legal dramas. Countless movies and shows have shown a subject connected to a polygraph (lie detector) that, with the flick of a needle, indicates the truth or falsity of an answer. Often accompanying the scene is some discussion by characters about how to "beat" the polygraph. Polygraphy appears in various guises throughout *Alias*, but the most advanced use of the technique appeared in season one, when SD-6 suspected Sydney of being a mole.

The reality of polygraphy is that it is essentially useless in accurately determining whether a subject is telling the truth. One of the few ways that it seems to have any sort of application is by exploiting the subject's fear of failure, a tactic that has dubious ethical implications and even more dubious validity. Numerous studies conducted by independent scientific bodies (such as the U.S. National Academy of Sciences) have shown that lie detector tests have unacceptably poor accuracy, especially in the face of any sort of countermeasures employed by the subject.

Use of polygraphs is widespread in sections of the U.S. government, particularly during recruitment, despite other U.S. government reports recommending against such use. One thing we do know is that no polygraph test has ever caught a spy in the United States; many innocent people, however, have had their careers destroyed on the basis of polygraph tests. Convicted spies Robert Hanssen and Aldrich Ames both passed CIA lie detector tests during their careers as double agents, and Ames has admitted that the advice given to him to beat the test was simply to relax.

It is worth noting that the use of polygraph results in U.S. courts is extremely controversial, and there is no widely accepted precedent for their admission. Polygraph results have only been admitted in some courts, and even when they are accepted, they are only used corroboratively (to support other direct, real or testimonial evidence).

PLAUSIBILITY

A polygraph test typically measures heart rate, blood pressure, respiration and skin conductivity. While a polygraph might measure these variables accurately, there is no reliable evidence to suggest that they are connected to truth- or lie-telling.

Given the failure of traditional polygraphy to reliably indicate the veracity of a subject's answers, some people are trying to use more advanced technologies to achieve real lie detection. The cutting edge of polygraphic technology was used in *Alias* when Sydney was asked to undergo a functional imaging test during the season two search for a mole in the CIA Rotunda.

The functional imaging test probably refers to a process called functional magnetic resonance imaging, or fMRI. fMRI is able to detect localized brain activity—in other words, it can tell what parts of the brain are active at particular times. It does this by detecting where blood is flowing within the brain. The theory behind using fMRI for lie detection is that certain parts of the brain will be more active when a person is lying. In reality, fMRIs are mainly used to diagnose and understand particular brain abnormalities. For example, different parts of the brain "light up" in dyslexics than in those who do not suffer from the condition.

Some of the current drawbacks of fMRI at the moment are that the scans take around twenty minutes or so, and the head needs to be very still during that time. It also happens inside a large tube in which the head must be completely or mostly contained. So Sydney sitting in a chair with a few electrodes attached to her head does not look like an fMRI. The electrodes on Sydney's head more likely suggest an EEG (electroencephalogram), which detects electrical activity on the outside of the brain. In combination with magnetic resonance imaging, EEG can be useful for locating brain activity.

However, none of this guarantees us anything about detecting lies. It is probably fair to say that fMRI is quite good at locating blood movement in the brain, but the meaning of that blood flow is not really understood, especially in terms of lie detection.

Some studies with fMRI have claimed to show different brain behavior when a person was lying than when they were telling the truth. The results essentially showed that it took more brain activity to lie than to tell the truth. However, the results showed this only on average for the group. The technique was not useful for detecting whether any particular individual was lying.

Perhaps the most serious problem with lie detection in Sydney's case is that she is a woman. Because polygraphy relies so much on blood flow, changes during different phases of the menstrual cycle or during pregnancy make polygraph results especially difficult to interpret for women. Even proponents of polygraphy admit that the techniques are poorly understood for female subjects, particularly since the majority of the research has been done on males.

Overall, science simply doesn't support the use of polygraphy in ascertaining whether a subject is telling the truth. —PLAUSIBILITY FACTOR: 3

REALISM

Sydney came out of the functional imaging test having "passed" but was still suspected by the interrogator because her responses were "too perfect." What we know about polygraphy so far suggests that it is relatively easy to beat a polygraph, so the fact that Sydney did so is not surprising. Whether this also applies to an fMRI test has not been tested yet but it is reasonable to think it could also be "beaten" in some way—cheaters are almost always technologically ahead of testers.

Modern technology will continue to be used in an effort to create a functional lie detector, probably because the mythology is so strong and the potential law-enforcement benefits so great. But so little is understood about the physiological processes involved in lie detection, especially in how it changes from person to person, that it is a safe bet to say there is no effective lie detection mechanism in existence at the moment, and there won't be for a long time, if ever.

So although the scientific basis of lie detection is extremely low, *Alias* gets a high score on realism because it reflects the real-life widespread misuse of polygraphy. Lie detection in the show works just as well as it would in real life—almost not at all. —REALISM FACTOR: 9

#3: FORCING THE TRUTH
Plausibility Factor: 6 out of 10
Realism Factor: 3 out of 10

CONTEXT

So if you can't tell if somebody is lying, why not just force them to tell the truth? This is the alternative method we see often in *Alias*, where truth serum is injected into a recalcitrant prisoner, whether CIA agent or enemy of the United States government.

PLAUSIBILITY

A variety of drugs have been employed for the purposes of eliciting the truth from a subject. A few of them are sodium thiopental (also known as sodium pentothal), scopolamine and alcohol. In the 1950s and 1960s, the CIA ran the MK-ULTRA Project to develop a truth serum effective against Soviet agents. Its efforts focused on giving LSD, barbiturates and amphetamines in rapid succession. The project was ultimately abandoned after mixed results. It certainly wasn't reliable enough to be used regularly, and the health risks associated with all these drugs are serious. —PLAUSIBILITY FACTOR: 6

REALISM

Sodium thiopental is a general anesthetic that causes cardiovascular and respiratory depression, hypotension (low blood pressure), apnea (pauses in breathing) and airway obstruction. Side effects include headaches, delirium after waking from the drug, prolonged sleepiness and nausea, all of which can last up to thirty-six hours. Along with a combination of two other drugs, it forms the sedative part of the lethal injection cocktail used to administer the death penalty in the United States. It doesn't work as a truth serum.

Scopolamine is hallucinogenic, and so any "truths" obtained while under it tend to be embellished. Used in large doses, it is toxic and can result in delirium, delusions, paralysis and death. In lower doses, it is quite useful for preventing nausea; many people use scopolamine patches to avoid seasickness. It also doesn't work as a truth serum.

Doctors have observed that patients on drugs such as barbiturates or benzodiazepines reveal far more than they would under normal circumstances, and this could be perceived as a kind of truth-telling, but it isn't obvious that a well-trained spy would be as susceptible to this effect. Furthermore, patients using all of these potential "truth drugs" tend to blurt out whatever is crossing their minds, whether a truth or an imagining.

Despite extensive efforts to find one, there is no known effective truth serum. Any effects that these drugs might have seem to come from the idea that subjects under the influence overwhelmingly believe they are unable to lie and hence tell the truth. The psychology behind this is similar to that of any purported effectiveness of polygraphs—the threat of being found out is sometimes enough to cause someone to confess. It has nothing to do with the actual lie detector or truth drug. —REALISM FACTOR: 3

#4: STAYING QUIET
Plausibility Factor: 9 out of 10
Realism Factor: 5 out of 10

CONTEXT
There are some really great headphones you can buy now. If you switch them on but don't play music through them, they still block external sound through a process called active noise control.

In season one's "Snowman," Marshall supplied Sydney and Noah with active noise control armbands for a mission. The idea was that the armbands would cancel out any noise within a few hundred yards as the agents went about their business.

PLAUSIBILITY
Sound travels as a wave, and active noise control devices work by detecting a sound wave and emitting another wave that perfectly cancels out the first, leaving absolute silence. Using this technology in modern headphones ensures you won't be disturbed by outside noise, allowing you to listen without distraction to the sound in the latest episode of *Alias*. —PLAUSIBILITY FACTOR: 9

REALISM
Unfortunately, three-dimensional active noise control would require an extensive set of microphones and speakers spread all around the agents to create the cancellation sound waves. Any noise created outside the zone of the microphones and speakers would not be cancelled; the only noises actually blocked would be those coming from the agents themselves, or whatever else was inside the zone. Still, it's a nice idea, and perhaps in the future we will get close to serious 3-D active noise control. —REALISM FACTOR: 5

#5: STAR MAPS
Plausibility Factor: 9 out of 10
Realism Factor: 9 out of 10

CONTEXT
In "A Broken Heart" (1-4), Sydney retrieved a circular crystal from a church's stained-glass window in Málaga, Spain. In "Time Will Tell" (1-8), Marshall discovered that the crystal, placed in Giovanni Donato's

ancient clock, revealed a star map, a snapshot of the sky taken from a specific location on Earth. Marshall was able to identify the location as Mount Aconcagua, near the border of Chile and Argentina.

PLAUSIBILITY

Although Marshall's deduction seems to be beyond the bounds of reality, our knowledge of astronomy is easily good enough to reconstruct the night sky from any point on the Earth at any time in history. You just have to know how the stars change their patterns over the years—with extremely good precision!

It's a computationally intensive task to find a place based on the stars visible at the time but certainly not beyond Marshall's abilities. A recent calculation done by Kate Spence of the University of Cambridge shows that the great pyramids of Egypt were probably built to line up with particular star formations visible at the time of their construction. In her paper published in the prestigious journal *Nature*, she worked the problem in "Time Will Tell" in reverse, calculating a date for the construction of the pyramids based on what the star patterns would have looked like. She made some assumptions about how the pyramid builders would have aligned the pyramids with certain star patterns on the day of the year corresponding to a religious festival. She then looked at what years had star patterns that would have given the actual configuration of the pyramids. She was able to date the construction of one pyramid within about ten years. Radiocarbon dating only allows estimates within a few hundred years. —PLAUSIBILITY FACTOR: 9

REALISM

With some heavy computing power, Marshall could have easily located where the star map encoded in the crystal was made. The only real difficulty is in believing that the map could have been precise enough to indicate an accurate location. But given the high precision of so many of Rambaldi's devices, I'll give him the benefit of the doubt and say that his star-mapping abilities were up to the task. —REALISM FACTOR: 9

#6: BUSINESS CARDS FOR SERIOUS NETWORKING
Plausibility Factor: 8 out of 10
Realism Factor: 6 out of 10

CONTEXT
Many subplots of *Alias* involve hacking into computer systems in supposedly secure locations around the world. Sometimes Sydney and Vaughn are able to make a hardware link to the system they are infiltrating, but other times they have a more tenuous entry point. In "Doppelganger" (1-5), Marshall designed a business card that, when placed on a computer monitor, could hack into the system.

PLAUSIBILITY
Putting aside the question of Marshall's computer-hacking ability, which has been demonstrated to be phenomenal, how could a business card contain the technology required to do the job?

In recent years, conductive inks have been made that allow the production of a circuit on a business card-sized piece of paper. In fact, the technology is sufficiently advanced that prototype inks that fit in desktop inkjet printers are now in development, and the industry is currently moving toward full-scale manufacturing. Of course, these printable electronics will be useful in far more areas than just espionage. A common device in many manufacturers' minds is the RFID (radio frequency identification tag), now being tested by some large retailers for tracking inventory and distribution. These RFIDs include a small antenna for communication with a reader, so it is entirely possible that Marshall could have printed an antenna that would pick up the emissions all computers give off. —PLAUSIBILITY FACTOR: 8

REALISM
The biggest obstacle to creating these devices in real life is providing enough memory and computational and battery power on the business card to do what is required by the plot. The business card would require more than an RFID, which is fundamentally just a passive device able to be probed by radio waves from a reading device. Marshall's invention would need to transmit and receive its own signals. And yet, there have been recent advances toward printable batteries and other printable electronic components. All of the technologies needed to make the business card work are being developed, but none are yet at the stage of miniaturization or reliability needed to guarantee successful hacking of

a computer system. And whether Marshall could have broken through the security on any computer he was hacking automatically stretches credulity—but he is the computer god, after all. —REALISM FACTOR: 6

#7: SARK'S RADIOACTIVE PERSONALITY
Plausibility Factor: 8 out of 10
Realism Factor: 2 out of 10

CONTEXT
How do you keep track of an enemy agent after releasing him back into the wild? In season one's "Rendezvous," one approach Sloane attempted was giving Sark a glass of expensive wine that contained a radioactive substance. The idea was that the radioactivity could be detected from a satellite, allowing SD-6 to keep track of Sark's whereabouts—at least until the radioactive material decayed away.

PLAUSIBILITY
Radioactive tracers are used in some medical scans to create images of the body, which allows doctors to evaluate how well various internal organs are functioning and to localize disease or tumors. The amount of radiation the body is exposed to in this process is typically similar to that from an x-ray.

In these tests, radioactive isotopes that decay away after a few hours or a few days are either injected into the bloodstream, ingested and absorbed through the stomach, added to blood removed from the patient and reinjected, or injected under the skin. —PLAUSIBILITY FACTOR: 8

REALISM
Even supposing Sark was given a more substantial dose than used in radioisotope imaging, the radioactive emissions from his body would spread out in all directions; a satellite could only pick up those emissions pointed directly at it, and even then only if they were gamma rays, a type of high-energy x-ray. (Other types of radioactive emissions, called alpha and beta emissions, would never make it up to a satellite and are extremely dangerous to have inside your body.) For the emissions to be detectable, Sark would have to have been so dosed up that there would be serious health risks. And even then, there are plenty of natural sources of radioactivity that would dominate Sark's signal.

In the episode, Sark managed to avoid being found by performing a

complete blood transfusion—which has its own set of medical complications and dangers! —REALISM FACTOR: 2

#8: QUANTUM BOMBS
Plausibility Factor: 1 out of 10
Realism Factor: 0 out of 10

CONTEXT
The bombs that appear in *Alias* are impressive for their sophistication
but none more so than those designed by Daniel Ryan in season three's
"Façade." With both Vaughn and Sark on a plane carrying a bomb that
would detonate if the plane fell below a certain altitude, the CIA convinced Ryan to send a code to deactivate the bomb.

Unfortunately, the CIA was duped, and Ryan's call initiated the
bomb's countdown. Meanwhile, Marshall had been working out a way
to deactivate the bomb using an identical one he had in his office. To
his horror, when the bomb on the plane was activated, so was the one in
Marshall's office. Marshall rapidly explained that the bombs were connected by quantum entanglement, which allowed for an instantaneous
link between them no matter how far they were separated.

PLAUSIBILITY
The physics of this scenario is pretty hairy stuff, so hang on! Quantum
entanglement is something that greatly troubled even the great physicist Einstein, who called it "spooky action at a distance." Still today,
many physicists (myself included!) are working to properly understand
the nature of quantum physics and the idea of quantum entanglement,
whereby two particles seem to be inextricably linked even though they
are in different places and have no tangible connection between them.

Experiments show that if you measure one of a pair of entangled particles, the properties of the other, if you were to measure it, are already
determined. It's like if two people on opposite sides of the world had coins
and they both flipped them at the same time. Say one person's coin flip was
heads; then the other person's coin half a world away would be guaranteed
to be tails. This is despite the fact that no signal could pass between them,
because no information can travel faster than the speed of light. It's a pretty
weird idea, but experiments show that it really happens.

It is this concept of entanglement that Ryan had supposedly exploited in his bomb design. If one bomb is activated, the other also activates,

even though there is no signal sent between them—attempting to shield the bombs from external communication would be useless. The concept of the quantum-entangled bomb is at least based on scientific principles. —PLAUSIBILITY FACTOR: 1

REALISM

Unfortunately, quantum physics just doesn't work the way it's described in "Façade." To continue our analogy: Even if the bombs were entangled, activating one bomb would just be like forcing one coin to be flipped. Unfortunately, the result of the coin flip would be random; there would be no way of guaranteeing the behavior of either bomb. Furthermore, it doesn't force the other coin to be flipped, so the bomb in Marshall's office would remain dormant.

No signal is actually sent from one entangled particle to the other when the first is measured (when the coin is flipped). All quantum entanglement talks about is how two separate measurements performed independently can be connected. To get one bomb to do something when the other is activated would require a conventional signal that travels from one to the other. Quantum entanglement just isn't going to help out.

The idea that quantum entanglement can be used to instantaneously transfer information around the universe is appealing and popular but fundamentally wrong. —REALISM FACTOR: 0

#9: WHAT MEMORY?

Plausibility Factor: 4 out of 10
Realism Factor: 3 out of 10

CONTEXT

At the end of *Alias*' second season, Sydney woke up in an alley in Hong Kong with no memory of the previous two years. She wasn't even aware those two years were missing from her life, and much of the third season involved Sydney's attempts to recover her memories of the missing time. We later discovered that the memory removal was intentional.

PLAUSIBILITY

Human memory is a complex and poorly understood phenomenon. We do know a few things about it, but far less than we would like, and memory research is an extremely active field.

It turns out that you can't even just talk about memory as one generic concept. There are at least three distinct types of memory that researchers have identified. These include short-term memory, explicit long-term memory and implicit long-term memory.

Short-term memory lasts a few seconds and is what we use to recall a phone number from the moment we look it up until we finish dialing. Explicit long-term memory is what most people think of as memory—it includes our recollections of people, places, knowledge and conscious acts from our past. Implicit long-term memories are instinctive or conditioned responses, such as how to walk, recognizing a cat or catching a ball.

Sydney still seems to retain all of her implicit long-term memory and seems to have no problems with short-term memory, so it is just a section of her explicit long-term memory that is missing.

One thing researchers do know about memory is that the brain changes physically as it forms memories. The brain sends signals within itself using various mechanisms, but one of its methods uses junctions called synapses that allow signals to be transmitted between nerve cells, and from nerves to muscles or glands. Synapses work by converting the electrical signals that travel through brain cells into chemical signals. As long-term memories form, particular synapses actually change in size and shape. Eric Kandel shared the Nobel Prize in Physiology or Medicine in 2000 for showing how memories are essentially located in the synapses. Stimulating synapses, he proposed, could strengthen them further and, hence, reinforce memory.

But we are not so much interested in how memories are formed as how Sydney could have had her memory erased.

If you know ahead of time that you want to prevent memories forming, there are possibilities. Propranolol, a type of drug called a beta-blocker, is usually used to reduce blood pressure, prevent migraines or treat abnormal heart rhythms. But it is also a key drug in current memory-altering research. It seems that propranolol taken during or immediately after a traumatic event can reduce the strength of memories of the event and disconnect emotional response. However, the effects of propranolol on memory formation are fairly weak and unreliable—people taking propranolol for hypertension seem to create memories without trouble. So this path does not seem a likely one for Sydney to have taken. She would have had to be using propranolol constantly through her two missing years, and even then she would have retained some recollection of her actions. It might have been useful for reducing the psychological and emotional impact of performing horrendous acts on behalf of the Covenant, but she would still remember them.

Some researchers are exploring the possibilities of selectively erasing old memories. One partial success hinges on the discovery that recalling a memory seems to open it up to manipulation, even if the memory is old. While the memory is being recalled, drugs can be used to block its consolidation and even go so far as to erase it. The research, done in rats and fish, has shown there is a second chance to alter memory, despite previous beliefs that memories are consolidated only once, at the time of formation. But in the same research, the scientists showed that only some types of memories are amenable to this sort of modification.
—PLAUSIBILITY FACTOR: 4

REALISM

Selective memory erasure is widely regarded by scientists as impossible. For a start, memory comes in packages. If you remove one memory, you might unintentionally lose something else important. After Sydney woke up in the alley, all of her memories from before the missing years seemed intact, even as far as remembering the location of the safe house and her contacts in Hong Kong. She also seemed to retain all her physical abilities.

Perhaps the most convincing reason to doubt that Sydney could have lost all memory of just those two years is that the brain is far too complex and interconnected to remove precisely the parts wanted without inadvertently turning her into a complete vegetable. And yet, our knowledge of memory and brain function is so primitive that perhaps more substantial memory manipulation will be possible in the future.
—REALISM FACTOR: 3

CONCLUSION: SCIENCE OR SCIENCE FICTION?

Overall, much of what happens in the name of science in *Alias* is unrealistic. But in nearly every case, it is based on something that is either actually possible or on the cutting edge of research. The ideas flirt with the boundaries of reality, which helps keep the show so engaging even for a picky science-type like me. Having a scientific background actually makes the show even more interesting because it challenges me to think about the real science behind the show—and there is almost always real science hiding back there.

Whether you're a science geek or you're just watching the show to drool over Sydney, Vaughn, Sloane, Sark or Irina, there is no doubt that modern science and technology drive the show in far more substantial ways than they do in most television programs. In terms of the science, *Alias* does a better job than just about any other drama on television because it at least tries to base its scenarios on real-world ideas and investigations. In a world where we have suspended disbelief far enough to believe in the characters' existence, we don't need full realism in the science—a plausible basis is enough.

And isn't that very plausibility what makes the show so appealing? Maybe—just maybe—the world of *Alias* could exist on the shadowy outskirts of our own.

David Harris is an Australian physicist and science journalist. He previously presented a popular radio show in which callers would challenge him to answer their scientific questions. In the same spirit, he wrote sixty-five episodes of a television series that answered children's science questions. He has also reported on science for newspapers and magazines, and is founding editor-in-chief of the magazine symmetry, *which focuses on the world of particle physics, synchrotron x-ray science and cosmology. He is currently based in California at Stanford Linear Accelerator Center, which copublishes* symmetry *with Fermi National Accelerator Laboratory.*

SALLY D. STABB, PH.D.

TORTURERS WANTED

Alias is a violent show, physically and psychologically. I remember in season two, in "Abduction" and "A Higher Echelon," Marshall was threatened with severe torture by Dr. Lee (known back then as "suit and glasses"). He also threatened Marshall's beloved mother. As an actor, you have to go places in your mind and soul for scenes like this in order to make the extreme fear feel truthful. Needless to say, that was a difficult day of filming. Yes, it's all pretend and fabricated on sound stage three at Disney in Burbank, California, but we all take a little bit of it home with us each day. I'm just glad Marshall hasn't had to do any of the torturing...although according to Sally Stabb, even Marshall would be capable of it.

> **NOW HIRING: Communications Specialists.** Great employment opportunities with an organization that fits your values. You'll help in the national security effort, learn marketable skills and work on a great team with strong leadership. On-the-job training provided; no previous experience or education necessary.

Of course, you would never answer an ad that said "Torturers Wanted." At least I hope not. But you just might answer the ad for the "Communications Specialist" and down the road find yourself threatening

61

someone's friends and family if he or she doesn't tell you what you want to know, or even beating the crap out of that person if the information is not forthcoming. You'd never do something that evil? You're too moral and too free-thinking? Only crazy sadists do this sort of thing? *Don't bet on it.*

Think. In *Alias*, it's not just Dr. Zhang Lee in the opening episode of the show, threatening Sydney with a sorry-we-ran-out-of-novocaine tooth extraction or, later, Sark strapping Vaughn to a zippy set of electrodes. Our heroes, working for the good guys, also do their share. Nasty interrogations are shown routinely. But hey, it gets to be a routine job—when you're a member of a tight little espionage agency. An insider in the cult of the spy. Let's take a look at how it all happens, shall we?

In Psych 101, we all learn about Stanley Milgram's classic study on obedience to authority. In case you don't remember it, two-thirds of the completely normal, sane, healthy participants in the study administered a full range of up to three hundred volts of electric shocks to a "learner" as punishment for incorrect responses when told to do so by a guy in a white lab coat. We learn about Zimbardo's famous experiment in which completely normal, sane, healthy men were randomly assigned to be "inmates" or "guards" in a simulated prison in the basement of a university psychology department building; the whole thing was called off after six days because the "guards" became too brutal and "prisoners" too disturbed. That's not real life? Can't happen today? *Don't believe it.*

The unpleasant reality is that we consistently underestimate how much our social groups control us. The heads of terrorist organizations know this. Cult leaders know this. Your very own military and intelligence communities know this. SD-6, the Alliance, the Covenant and the CIA work the same way.

They're *all* cults at some level. So if you join up, you become a cult member. Perhaps it's easiest to think of Sloane as the charismatic, messianic-delusional, manipulative leader of a group of unknowing followers who do his bidding without knowing his endgame. Maybe we can wrap our brains around the Covenant as an evil, coercive gang bent on destroying the world with Rambaldi technology, using mind control and torture to help them along the way. But surely (the post-SD-6) Sydney, Vaughn, Jack, Dixon, Marshall and Will are not really cult members. After all, they're fighting the good fight, and we can't truly call the CIA a cult. Or can we? Perhaps a look at the evidence is in order.

MEMBERSHIP RECRUITMENT

All cults recruit members who are usually young (for example, current CIA rules are that you can not be trained for espionage work unless under age thirty-eight) and ideologically vulnerable. Sydney's entrée is shown in flashback as she gets a business card from a nice, friendly, clean-cut looking recruiter on campus. She recounts to her fiancé Danny: "I fit a profile...I felt I didn't belong...since Mom died, I hoped for someone to give my life meaning. That's you...but I met the CIA first."

This is not much different from what is seen in terrorist groups, where expatriated, often educated but aimless youth become drawn back to their religion and countrymen while away, are befriended by others who just happen to be extremists and then adopt their beliefs. In *Alias*, all the main agents seem to be twenty- or thirty-somethings; those who are older and have survived have been in the biz since they were young.

The other recruitment option is to grow your own at home. Children are often raised in cults. Members of terrorist groups such as al-Qaeda put their sons into madrasahs, some of which are mere excuses for raising suicide bombers in the name of the holy jihad. In *Alias*, the KGB's prototype of "Project Christmas" is picked up by the CIA and developed for similar purposes—to raise loyal spies from kiddie level on up. Sydney, of course, was one of these children.

LEGITIMACY

Once on board, cult members, like their leaders, believe they are either saving the world or creating a new world order. A fundamental clash of good and evil is to be resolved in an apocalyptic confrontation; unbelievers will all die and the believers will survive for the rebirth of a purified world. This vision of a divine new world is the inspiration for Sloane's pursuit of the Rambaldi prophecy. The ultimate power of Rambaldi likewise draws the Covenant, whose members speak of a "second coming," a savior who must be created from Sydney's eggs and Rambaldi's DNA. There are cryptic mystical predictions such as, "The Passenger and The Chosen One will battle. . . ." From the CIA's point of view, their mission, equally fervent, is to prevent the Rambaldi prophecy from ever being realized. The CIA's brave new world is one purged of the evils of those represented by Sloane and the Covenant. This visionary ideology is a big part of what keeps Sydney, Vaughn and Jack working for the CIA. It is what brings Dixon back in and what keeps Marshall in government work when he could no doubt make a private fortune in industry.

Modern cults incorporate a scientific aspect for legitimacy, and the organizations in *Alias* are no exception. High technology is engaged in the service of the epic battle between good and evil. The allure of the ancient Rambaldi legacy is partly due to its surprising link to current or even future science: underwater topographic maps, the heart machine or embedded memories that have been passed along genetically and can be "revived" through neurochemical green gook. In addition, there are nuclear and biological weapons that the Alliance/SD-6/the Covenant often attempt to acquire. The fact that global extinction is a realistic, empirical possibility on Earth today both enhances the realism of *Alias* and hooks what may be some viewers' deepest fears about violent terroristic and religious cults.

FITTING IN

Related to the ultimate confrontation of good and evil, all cults cultivate a deep "us versus them" mentality. Cult leaders and high-ranking members seek to create an in-group, a consensual social environment that reduces uncertainty and provides identification for their followers. Anyone not on the inside is designated as one of "The Others," an outgroup to be denigrated, despised and destroyed. Early on in the series, Sydney realized how her SD-6 counterparts (who do not yet know they aren't CIA) perceive Sloane: "They don't know how evil he is." She then vowed, periodically throughout the series, to kill him. Sharp lines are thus drawn between those who deserve to exist and those who don't. "The Others" are set up as the source of all distress, thereby justifying violence against them. Within this "ideology of antagonism" (Staub, 183), anything good that happens to "the Other" inflames hostility, and the world would be a better place without "the Other." Countless examples of this dynamic are seen in *Alias*...when we can tell who is in which group. Part of what keeps *Alias* interesting is that we don't always know who is a bad guy; loyalties switch, there are double agents and multiple betrayals. Who is us? Who is them? But Sydney, Vaughn, Dixon and Will are consistently reassuring touchstones in locating the good guys. And of course, the Good Guys R Us.

While conversion to a cult often involves very honest and earnest beliefs on the part of new members with whom the organization shares its values, these internal processes are manipulated and held in place by a whole series of external consequences and controls. "Engineering" or "brainwashing" converts involves psychological, physical and often financial influence. Social roles, rules and boundaries are restructured. Sydney can't talk to her friends about her work. She can't be a normal friend; she can't have a normal romantic relationship with anyone. She must live in constant fear that her friends may be endangered by her participation at SD-6 and then the CIA. If they know too much, they may be killed (Danny) or tortured (Will). Dixon wrestles with these threats as well, as his wife is killed and his children abducted in revenge for his CIA participation. This makes it tempting for all of them to remain even more firmly inside the group. Sydney and Dixon can talk to Jack or Vaughn because they are fellow followers in the CIA organization. Outsiders become dangerous, not to be trusted. You never know who your real friends are once you step outside the comfort of the cult.

LA FAMILIA

Cults also try to ensure the loyalty of their members from the inside. It is not uncommon for members to be encouraged to rat on each other for potentially treasonous actions. So you may not even know who your allies are within your organization. Everybody is always scoping out everyone else:

> JACK (to Vaughn): Why did you pull my file?
> VAUGHN: What were you doing checking up on me checking up on you? ("Color-Blind," 1-7)

In a two-faced turnaround, the CIA therapist, Dr. Barnett, tells Vaughn: "It's all confidential...but I have reports...." At various points in the series, Sloane has Jack investigated at SD-6, and Dixon has Sydney checked out. At the CIA, Jack has Vaughn investigated, Lindsey has Jack investigated, Jack has Lauren investigated, and the list goes on. The CIA, FBI and NSC, who are supposed to be allies, snoop on each other, too, checking out suspicions, playing out turf wars and one-upmanship games.

Truthful data is at a premium in cults, but not easy to come by, because cults systematically control the flow of information to which followers have access. Leaders, and sometimes those higher up in the cult hierarchy, often have total power over the distribution of information and selectively share that data on a "need to know" basis with followers. Jack is very high in the CIA chain of command (perhaps higher than we have been told thus far). He can get to computer files, documents and resources that most others cannot. He only allows Sydney, Vaughn, Dixon and others access to information when he considers the time right. Kendall has access to an entire facility (the Black Hole in Nevada) that is secret from most of his own CIA people. Different tasks are compartmentalized within the CIA, and agents in these projects may not be aware of each other's activities—although their superiors will be. Sloane, while with SD-6 and the Alliance, did likewise. When the Covenant tried to brainwash Sydney, it attempted to take total control of information released to her, breaking down her old personality and values and hoping to replace those with an entirely new identity and set of beliefs.

Once in a cult, information is slanted by the use of unique language, which is used to solidify group identity. Code names, abbreviations and specialized terms ("Op Tech") serve this purpose, as well as having military security functions. "The Chosen" and "The Passenger" are both names endowed with special, powerful meanings known only to insiders. When Vaughn goes out into the field and becomes "Boy Scout" he (and we, as vicarious viewers) plays on the human desire to transcend and escape one's own identity and destiny. In fact, changing names and creating new personal information—having an alias—seem to be part of the attraction of spy stuff in general. Who among us hasn't daydreamed of becoming someone else, somewhere else, and starting all over again? Cults provide this opportunity. The CIA and the Covenant provide this opportunity.

LEADERSHIP SKILLS A MUST

Strong leaders are key to the success of cults. In religious cults, charismatic leaders are necessary, and such groups often fall apart when their leaders leave. Sloane is a classic religious charismatic leader: persuasive, possessed of divine guidance (according to himself) and obsessed. While in control of SD-6, for example, he did all the things we see cult leaders do: he was not accountable to others and could do things mere followers could not. He could induce guilt, threaten or enforce rules in order to control members. He had the power to inflict suffering and to end suffering. He presented himself as spontaneous and mystically enlightened to his followers, while they had no knowledge of his heavy manipulation behind the scenes. He could inflame the passions of SD-6 members, keeping them emotionally agitated, anxious or righteously angry. Members who dared to critique him would be encouraged to reconsider their *own* faults, thus making *them* the ones who were deficient or evil in some way. Sloane shared his special, occult and privileged information only with clearly loyal members (Jack; and even then, not completely). Higher authority in religious cults goes unquestioned. Setting aside Jack's double-agent status, no one at SD-6 thought someone else besides Sloane should be in power. Whenever it happened, those who found out that they were lied to about Sloane's true nature and the mission of SD-6 were terribly upset and shaken; this included Sydney, Dixon and Marshall.

In political/terroristic cults, strong leaders are valued and encouraged, but these organizations often survive a change in leadership. Seats at the Alliance table shift, but for a long time the Alliance stays intact, with multiple units across the globe. This was revealed to a startled Sydney early on, when Vaughn showed her the Alliance map. The CIA in *Alias* functions more in this political cult mode. Kendall leaves temporarily, and the CIA itself survives, despite the passing reign of the unsavory Robert Lindsey. Jack is always there in some position of power and authority. At the CIA, interestingly, Sydney, Vaughn and Jack all question the highest level of the CIA leadership. However, none of them question the CIA's ultimate mission—and the authority to carry out that mission.

In all cults, leaders and followers are locked into a cycle of mutual need to regulate uncertainty. As a follower, Sydney looks to her father, Vaughn (as her handler), Kendall or even her mother Irina (more dangerous) for guidance. She used to look to Sloane, too, before she knew the truth about him. Sydney is especially vulnerable to the kind of influences leaders show in cults (or SD-6 or the CIA) because she has a long-term, old and deep insecurity from her chaotic upbringing.

On their own side, cult leaders need to see themselves as infallible. Jack struggles with this, as he still berates himself for being deceived by Irina decades ago; he works tirelessly to protect Sydney, as well as to gain and then maintain her trust. Sloane is routinely sent into bouts of intense action whenever he cannot see or control all events around him.

ALL IN THE FAMILY

Speaking of chaotic upbringing, if *Alias* isn't Dysfunctional Family Feud in spy gear, I don't know what is! This is another domain in which cultic influences are echoed throughout the organizations in *Alias*. In cults, family relationships are frequently manipulated and often broken. Cult leaders often try to split families apart so that loyalty will remain only to them, or in order to coerce members to obey. Almost every family relationship presented in *Alias* has been warped in some way by the CIA, SD-6, the Alliance or the Covenant. Women who are double agents marry men in order to further the gains of the group to whom they owe original loyalty: Jack/Irina, Vaughn/Lauren, Will/Francie. (Oddly, this never happens in reverse, though.)

Family members are routinely threatened or made to do things without their consent. In addition to the death of Dixon's wife, the kidnapping of his children and the murder of Sydney's first fiancé by SD-6, there is the computer programmer Kaplan, who was taken by the Covenant, separated from his wife and children, who are held hostage, and thereby made to do the Covenant's bidding. Kids are manipulated to fit the long-term goals of these organizations. The CIA's "Project Christmas," in which Sydney was raised, and its KGB counterpart fit this mold as well, as do some current terroristic cult practices. Parental authority over children is undermined; parents may be shamed or humiliated in front of children so kids will switch loyalty to cult leaders. Children are often abused in cults, and although in *Alias* children are certainly scared, often tied up and gagged, the more aggressive forms of abuse are not shown. (Ratings might not hold up so well if children, not just adults, were tortured.)

Cults attempt to become "fictive families" (Whitsett, 492) and demand a level of commitment similar to that seen in abusive families. Sloane often talked about SD-6 as a family early in the series, waxing moony over his love for Sydney as a daughter. The CIA folks also try to promote this kind of environment. In cults, however, family, usually the center of love and devotion, becomes a battlefield. This is clearly seen throughout *Alias*, as family loyalties are questioned, tried and often but not always betrayed. Sydney swings back and forth between trust and doubt regarding both her parents. She is justifiably angry when her father withholds personal information about her in the interests of the CIA. Here's a typical series of comments from Sydney to her dad from early in the second season:

"I should have believed you."

"I'd like to believe you but I don't trust you at all."

She agonized about her relationship with her mother when Irina resurfaced, alive. Sydney had to rework her entire history and identity when Irina was back on the scene. A source of both intense suffering (Irina shoots Sydney) and connection (stories of her childhood, small gifts, cooperation via useful information), Irina's unknown loyalties and Sydney's devotion to the mission of the CIA make for a twisted family picture indeed, to say nothing of the fireworks when Irina, Jack and Sydney were on a joint operation together in Kashmir! Bickering parents must be told how to behave by their uppity daughter, and the family that happily kills together can't get beyond their own past histories and organizational allegiances.

Sloane appears to have an uncorrupted love for his wife, to the point of faking her death in order to keep from having to kill her for real in order to obtain a seat at the Alliance table. Being at the head of his organization's hierarchy, perhaps he can afford to try to keep his family relationships intact, a luxury that others below him cannot share.

Both Sark and Vaughn have had fathers who have been killed as a result of their involvement with their respective espionage agencies. Vaughn's father, killed in the line of duty protecting Sydney's sister as a child, is glorified by the CIA, and his dutiful son carries on the sacred mission. Sark, on the other hand, is portrayed as the rageful, neglected child who had a hand in his own father's murder, with motives for his father's fortune and for revenge. The point, however, is that both these father-son relationships have been substantially altered by their entanglement with these cultlike organizations.

THE KICKER

Of course, if all the cult techniques already described aren't enough to keep everyone in line, obedience to the cult's leaders and mission may be enforced by greater punishments.

There is always torture.

Torture or death may come to those who attempt to leave or betray the group. While this happens in *Alias*, interrogation and torture are most often illustrated in their use against out-groups, whoever they may be. The CIA, SD-6, the Alliance and the Covenant all torture each other when it is deemed necessary. Interrogation's purpose is to get information; torture's purpose is to demoralize the victim, make an example of him or her, to break the will. But it is a slippery slope between the two, and one often merges with the other.

There is some evidence that certain individuals may be more likely to accept torture training than others. Good torturers do like clear systems of hierarchy, order and predictability. They like to be led, as well as to have power over those lower than they are. They may also want to progress through the cult or military system, as does Sark. He is always number two to someone, and is referred to as "a dog who always comes back to his master" by Sloane; he is likewise controlled by Irina and Katya. He will willingly torture to show his loyalty and to advance.

In cults, as in terrorist groups and military/intelligence agencies, however, torture can be taught. Most torturers are not warped sickos who get off on pain; they are technicians. Interrogation and torture training develops progressive changes in thought patterns and socialization forces, resulting in individuals who are ready to harm others. Here's how it's done.

First, there will be sanctions for not doing it. If torturers don't follow through, the torture technique is likely to be turned against them. So that's motivation number one. Motivation number two is the greater cause or goal—the end justifies the means; information must be extracted so that the overall mission, which is Right and True and Just, can be completed. Motivation number three is the rationalization of one's own horrid behavior. Since evidence from the victim is needed to vindicate the torture itself, it must continue until that information is obtained.

Torturers also have to distance themselves from their victims, often by thinking of them as less than human. They are scum, they are beasts, the lowest of the low. The more inhuman the victim becomes in reality, for example by unearthly, animallike screaming, the easier it is. Torturers can also create distance through language, often using euphemisms. They don't interrogate or torture; they go to "The Conversation Room." They don't kill innocent women and children when they bomb enemy targets; rather, the enemy incurs "collateral damage."

Among the other dynamics that allow torture to occur are those most shameful to admit. The feeling of power is heady. The more you do it, the easier it gets; either through desensitization or learning to like it, or both.

Interrogation techniques that involve threats or are psychological in nature actually tend to be more effective than corporeal means. People often become acclimated to bodily pain; severe pain often elicits inaccurate info, just to get torturer to stop. Remember Sydney's stint in the CIA detention center courtesy of Director Lindsey? Duped by the big, sloppy, childlike cellmate ("Campbell") next to her, she talked rather than see him tortured. Lindsey gloated, "Your psych profile shows your weakness is empathy. It's harder for you than physical torture."

Interrogation and torture occur in many *Alias* episodes. Almost the entire spectrum of techniques is used. Most of these strategies induce a profound sense of powerlessness, hopelessness and helplessness when the victim's life becomes dependent on the interrogator's/torturer's whims. This is considered a highly desirable state of affairs for the torturer, conducive to either of the favored goals of gaining information or of destroying the victim's sense of self, identity and worldview. Common ways of inducing people to give up information include:

- threats of awful things happening to the victim, his or her family and friends; betrayal; physical torture or more intense torture. The more vague the threat the better, thus allowing the victim's imagination to run wild.
- use of drugs and/or hypnosis. The CIA explored these options extensively in the 1950s through the 1970s. This included LSD (not effective), marijuana and sodium pentothal ("truth serum"), which lowers inhibitions but does not alter deep-seated convictions.
- isolation
- monotony/sensory deprivation
- exposure to extremes of heat and cold
- exhaustion
- restraint
- humiliation
- deprivation of food, water, clothing, sanitation
- unpredictability of life/death, light/dark, favors/punishments, food/starvation, time; uncertainty itself is a motivational force.
- shaking (nice because it doesn't leave marks)
- slapping, hitting, shoving, punching, kicking
- being forced to stand or to sit in awkward positions for days
- electric shock (often to genitals)
- pins, needles, cutting (including amputation)
- burning
- whipping (back, soles of feet, etc.)
- other forms of sexual torture (I won't go into the details, but suffice

it to say that the author had some nightmares after reading first-hand accounts of this material.)

New technologies that are not as invasive as the techniques noted above are being developed to try to detect lying and to be used in interrogation (MRI brain scans, infrared scanners for facial heat), but these are controversial and not field tested. Old-fashioned lie detectors don't work. And as Knight says, "A machine has yet to be developed that makes the human interviewer redundant." On *Alias*, the human "interviewer" is very much a presence, always ready to serve in the cosmic clash between good and evil.

REALITY BITES

And now for a shrinky digression: *the most unrealistic part of* Alias *is that no one suffers lasting effects from his or her torture or interrogations, or from being the one who tortures and interrogates.* The range and intensity of symptoms that would occur given the degree of harm that Sydney, Vaughn, Jack or any other *Alias* character has suffered would be mondo serious. Depression, exhaustion, numbing, sleeplessness with nightmares, impaired memory and concentration, anxiety, hyperarousal, social withdrawal, apathy, headaches, intrusive memories, rages, impaired relationships, dissociation, alcohol or drug (ab)use and sexual difficulties would top the list. No one is immune to these, regardless of his or her training or preparation. You can compartmentalize, deny or dissociate—but you will not be well.

The one possible exception to the *Alias* rule that torture and interrogation have no lasting effects is when Sydney came out of her two-year amnesia. This is the only thing that really bothers her on a long-term basis. Has she been "brainwashed"? What did she do in the two years she was with the Covenant? Techniques of "brainwashing" overlap with torture/interrogation and with cult dynamics. Torture is used to break down the former self, and then, through control of information, systems of reinforced and punished beliefs and hypnotic suggestion, a new personality is constructed.

During her period of amnesia recovery, Sydney agreed, reluctantly, to go into therapy. This is the only time in the show she did so voluntarily. Here other survivors talked about their post-traumatic stress disorder symptoms, and Sydney was shown to have flashbacks. These ended up being helpful, though they were scary and didn't last long; a pretty darn naïve scenario. We also discovered that while initially there was the suggestion that Sydney had been converted and had shed her identity and become someone else, we found out eventually that she "never broke" and that she pretended to be with the Covenant the whole time. Her lack of memory for the whole two years was attributed to a previous hypnotic induction by her father when Sydney was a child. Jack supposedly "installed" a "fail-safe" mechanism in her brain so that she would never give in. The ability to do this in real life is questionable.

What is not questionable is that on *Alias*, the good guys do all the same stuff that the bad guys do, but are perceived as okay and justified in their actions. We want to believe that Sydney, Vaughn and Jack are good and that their cause is the right cause. This ability to rationalize makes the behavior of these CIA members seem okay, even though it is the mirror image of SD-6, Alliance or Covenant members' behavior. When we do this, violence is in fact more likely and more to be condoned. *As viewers, we're indoctrinated into the cult of the CIA just as the* Alias *characters are.*

So keep in mind what Philip Zimbardo, past president of the American Psychological Association, has written: ". . . when systematically practiced by state-sanctioned police, military or destructive cults, mind control can induce false confessions, create converts who willingly torture or kill...work tirelessly, give up their money—and even their lives—for 'the cause'" (310).

Still, I'm not sure I've convinced my readers that it's not just messed-up, dysfunctional people who can torture. You'd never fall for that flakey, new-agey cult caca. I'm pretty sure you'd like to believe you are strong, independent, a master or mistresses of your own fate. You'd be in that one-third of participants in Milgram's study who didn't give all the shocks. You're a good person, on the side of what is Right, True and Just. You don't thoughtlessly conform to group pressure. You make your own decisions, untainted by the influence of others or ideologies.

Wanna find out for sure? Go ahead and answer that ad!

Hey, kids! For more fun via the Internet, check out these Web sites, where the now declassified early CIA interrogation manuals are available! This is a Web address to the revised manual declassified in 1983 called the *Human Resource Exploitation Training Manual*: www2.gwu. edu/~nsarchiv/NSAEBB/NSAEBB27/02-04.htm. An address to the KUBARK manual is listed below: www2.gwu.edu/~nsarchiv/NSAEBB/

NSAEBB27/01-01.htm. Both of these links were obtained from the National Security Archive, which can be found at www2.gwu.edu/~nsarchiv/nsa/the_archive.html.

Thinking about doing something better than just satisfying your prurient interest in nastiness? Try:

- The International Policy Institute for Counter-Terrorism: www.ict.org.il/
- The Coalition to Stop the Use of Child Soldiers: www.child-soldiers.org/
- The Global Security Organization: www.globalsecurity.org/
- The Center for Victims of Torture: www.cvt.org/

BIBLIOGRAPHY

Beit-Hallahmi, Benjamin. "Apocalyptic Dreams and Religious Ideologies: Losing and Saving Self and World." *Psychoanalytic Review,* 90 4 (2003): 403–439.

Berkowitz, Leonard. "Evil Is More Than Banal: Situationism and the Concept of Evil." *Personality and Social Psychology Review,* 3 3 (1999): 246–253.

Bohm, Jonathan, and Laurence Alison. "An Exploratory Study in Methods of Distinguishing Destructive Cults." *Psychology, Crime and Law,* 7 2 (2001): 133–165.

Bowden, Mark. "The Dark Art of Interrogation." *The Atlantic Monthly* Oct. 2003: 51–76.

Brothers, Doris. "Clutching at Certainty: Thoughts on the Coercive Grip of Cult-like Groups: Comment." *Group,* 27 2–3 (2003): 79–88.

Centner, Christopher M. "Cults and Terrorism: Similarities and Differences." *Cultic Studies Review,* 2 2 (2003).

Darley, John M. "Methods for the Study of Evil-doing Actions." *Personality and Social Psychology Review,* 3 3 (1999): 269–275.

Dingfelder, Sadie F. "Fatal Friendships." *APA Monitor on Psychology Magazine* Nov. 2004: 20–21.

Knight, Jonathan. "The Truth About Lying." *Nature* 15 Apr. 2004: 692–694.

Langone, Michael D. "Cults, Conversion, Science, and Harm." *Cultic Studies Review,* 1 2 (2002): 178–186.

Lewis, James R., and David G. Bromley. "The Cult Withdrawal Syndrome: A Case of Misattribution of Cause?" *Journal for the Scientific Study of Religion, 26* 4 (1987): 508–523.

Lifton, Robert Jay. "Beyond Armageddon: New Patterns of Ultimate Violence." *Modern Psychoanalysis,* 22 1 (1997): 17–29.

———. "Doctors and Torture." *The New England Journal of Medicine, 351* 5 (2004): 415–416.

Miller, Arthur G., and Anne K. Gordon, and Amy M. Buddie. "Accounting for Evil and Cruelty: Is to Explain to Condone?" *Personality and Social Psychology Review,* 3 3 (1999): 254–268.

Mullin, Barbara-Ann, and Michael A. Hogg. "Motivations for Group Membership: The Role of Subjective Importance and Uncertainty Reduction." *Basic and Applied Social Psychology,* 21 2 (1999): 91–103.

O'Rourke, Norm. "Vigorous Shaking of Political Prisoners as a Means of Interrogation: Physical, Affective, and Neuropsychological Sequelae." *Politics and the Life Sciences,* 18 1 (1999): 31–36.

Pomerantz, Jay M. "Analyzing the Terrorist Mind." *Drug Benefit Trends,* 13 12 (2001): 2–3.

Ross, Colin A. *BLUEBIRD: Deliberate Creation of Multiple Personality by Psychiatrists.* Richardson, TX: Manitou Communications, Inc., 2000.

Schwartz, Lita Linzer, and Florence W. Kaslow. "The Cult Phenomenon: A Turn of the Century Update." *American Journal of Family Therapy,* 29 1 (2001): 13–22.

Staub, Ervin. "The Roots of Evil: Social Conditions, Culture, Personality, and Basic Human Needs." *Personality and Social Psychology Review,* 3 (1999): 179–192.

"True Lies." *Nature* 15 Apr. 2004: 679.

Walsh, Yvonne. "Deconstructing 'Brainwashing' within Cults as an Aid to Counselling Psychologists." *Counselling Psychology Quarterly,* 14 2 (2001): 119–129.

Whitsett, Doni, and Stephen A. Kent. "Cults and Families." *Families in Society,* 84 4 (2003): 491–502.

Wilson, John P., and Beverley Raphael, eds. *International Handbook of Traumatic Stress Syndromes.* New York: Kluwer Academic Publishers, 1993.

Zimbardo, Philip G. "Mind Control: Psychological Reality or Mindless Rhetoric?" *Cultic Studies Review,* 1 3 (2002): 309–311.

Sally D. Stabb is an associate professor of counseling psychology at Texas Woman's University and a licensed psychologist. Her teaching and research interests include gender and emotion, sexuality, qualitative methods and other nerdy stuff. When not doing the professor thing, she enjoys travel, ethnic food/music/art/dance, reading, scuba diving, cooking, Scrabble and spending time with her sig-o (Martin) and her girlfriends. She is a serious amateur (twelve plus years) in the study of Middle Eastern dance.

TRACY S. MORRIS

GEEK CHIC

This introduction is surprisingly difficult to write. What can I objectively say about my portrayal of Marshall J. Flinkman? I will say, it's always been a welcome challenge to balance his single-minded, techno-geek persona with the sweeter, more vulnerable aspects of the character, like his insecurity and his lack of people skills. I think that's why there has been such a positive response to Marshall: he's a real person. When Marshall's on a mission, it's like we're all on that mission. It's real—he's in danger, and we feel for him in ways we don't for super-capable Sydney. We've all met someone like Marshall...at work, or even at home. Marshall is appealing because he reminds us of ourselves. Oh, alright—maybe it's just the hair. . . .

BLAME MY COFFEEMAKER.

That's my excuse.

It's a complicated little gadget. It's supposed to turn itself on and off, brew my java, do the dishes, walk the dog and make me lose fifty pounds.

Well, it is!

But I can't even get it programmed, and frankly, that's a little embarrassing.

That's why I like Marshall. I realize that I should love *Alias* because of the butt-kicking action, that somewhere down deep, I should feel proud that there are strong female leads in dynamic blah de blah blah. Been there, done that. Buffy anyone?

Marshall. The slightly goofy, ever-so-smart technophile who designs those easy-to-use, friendly-yet-lethal gadgets that Sydney employs each episode to overthrow third world despots in her quest for Rambaldi artifacts and Kool-Aid hair dye.

I'll admit Marshall wasn't my favorite character at first. With an ensemble cast, it's hard for everyone to get face time. Between wincing at Sydney's accidental adventures in dental hygiene and keeping up with the scorecard of new characters, Marshall was barely a blip on the radar.

However, by the second episode, Marshall made me sit up and take note with his introduction of the sleeping disk: "I accidentally touched this the other day, and I fell and knocked my head on the desk and was out cold for twenty minutes. You guys should see this." At which point he pointed to a bandage on the back of his head.

More great moments like that followed: Marshall's inflatable couch, his conspiracy theories linking Eliza Doolittle and Dr. Doolittle, his casual mentioning of monkey documentaries.

I couldn't help it; I was hooked. I think Marshall is, to use his own word, superswank. He may be quirky, but I'm a sucker for quirky. Especially smart quirky.

Marshall is Q to Sydney's James Bond. Only much cooler. Throughout the 007 series, Q remained the most basic of stock characters. Like the six-foot-tall Ninja Turtle that I had taped to my door as a little girl, Q was a cardboard character who remained in the background. Besides, Marshall can invent circles around Q.

Sure, Q came up with some great toys. But did he ever stop to take into account how much weight a rocket launcher adds to a car? Or what that extra weight would do to the fuel mileage? During each Bond film, I kept waiting in breathless anticipation to see if 007 was going to run out of gas during the critical chase scene. Marshall would not only design the car with the rocket launcher, he would figure out how to make it lighter and find a more efficient fuel so that Sydney wouldn't run the risk of getting stranded in the middle of Moscow with the plans for the latest supersecret weapon of mass destruction stuffed in her bra.

So what makes Marshall my character of choice on *Alias*? Why do so many other terrific ones walk home with the consolation prize? Sydney is a great actionista (as opposed to a Sandinista, who she might be overthrowing in any given episode), but in the end she's just Mrs. Peel with a slightly better arsenal and a lot more hair dye. Vaughn is too mercurial in his affections. And Jack...Jack is a completely different essay.

The answer goes back to my coffeemaker: Marshall could program it so that even I could use it.

Coffeemakers worry me. We need them to fuel our caffeine-driven lives, but they deny us this basic desire, smugly, by refusing to be easy to use.

Electronics don't bother Marshall. In fact, I bet that he could rebuild my coffeemaker so that it could also make julienne fries while it was concocting an extra frothy mocha deluxe latte.

Sydney speaks seven or eight languages, knows kung fu, chair fu, cell fu and fu fu, and performs them while looking great in leather. But she probably can't program her TiVo. I'll bet she calls Marshall to help:

"Marshall, I can't go find Rambaldi's used toothbrush if I miss *Smallville!*"

That's what makes Marshall a champion to the everyman. Most of us don't have a friend like Sydney, and don't really want one. I don't need someone to come busting into my workplace to beat up my boss and overthrow him, freeing me from the tyranny of my nine-to-five job. Being liberated from my nine-to-five means I'm also liberated from my pesky paycheck. And look at what happened to Francie and Will! But if there was someone who would just come busting into my home (gently, by using the doorknob) and hook up my entertainment system, I would call that man my hero.

And I'm not alone. As technology takes over our lives, the geeks have replaced the jocks as our idols. Call it geek chic. Geeks aren't just working their way into our culture. They're here. Geeks are the outsiders, and being an outsider is cool and sexy (but only if you can program my computer, show me how to use my DVD player or look like Keanu Reeves).

Part of what makes geeks sexy is the sweet vulnerable side that they're not afraid to show (unlike the bad boys of the world). Marshall is at his sweetest when he is, like in "Cypher" (2-3), disclosing his not-so-secret crush on Sydney: "Because if you're stuck in the ducts when the rocket launches, then, well, boom. And I'd miss you."

Television has plenty of examples of this kind of sexy vulnerability in characters. Think of Willow on *Buffy the Vampire Slayer*, Mulder on *The X-Files* or Jared on *The Pretender*.

Vulnerability equals cuddly. As one person put it on a message board: "Marshall is my own personal Ewok."

Now, everyone on *Alias* is technologically savvy. Sydney's TiVo aside, she can still crack a safe just as casually as she cracks some heads. Even faux

Francie (Fauxrancie?) was able to hack the CIA's database using a Web site for bouillabaisse. (Don't you hate it when something like that happens?)

But among the chic of the beautiful spy people, only Marshall is a true geek. Consider the evidence.

First, his mother fixation. In "The Abduction" (2-10), Marshall was still living with his mother. I'm certain that he made enough money on SD-6's payroll to afford his own apartment, so I can only assume that he chose to live at home. Marshall asked Sydney to bring back touristy snapshots from her assignment for good old mom so that he could pass them off as his own. And when he finally got sent on a mission of his own, the first person he called upon returning home? You guessed it! Mommy dearest.

Second, his social awkwardness. Marshall has to speak in front of the rest of his spy buddies a lot. Think about it. He comes up with a new gadget or three every time there is some world crisis. Then he has to explain how they work. This is a guy who studies polar bear hair for its insulating properties. He builds lock picks into medals, and cameras into tubes of lipstick. He must come up with a new toy every five seconds.

Despite all this, he's still a social toddler. Every time he talks his way into a verbal cul-de-sac or does something silly like accidentally cutting off his own tie, his coworkers wince in sympathy or roll their eyes in frustration. It's as if they want to pat him on the head and send him back to his office with the adult equivalent of a boppy pillow and a paccie.

There were probably times that Sloane used to sit around on a slow day (because he could, and he's eeeevil) inventing emergencies just to see if Marshall could actually build a cell phone into that little Monopoly dog, and then watched the fun as he tried to explain it to Jack.

Lastly, the name. Marshall Flinkman. Need I say more?

Yet for all his geek moments, Marshall is still cool. This is where the chic part of geek chic comes into play.

In "A Higher Echelon" (2-11), when Marshall was captured by an enemy and faced hideous torture, he survived by using his brains and his wits. First, he bought himself time by agreeing to reconstruct a coveted computer program. Then, he sent a distress signal to his friends under the cover of downloading some mp3s.

Later in the same episode, he saved both himself and Sydney, his would-be rescuer, by using a jacket that he had converted into a parachute to aide their escape. (Forget the CIA; he could make a mint marketing that to base jumpers!)

Even during those briefings when Marshall is at his geekiest, you don't feel bad for him. Yes, he may be socially hobbled, but his technological wizardry shines through. In the end, he's no social pariah. His quirks become endearing. His personality becomes sweet. His character becomes cool. His geekiness is his best asset.

Let's face it: *Alias* is really about the quest for the ultimate geek. I'm talking, of course, about Rambaldi. The Nostradamus/Leonardo da Vinci hybrid character who was writing code before computers, analyzing DNA before Mendel and putting orchids into stasis pods as a hobby.

In the quest for the ultimate geek, Marshall has more than held his own. Why? Here's my theory: Marshall *is* Rambaldi.

Consider it: *Alias* hints that Rambaldi unlocked the secrets to eternal life. He was a genius (he foresaw cellular phones during the Italian Renaissance), and he was apparently fixated on Sydney.

Marshall toys with Rambaldi-esque inventions. And he's pretty attached to Sydney. If Rambaldi managed to survive to this day, he would want to hide from the CIA, the KGB, K-Directorate, SD-6 and the Covenant. Not to mention any other Johnny-come-lately superspy group with sinister capital letters and an unhealthy interest in him and his inventions. What better place to hide than in plain sight as a modern-day genius tinkerer?

We live in a society where our telephones are smarter than we are, and figuring out our digital cameras makes us want to hide in the closet. They sit on our shelves, collecting dust and accusing us. *You don't even use me. If you were smarter, you would figure me out.*

And every week, there's Marshall (whoever he may be), reassuringly inventing gadgets that can reprogram the International Space Station with the touch of a button, and without a technical manual the size of the *Encyclopedia Britannica*.

Marshall doesn't need a sports car with a rocket launcher in the trunk. All he needs is a few tools, and a coffeemaker.

When not watching Alias *or being intimidated by gadgetry, Tracy S. Morris is a writer of funny fantasy, silly science fiction and the occasional serious news story. Her first novel,* Tranquility, *a Southern/science fiction/mystery/oddity novel, is available from Yard Dog Press, along with Bill Allen's Gods and Other Children. Her fantasy humor chapbook,* Medieval Misfits, *is also available from Yard Dog Press.*

Tracy lives in Fort Smith, Arkansas, with her husband, dog and three hyperactive ferrets. The ferrets are in charge. You can find out more about Tracy's work at her Web page, www.tracysmorris.com.

ROBERT STOKES

ALIAS AND THE REAL DEAL
A REALITY CHECK

All of us actors on the set often joke about the plausibility of Alias. I mean, "Wheels up in an hour"??? How can Syd, Vaughn and Dixon get packed and ready to go in an hour? How can you pick your outfits out so quickly? Who's in charge of snacks for the plane? But Alias is, after all, television. I usually tell people that the show should be taken with a grain of salt: it's hyper-realism, folks, based on actual research but taken to the next level of fantasy. Robert Stokes has good critiques, but even he comes to the same conclusion we did: Don't analyze it too much—just sit back and enjoy the ride.

LIAS, THE ABC-TV HIT ESPIONAGE DRAMA, has to be a wet dream for CIA officials—and I'm not referring to actress Jennifer Garner, who plays the kick-butt, covert agent babe for the Agency's L.A.-based counterterrorism operation.

I'm talking about the unlimited resources in money, superhuman field agents, high-tech magic, logistics and material that the *Alias* CIA counterterrorism chief has at the snap of a finger. You can bet the ranch that if ex-CIA director George Tenet had anything approaching that level of assets, plus better liaison with the FBI, it might have been an entirely different story on 9/11.

Tenet was having breakfast on Capitol Hill when he got word of the first plane hitting the north tower of the World Trade Center that bright

September morning. His response: "I hope it doesn't turn out to be that guy from Minneapolis who was taking flying lessons but didn't want to know about takeoffs or landings."

Under the law, domestic terrorism is the FBI's responsibility, but CIA's Tenet clearly did not walk back the cat on that intelligence.

However, in creator J. J. Abrams' *Alias* CIA, Sydney and her lover/ fellow field agent, Vaughn, would have said, "Screw the rules," and already nailed the dude days before 9/11 and had him in a "black, level 6" (unlisted and highly classified) Department of Defense interrogation facility. He'd have been spilling his guts within hours of the first reports that came over Director Dixon's desk. In *Alias*, the CIA does not provide its detainee list to the ACLU or the International Red Cross and does not apologize for it.

Okay, I understand this is Hollywood's take on the CIA and its hot flashes for the James Bond-style Black Ops. But if Abrams is trying to figure out why the ratings went south during season three (despite eight Emmy nominations, viewership dropped 9 percent), he might consider dialing back on the fantasy missions and crafting episodes closer to the real deal.

With apologies to *Alias* addicts everywhere, let me point out some of the more egregious gaps between the flawed, problematic grind of real-world espionage operations as practiced by the CIA and the other-world reality of missions impossible conducted by Agent Sydney Bristow and company each week on ABC.

Transportation: *Alias'* agents have a fleet of corporate jets at their disposal 24-7 for last-minute jaunts to exotic ports of call. Compare this to the reality of CIA agents who must fly commercial coach or depend on the Department of Defense for rides. This is often on a space-available basis in the mind-numbing fuselage of military C-141 and C-17 transports that offer collapsible plastic seats and military Meals, Ready-to-Eat (MREs) for snacks. Ditto for helicopters. The transportation budget for CIA agents in *Alias* could feed the entire African continent.

Languages: According to new CIA director Rep. Porter Goss, one of the reasons the real CIA has not been able to gather better "HUMINT" (human intelligence) for many years is the lack of field operatives who speak foreign languages like a native and are up to speed on the culture of the country they are spying on. Not so with Sydney and Vaughn, who seem to be fluent in the language of every country they parachute into, ranging from Russia, North Korea and the Arabic Middle East to Japan, China and the former Yugoslavia. As an added bonus, Sydney even reads lips. I didn't know they taught that at "The Farm." Next season, Agent Bristow may even show off her "remote viewing" (mind reading, in the civilian vernacular) capabilities.

Martial Arts: It's true that field agents are given some basic training in self-defense at "The Farm," the CIA's Virginia field training facility, but no one without many years of daily training, including a black belt in a hard-style karate, would be able to do the types of lethal kicks, sweeps, joint locks and takedowns that Sydney Bristow demonstrates. I am a Ni-Dan (second-degree black belt) in Seido, a Japanese hard karate style adapted from Mas Oyama's Kyokushinkai. It took me fifteen years of training to earn it.

Unlimited Funding: How does Jack Bristow, Sydney's veteran covert agent dad, come up with the stacks of greenbacks conveniently stashed in a secret storage bin safe off the property to finance a $3 million operation to break Sydney out of a highly secure DOD interrogation facility unless he's skimming off the books? Is there anyone in *Alias'* CIA watching the bottom line? Doesn't seem so. Perhaps Abrams is implying that because the majority of the U.S. Intelligence budget is for "Black Ops," and therefore only available to those with a Need To Know, no one is checking that closely. Not so in the case of convicted spy Aldrich Ames. Ames, the CIA spy who was caught selling secrets to the Russians in 1994 and given life without parole, was earning a GS-14 salary at the time of his arrest—less than $80,000 a year. No wonder he was moonlighting. The reason Ames got caught: his uptown lifestyle that included driving a new Jag and buying a $600,000 house with cash.

Technology: This aspect of *Alias* is probably closest to the real-time technology now available to most intelligence agencies due to the miniaturization of audio listening devices, buttonhole cameras, microchips and spy satellites circling the Earth. What is not so real is the operational perfection of the Op Tech toys produced by Marshall, the dweeby tech genius of *Alias.* Murphy's Law generally rules in terms of technology on an operation. If there is a possibility of a screwup, it will happen. And then there was the episode with the inflatable Kevlar that drew the lethal response from the security system, saving Sydney and Vaughn's butts. Okay, Marshall. If you say so.

No Liaison with Local Station Chiefs: When Agent Bristow is dispatched on an operation, she never checks in with the local chief of station. In the real CIA, this would be considered a huge breach of protocol. Anytime a field operation is launched in a foreign city, it's standard procedure to alert the local station chief. These are sensitive turf issues. There are times when "NOCs" (nonofficial cover), deep cover CIA agents, operate without the knowledge of local Agency assets, but that is normally a long-term operation and not a tactical smash-and-grab foray.

Alias' *Los Angeles Base of Operations*: Being based in L.A. is certainly convenient for the *Alias* CIA, its cast and its creator, Abrams, who lives there, but in reality it would never happen. All tactical and strategic CIA operations originate from the headquarters in Langley, Virginia. For legal and pragmatic reasons, the CIA would not have a major operational activity in a U.S. city except for a one-person liaison office in major hubs, i.e., New York, Chicago and L.A. When Sark was masquerading as a CIA agent in North Korea, he told a potential defector, "I'm based in the Portland office." Was that a deliberate lie or a boner on the part of the scriptwriter?

Alias' *Tactical Ops*: When the real CIA conducts a snatch operation or an op where the target is heavily armed and dangerous, it calls on its paramilitary assets to provide the firepower—backed up by Navy SEALs; Army Delta Force; or Grey Fox, a supersecret paramilitary team under Task Force 121, a secret man-hunting unit formed by Defense Secretary Donald Rumsfeld for the war on terrorism to find Saddam Hussein, Osama bin Laden and other high-value targets. There is a distinct difference between covert CIA agents who conduct traditional spying operations against target countries and paramilitary types who operate in quasi-combat roles in places like Afghanistan, Iraq and Bosnia. But in the world of *Alias*, the two agents are morphed into one. One of the legendary CIA agents who combined combat experience with clandestine tradecraft was William Buckley. But even his twenty years of spy and survivor skills were not able to prevent him from being captured and tortured to death in Beirut in March 1984.

Bomb Defusing with the Clock Ticking: This scenario clearly ratchets up the drama of *Alias* episodes and is intended to move the audience to the edge of their Barcaloungers. Added to the moment is the stuttering and hand wringing of Marshall, as he directs "Mountaineer" or "Boy Scout" to cut wires on the bomb to stop the relentless countdown to disaster. But whoa, folks! In real life, bomb disposal experts use the same approach with most devices: If it's ticking, they're outta there. If it's not ticking, they attach a "disrupter" to the explosive device. The disrupter uses a high-speed water jet—fifteen feet per second—to separate the detonator connection from the explosive charge. As a general rule, live explosive devices cannot—and should not—be disarmed manually. Those who have tried are no longer around to explain why they failed.

Wall of Honor: After Sydney returned from "the dead" in an episode, she and her father, Jack, passed a list of names of agents in the foyer of the *Alias* L.A. headquarters. As the camera focused on Sydney's name, Jack said, "I'll make sure they remove it by tomorrow." I know it makes for high TV drama, but the reality is that back at the CIA's Langley headquarters, while there is a plaque in the lobby that honors agents killed in action, no names are used—only stars. Identities of real CIA agents are considered secret even in death.

Execution of Arvin Sloane: Most *Alias* fans would gladly turn the tap on the lethal injection of Mr. Sloane, the amoral double agent with a heart of stone. But what kind of a message is the show communicating here, that the U.S Government has the power to interrogate and execute people guilty of violating national security without due process? I'm the first to concede that the recently revealed strategy of "extraordinary rendition" used by the CIA to snatch terrorist suspects and ship them to a foreign country for hard-core interrogation does not place the U.S. in the most favorable light. But the process of the Sloane "execution" portrayed the U.S. as a country that's nothing more than some macho Latin American junta run amok. Not only was this Star Chamber execution asking the viewer to suspend belief way past cool, but the cocktail given to Sloane by Jack Bristow to neutralize the fatal poison is way over the top—shades of the zombie movies. All we needed was a Haitian drum soundtrack and the ghost of Papa Doc.

Alias' Agent Relationships: There is a cardinal rule in almost every intelligence organization throughout the world: there is to be no involvement, sexually or emotionally, between clandestine operatives. Sure, it happens, but once the relationship is out in the open, there is no way that the CIA or any self-respecting intelligence agency would permit a male and female agent to continue working together, particularly in a sensitive and dangerous undercover role. Yet in *Alias*, Sydney continued to go on missions with Vaughn despite her anger with him, especially after he chose not to wait for her during her two-year hostage sojourn.

All this said, I concede that like *Alias* addicts everywhere, I am ready to suspend belief and get on with the new season, desperate for a new fix from the exploits of Sydney, Vaughn and company.

What sinister surprises still await Agent Bristow and the rest of the newly formed CIA Black Ops group APO? Will Jack turn out to be the ultimate double agent after all, still conniving with not-really-dead double-agent wife Irina on some sort of Manchurian Candidate gig to use their daughter, Sydney, for some nefarious means to an end?

We're waiting, J. J.

Robert Stokes is a novelist, playwright and former journalist with Newsweek *and* Life *magazines who served in Army Intelligence in the 1960s in West Germany. Stokes is collaborating with Martin Kaiser on a memoir entitled* Odyssey of an Eavesdropper: The King of Electronic Countermeasures, *to be published by Carroll and Graf in 2005.*

J O D Y   L Y N N   N Y E

WHY SYDNEY HAS NO SOCIAL LIFE

This should be required reading for all new (and even returning) writers on Alias. This is all the work that would have to go on behind the CIA scenes, as it were. I never truly thought about how much time and effort would actually be required to be a top-notch field agent. I guess it's a good thing Marshall's mostly stuck in the office! Keeps it simple!

THE MISSIONS WE ENJOY SEEING on *Alias* are like the tip of the iceberg of Sydney Bristow's efforts for the CIA (or, formerly, SD-6): only 10 percent of the actual preparation and execution makes for good viewing. Behind every successful caper pulled is a tremendous amount of research, training, briefing, fact-checking, debriefing, recovery and follow-up. The fact that Sydney has not been killed, maimed severely (apart from a two-year memory lapse), fallen irretrievably into enemy hands or gone out of her mind is a tribute to the excellence of the wide-ranging team of experts behind her, natural resilience and rigorous training—although being a fictional character in a show improbable enough to be termed "spy-fi" likely helps.

Naturally, an agent who is going to be in the field and doing as many things as our heroine is must be conversant in many arts and sciences, few of which she is likely to have learned during her upbringing, no matter what her father did for a living. A good basic education is invaluable for a potential agent, but it is also necessary that she come equipped with natural strength, flexibility (both of mind and body) and a willingness to learn more very, very quickly.

BASIC TRAINING

Before her first mission Sydney Bristow would almost certainly have gone through a boot camp of sorts lasting six months to two years. We saw very little of her initial involvement with SD-6, so we don't know if she had to maintain an ordinary-seeming life as a cover for her earliest training, or spent that time at a facility far away from her home. If the former, then she would have had to set up a domestic arrangement that fit her cover, with an eye toward security that would prevent casual visitors from receiving any inkling of her secret training. She would have needed to take care with her preparations and inspect her living quarters on a regular basis to insure that it wasn't under electronic or physical surveillance. If the latter, a suitable excuse for her extended absence would have been required, as well as the creation of documents to back it up: letters home, for instance, from a study abroad program.

During her training, Sydney must have become an expert in basic unarmed martial arts, at a minimum karate and aikido, and Krav Maga, a specialty of the Israeli Defense Forces. These would have built upon her natural abilities through training in single exercises, katas and open bouts until she automatically reacted to defend herself without having to think. She would also have needed a grounding in armed martial arts as well, probably kendo, skills with knives and other edged weapons, bo sticks and lesser blunt instruments, and throwing weapons of all kinds. Fencing was likely also included, to keep her supple and strong and to teach her to watch her opponent's eyes rather than his weapon. Once she reached a certain level of expertise in these skills, she would need to train constantly to keep them fresh. She would also be working on strength training. A course of free weights every other day would prevent her muscles from weakening, while the interval would keep them from becoming overstressed.

While her body was being trained, she would also have begun to study armaments. She has shown throughout the aired seasons of *Alias* that she is an expert at loading and firing almost anything with a trigger. Sydney would have been instructed in guns, from popguns all the way up to railguns, studying their structure, types of ammunition, weaknesses and quirks, as well as which end the bullet comes out. She would need to know how to assemble, disassemble, load, repair, improvise ammunition for (when possible) and clean and maintain any kind of gun. Examples of weaponry from every nation would be at her service, along with experts to show her how they work. She would need to learn to identify ammunition by sight, quickly recalling its destructive and penetrative potential. All these skills can only be achieved by practice and constant re-familiarization.

Her training would include not only how to load and fire these weapons, but also how to identify each by the sound of a bullet fired out of the gun, muffled and unmuffled. She would learn to identify each silencer by type, and to count bullets while she is under fire. She has demonstrated that she knows not only to count bullets and ascertain how many are usually in a magazine for the kind of weapon being used, but to listen for the sound of said magazine being ejected and hitting the floor, muffled and unmuffled by carpet or other softening agents, and the sound of a new cartridge being shoved into place. All of these skills can be vital for a field agent's survival, and Sydney's abilities have saved her life time and again.

She would need to maintain skills in marksmanship, rating at least "expert" in frequent tests, and receive updates on recently introduced weapons. She would also work out where on her person it would be best to carry certain devices, balancing ease of access against how heavy or awkward a device would be to convey to her target site.

Besides pistols, rifles and automatic weapons, she would have to have a basic knowledge of munitions. She would certainly have been shown examples of how they are constructed in all of the countries within the Geneva Convention and, more importantly, outside of it, because a field agent without help is far more likely to have to defuse a bomb planted by someone who belongs to an enemy nation or terrorist force than one planted by an ally—although this is not certain in today's atmosphere. One of the elements of grave importance is that the wires used in timers that lead to positive, negative and ground are different colors in different countries, so snipping a black wire might have just the opposite effect from the one she intended. Sydney would be best served by learning how *not* to set off a suspicious device, and how to get away from it before it can explode. Discretion, as the cliché goes, is often the better part of valor, and certainly the best part of survival.

There are also times when Sydney *does* need to blow something up. When Marshall has not furnished her with one of his nifty little devices, or it fails or has been taken from her, she must know how to improvise.

Instruction in destructive chemistry is likely to be offered to an agent who has been assigned such a mission. She would need to know a good deal about the destructive force of each type of explosive, along with power supplies, fuses, the friability of explosive agents and hundreds of other facts, such as how to tell when aging TNT is more dangerous to attempt to move than to wire to a timer.

Certain other basic chemistry skills are necessary for a secret agent. It's really embarrassing to find oneself poisoned or given knockout drops by someone who one was planning to knock out or kill oneself. She needs to be familiar with the smell and appearance of soporifics, hypnotics and hallucinogens, and to be wary of the drugs that cannot be seen or tasted, such as Rohypnol. Sydney would have to put in some time in a chemistry lab learning reactions.

Finally, Sydney would also have been trained in surveillance, both electronic and line-of-sight. She might keep in practice by picking a subject at random and following him or her. Equally, she must ensure that she is not followed, overheard or observed, either by fellow agents practicing their skills, or by enemy agents.

DEPARTMENT Q

Let's just assume that a beginning field agent is not James Bond. *Most* agents are not James Bond. They obey instructions, they follow the mission and they do not get distracted by extraneous circumstances. Therefore, when they are issued a piece of specialized equipment, such as one of Marshall's inventions, they are expected to return it to the point of issue intact, if not in perfect working order. If such a thing is not possible, explanations WILL be required, and will have to be in the field report. Sydney would receive a detailed briefing, when there is time, on each item she is issued.

If she discovers a fascinating and useful device in the course of a mission, she would be expected to turn it in in the best condition possible and deliver a debriefing of any information she has gleaned about it.

SURVIVAL

Penalties are most often severe for anyone caught committing espionage within international borders. Being shot on the spot is not uncommon.

Being imprisoned and held for possible exchange for prisoners held by one's own government would be a more fortunate circumstance, though the agent must anticipate that she will be subject to harsh treatment and torture. The job of field agent automatically entails danger; Sydney understands that she might be captured or killed on any mission, but if she let that fear overwhelm her, she would no longer be effective in the field. It takes an extraordinary mind, already attuned to survival, to be a field agent. It's up to the Department to have trained her in the skills that will let her do so.

It is an agent's duty to escape from captivity if possible, thereby obviating the necessity for the Department to negotiate for her release. Survival training would help Sydney learn to be resourceful, to adapt any tool at hand to a weapon or a means of communication, or to help her achieve basic food and shelter. She would learn everything a Scout does: how to make fire, how to find water, how to make her way to a designated point based on the stars, sunrise and sunset.

Rope skills are also vital, including all knots. An agent has to be able to deadlift at a minimum his or her own weight, if not more. Practical application includes hauling oneself up and down cliffs, buildings, ropes or in and out of places where there is no other access than a small hatch at the top of a sheer wall. Training would likely be accomplished using standard Army field packs in order to simulate heavy equipment. She would have taken Ranger School to enable her to make parachute insertions into enemy territory, possibly including HALO (high-altitude, low-opening) jumps, and has certainly had experience with parasails. Skills would include knowing how to free herself from a snagged chute and how to land on various types of terrain. She would have to know how to swim well for at least one mile, in cold water, and how to remain underwater for over a minute.

The Department also has resources for more specialized skills. Training on safe-cracking, picking locks and outwitting computerized security systems might be handled by a reformed burglar, in the same way that a hacker often finds him or herself employed by the very computer company whose hard drives he or she has been blithely dancing through. Thanks to Marshall's techno-toys, Sydney only has to be able to recognize basic interface equipment in order to attach a gizmo that will download or upload programs—information covered in the standard briefing—but the means of accessing such secure locations can only be accomplished if she is trained to get in where no enemy wishes her to go.

Sydney has to know life-saving techniques such as CPR and basic first aid. She has often been in a situation where she has had to bind her own wounds or those of a fellow agent or rescue subject.

PASSING FOR NORMAL

At a minimum, Sydney needs to speak four languages well besides English: Parisian French, Russian, one or more dialects of Chinese, and Arabic. According to her official files she speaks at least thirteen. Her initial training would cover basic conversation in these four with native speakers. She would need to become and remain familiar with each of these languages. Rapid immersion courses would be tailored to the specialist topic one is discussing with a foreign subject, teaching technical and accepted terms dealing with such specifics as diplomacy, guns, drugs, diamonds, smuggling humans, kidnapping, arson and various other subjects. She would need to be equally conversant in making and understanding threats. To pass without detection among the average "man on the street," Sydney would also need to master the niceties of making small talk in these languages. Subtleties of language cannot be overestimated, because it is these small things that usually reveal one as a nonnative speaker. Languages change from day to day to accommodate new concepts and products. Reports from bureaus around the world would be coming into the CIA daily with news and other cultural information, to be incorporated into language lessons. Other languages would be added according to need. While fluency in one language other than one's mother tongue increases the facility for learning others, a linguist still needs to practice each individually to avoid accidentally using words or phrases from others (the "how you say...?" factor).

Current events are very important for an agent to understand. Briefings would be provided weekly, if not daily—if, indeed, not hourly. In volatile international situations, such as the ongoing crisis in the Middle East, constant monitoring of people and places involved, and diplomacy and other interventions, must be maintained. These reports would be widely available throughout the Department on a general basis. Specialized, detailed mission briefings would be provided to agents depending upon specific assignments. Sydney would have to absorb all of the pertinent information, keeping the subtleties of each country and culture in mind.

Camouflage and concealment on the ground is vital, though odds are unlikely that Sydney would find herself in a rural situation. It is much more likely that she would have to conceal herself within an urban environment, to blend in with the crowd if possible, and then to find places of concealment in buildings. A study of architecture with an emphasis on ventilation ductwork and plumbing access would give her an insight into places that most people would overlook.

DISGUISE

Most of the things that Sydney Bristow gets away with are purely dumb luck. Because of the advent of face-recognition technology, someone with features like hers—eyes set fairly close together, a strong jaw and prominent lips—is going to be very easily detected with even a low-resolution brand of face-recognition software, or the passing glance of someone who has seen her before. A course in theatrical makeup would give her good grounding for more subtle disguises that will fool the naked eye of a guard or an acquaintance. As long as technology is out of the reach of many of the CIA's targets, or taken for granted by the ones who have it, then it will continue to be possible to use simple techniques to pass unscrutinized. Cheek pads, nose shadowing, latex, fake scars, built-up features, wigs, the modern equivalent of nose putty, contact lenses and spectacles: all of the tricks of the theatrical trade would be at the hands of the field agent. Such things can be improvised and should be when necessary. Many of the chemical compounds that are used to make theatrical makeup are fairly simple and could be synthesized on the spot using materials from any corner drugstore in most areas of the world.

To assist in carrying off a subterfuge, acting lessons would also serve the field agent well, teaching her to be aware of her personal physical quirks and allowing her to subdue them to make herself less recognizable. Attitude helps. Sydney has often plunged right past guards who might have recognized her as an intruder had she not shown them by her demeanor that she belonged there. Confidence provides entrée where timidity invites detection.

Clothing should always be appropriate to the situation. Gone are the days when government agents could be identified by their white socks and dark suits. Nor are they all men anymore. Sydney dresses in high fashion where appropriate. Her model-like physique allows her to wear provocative outfits that keep observers from paying attention to the identity of the woman beneath the clothes. Because she is slender she can also fit into nearly any uniform she can capture along the way.

Most of the time she will want to pass as unobtrusively as possible. For that the CIA would provide her with briefings as to how women dress in the specific locale, with details of makeup, hair and jewelry. It's not out of line to suggest that some of the latter might be Marshall's gizmos in disguise. Sydney might also be able to consult with experts in the locale to which she has been assigned, for details in how to carry off wearing a specific outfit. Acting proficiency alone will not suffice when encumbered with an unfamiliar garment such as a burqa or a sari.

The Department's clothing allowance would hardly extend to a couturier wardrobe, but tailors and designers on staff or from a trusted outsource company could make look-alike garments to measure. Such manufacture is painstaking and complicated. At least two fittings, probably three, would be necessary for any unusual outfit. For covert operations, Sydney has worn jumpsuits of nonreflective fabric with non-Velcro fastenings on pockets and pouches. Her garments need to be thin, light and soft, since she often wears them underneath street clothing or more formal attire and on occasion has to discard them after obtaining her mission's aim. Such jumpsuits, which can be crunched up into a very small volume, aren't available off-the-rack.

TRANSPORT

Defensive driving is a necessity for a field agent. Being a safe driver is a basic requirement. Although agents who are often in hot spots become adrenaline junkies, it can draw too much attention if one is a hot dog behind the wheel. The aim is to keep a low profile, driving the way that the rest of the traffic does, which means in London one drives "deferentially," in Milan anything goes, and in Pasadena...anything goes. Fleeing and eluding, or, by nature, stunt driving, would also be overseen by specialists, to give the agent confidence behind the wheel. Basic courses would have been included in the first six-month training period, and renewed after that by expert instructors, as needed. Refresher courses in new road signs and driving rules would be offered according to assignment.

Every field agent needs to, of necessity, know how to fly a plane or a helicopter, and drive all motorcycles from Vespas up to Harley-Davidsons, an all-terrain vehicle, a jet ski and a hovercraft. She must also be able to manage a boat, whether motorized, sail or row, and any kind of motor vehicle, including trucks—especially those with manual transmissions, as that is what is in use in most of the world. She must be able to drive left-hand or right-hand drives, over all types of terrain without flipping over, in all weathers.

An agent would be required to be up-to-date on types of aircraft being built; the specs would be provided by the manufacturers. Knowing how much a device costs is not as important as knowing how much fuel it will hold, how much it will expend by the hour and how to make it go. Of primary importance is knowing how much runway a jet will need. Most frequently, one will be taking off from a location in which the jet was successfully landed previously, and can rely on having sufficient runway space. Being able to determine whether or not the place one is planning to land it is of adequate size, however, requires knowing how to read flight maps and identify potential landing sites in an emergency, as well as spotting small airports. Fortunately for the American field agent the default language of aviation worldwide is English, with few exceptions—but an agent on assignment should be prepared for those exceptions. A working knowledge of the above-mentioned basic languages and a smattering of Korean should suffice, though when one is going to land in a hostile environment such as Korea, one is probably not asking for landing permission from ground control.

MISCELLANEOUS

Mental focus must come naturally to a field agent. She must learn to concentrate on the task at hand to the exclusion of all else, and not be distracted by extraneous circumstances. When she runs into other agents whom she knows to be working for other nations or organizations, it is not necessary to stop them from whatever it is they're doing unless their mission interferes with her own. That said, it is always wise to report the other person's presence to the field office. Knowing when to interfere, knowing when to step forward, is a matter of experience. Knowing that one *should* is a matter of training.

Other vital skills include instant memorization, since it's considered amateurish to ask someone on whom you're eavesdropping to repeat instructions or to speak more slowly and clearly. Also useful is a knack for memorizing and being able to reproduce touch-tone telephone numbers one has heard being dialed. Marshall's devices might not always be available to read the entire dialing history of a telephone, and like many circumstances in espionage, you only get one shot. Hopefully. (As opposed to firing squads, the traditional penalty for unsuccessful spies, which usually have more.)

Let's examine a typical day in Sydney's life. At a conservative estimate, taking into account eight hours for sleep, Sydney's daily regimen would require an hour or more for personal grooming, and two to three hours for meals. A sweep of her premises and car for listening or surveillance devices would eat up an hour two or three times a week, or more frequently during periods of higher national security alert. Understanding the traffic patterns of the Los Angeles area, Sydney would have to set aside a minimum of an hour round trip for travel time between her apartment and the CIA campus. Once she arrived in the office, she would review messages or directives from her superiors, then spend an hour or more reading the current news to keep up on world affairs and reading, viewing or listening to secure briefings for her next mission. If she had recently returned from a mission, she would need to devote as many as several hours per day for one or more days to debriefings, thereby putting her other activities behind schedule.

Her other activities would include one to five hours of physical training, self-defense and target practice, an hour or so for language practice, both in languages in which she is currently fluent and intensive immersion in new languages she will require for future missions, and memorization of pertinent facts, building layouts, faces and names, and techniques. She might also be called upon to test equipment, stand still for garment fittings, be trained in the use of new weaponry or other equipment, or assist in the interviewing of a contact or suspect in the custody of the CIA, each of which would take up at least a half hour of her day. At this point, Sydney is looking, at minimum, at only two hours out of every twenty-four not eaten up by work or basic survival activities.

Her previous cover of pretending to be a college student involved further study, not to mention homework and sitting for exams. Admittedly, Sydney missed a lot of school. Her second cover as a traveling executive for Credit Dauphine, an international bank, was much better, since it did not require further time commitments. Still, once you add in time to grocery shop (an hour or more a week), do laundry (two to three hours), maintain a vehicle (up to half a day monthly) and clean an apartment (an hour daily), there is almost no time left in which she might conceivably interact with other human beings not inside the Department. Coffee with a personable man she might meet at the Laundromat or over the tomato bin in the supermarket would have to be balanced against the time it would take to run a security check on him, whether she ought to cut into her precious sleep time in favor of a date and whether that time might be better used toward her next assignment.

In the best interests of her country, and for the sake of a higher calling, Sydney has devoted herself to making what some would see as the supreme sacrifice for a personable young woman: the death of her social life. It looks as though poor Sydney's only hope is that there's one more Rambaldi device out there, one that can slow the rotation of the Earth and stretch her days out to thirty hours, or perhaps a leisurely forty-eight or more.

Fortunately, in *Alias*, an invention like that is no more unlikely than her schedule.

Jody Lynn Nye lists her main career activity as "spoiling cats." She lives northwest of Chicago with two of the above and her husband, author and packager Bill Fawcett. She has written over thirty books, including The Ship Who Won *with Anne McCaffrey; a humorous anthology about mothers,* Don't Forget Your Spacesuit, Dear; *and over seventy short stories. Her latest books are* Strong-Arm Tactics *(Meisha Merlin) and* Myth-Taken Identity, *cowritten with Robert Asprin (Meisha Merlin).*

PSYCHOLOGICAL PROFILE: SUBJECT J. J. ABRAMS

I know Misty K. Hook's analysis of J. J. was intended to be tongue-in-cheek, but I have to say I was still a bit shocked by the findings of this detailed analysis. I've known J. J. for six years, and all I can say is that he is a talented, caring, altruistic, fearless leader who trusted me to help bring his vision to life. (Oh, and his parents are also really sweet.)

MEMORANDUM
DATE: January 17, 2005
TO: Special Agent Misty K. Hook, Ph.D.
FROM: Section Chief, PsyOps
RE: Psychological profile of J. J. Abrams, creator of *Alias*

As you know, during our staff meeting of January 14, concerns were raised about the television show *Alias*. It was stated that the show provides unacceptable illumination of the inner workings of the Central Intelligence Agency and is extremely accurate about the mental status of our field agents. Attention has focused on J. J. Abrams, the creative force behind the show. It was suggested that either he is making uncannily precise guesses about our operations (particularly about the little-known existence of Black Ops sections) or that he may have a mole within the agency who is feeding him information. In order to assess the level of risk, we need for you to complete a psychological profile of subject Abrams in order to determine if he is a threat to the CIA and, if so, how best we can intervene.

MEMORANDUM
DATE: January 18, 2005
To: Section Chief, PsyOps
FROM: Special Agent Misty K. Hook, Ph.D.
RE: Psychological profile of J. J. Abrams, creator of *Alias*

Given the covert nature of the assignment you suggest, I will be unable to speak directly with the friends, family, coworkers and employees of subject Abrams. As such, it will be exceedingly difficult to provide an accurate assessment of him. I recommend utilizing an alternate plan, perhaps the covert observation we usually employ.

MEMORANDUM
DATE: January 20, 2005
To: Special Agent Misty K. Hook, Ph.D.
FROM: Section Chief, PsyOps
RE: Psychological profile of J. J. Abrams, creator of *Alias*

The usual covert observation will not work in this situation. We really need the profile. You're the psychologist—find a way to make it work! You have a week from today.

MEMORANDUM
DATE: January 26, 2005
To: Section Chief, PsyOps
FROM: Special Agent Misty K. Hook, Ph.D.
RE: Psychological profile of J. J. Abrams, creator of *Alias*

Given the limitations of the assignment, the following psychological profile is based upon basic biographical knowledge, public interviews and the creative output of Abrams himself. My research led me to believe that much of his psyche is embedded within his artistic creations. As such, it was this area that provided me with the richest data. As requested, my conclusions and recommendations about future directions regarding this situation are included after my general profile.

BASIC IDENTIFYING INFORMATION

Jeffrey J. Abrams (usually called J. J.) is a thirty-eight-year-old, married, Jewish, Caucasian male. He is the son of Gerald, a TV and movie producer, and Carol, a law professor and award-winning producer and writer. He has one sister, Tracy, who has done some screenwriting, including working alongside her brother on *Felicity* (despite the overshadowing nature of J. J.'s success, there is no evidence of sibling rivalry). Although the family is somewhat close in terms of visiting each other and they put on a good public face, psychological underpinnings of dysfunction are present. The time-intensive and prolific nature of his parents' careers led to benign neglect in terms of the general care and nurturance of J. J.'s psyche (see section on diagnostic rationale for more on this).

Subject Abrams was born in New York but was raised in Los Angeles. From all reports, J. J. began to get interested in the entertainment industry at the age of eight when his grandfather took him on a tour of a studio. Given his parents' work in the industry, it is likely that he became interested in entertainment earlier and for a much more psychologically validating reason (i.e., their interest and approval). However, it is significant that this is the accepted story about how he developed his vocational interests. J. J. closely identified with his grandfather, since he fulfilled the emotional void left by his parents. He regarded him as the significant father figure and someone who helped him develop his self-image. He has been quoted as stating that it was his grandfather who made him appreciate his Jewish heritage.

Subject Abrams attended Sarah Lawrence College in Bronxville, New York, but dropped out before receiving his degree. He started working in the entertainment industry, first with sound effects and moving later to being a writer, director, producer and sometime actor and composer. He was a writer for such popular movies as *Regarding Henry*, *Forever Young* and *Armageddon* but came to real prominence with his creation and direction of the TV shows *Felicity* in 1998, *Alias* in 2001 and *Lost* in 2004. He has a wife and two children. Interestingly, I could find very little information on any of them.

GENERAL DIAGNOSIS

Subject Abrams has a mild form of Bipolar I Disorder with recurrent manic episodes. While he does have depressive periods, his most frequent mood is manic. Many colleagues and interviewers have described him as exceedingly talkative, exhibiting racing thoughts, easily distracted, having increased goal-directed activity and psychomotor agitation and demonstrating a decreased need for sleep. Additionally, the empirical evidence documenting solid correlations between creativity and mental illness (usually depression or mania) provides a further basis for my diagnosis. There are times that you can see bipolar tendencies reflected in the tone of individual *Alias* episodes. Sydney Bristow (the main character) frequently shows her depressive side while many of the action sequences have a kind of manic presence to them. Given the mildness of subject Abrams' disorder, the frenetic pace at which he lives often comes across as extremely productive and admirable. It is doubtful that those around him see his disorder as harmful. Instead, they accept his "down" periods as inevitable and depend upon his mania as a way to get many things done at once.

DIAGNOSTIC RATIONALE

At this time, the bipolar disorder is not adversely affecting subject Abrams, at least professionally. He is a man who is incredibly creative and productive; he uses his mania toward professional gain. In fact, all evidence suggests that he is a workaholic. Anyone who has as many projects going on simultaneously as Abrams does must live his job. However, his workaholism, while quite lucrative, can cause his personal life to suffer. Although Abrams is married and has children, they don't see him frequently, and, when at home, he has difficulty focusing his attention upon them. Additionally, subject Abrams has difficulty forming and maintaining close personal friendships. While he does have many colleagues and some "good" friends, his work schedule leaves little time for socializing, thereby giving him a culturally acceptable rationale for his psychological distance.

This difficulty with romantic and emotional intimacy provides evidence to support the fact that subject Abrams is still trying to settle some unresolved aspects of his psychosocial development. The inconsistency in his caregivers and subsequent avoidant attachment to his parents led to a lack of trust in people, heightened insecurities and distrust of the world around him. This was then followed by difficulty in being truly intimate with others, fear of commitment and a belief that relationships result in heartache. Although both parents were equally unavailable to him emotionally, he is more distrustful of women. This is due to the high expectations placed on women as nurturers (see sections below for further details on this).

DEVELOPMENTAL REGRESSION

As is common with people who suffer setbacks in developmental milestones, subject Abrams' development has regressed to a point during early adolescence. The nature of his bipolar disorder makes him intense and emotionally labile (exhibiting rapid mood fluctuation)—characteristics of the adolescent period. It is clear that part of his ego is mired in adolescent delights: the joy in the simple things, comic books and the utmost loyalty to the friends who bolster his self-esteem. His logo—the one that designates a J. J. Abrams show—is "Bad Robot," a clunky, amateurish robot that is reminiscent of the Transformers toys that were popular when he was a boy. This toy serves as an illustration of subject Abrams' ego identification with a time in his life when he was emotionally successful.

An avid following of the comic books of his youth is another symptom of his developmental regression. All the signs are there in the *Alias* universe. The comic books he read as a child were filled with huge action scenes, despicable villains, exotic locales, intense character development and irritating cliff-hangers. *Alias*, especially during its first season, contained all of those elements. Sydney Bristow, a serious globe-trotter, battled evil people in fights that sometimes were so choreographed that you could almost see the "Wham!" illuminated in the dust unsettled by her superpowered kicks. Each show ended with Sydney stuck in a jam that was resolved the following week. However, as subject Abrams did some personal growth, as the series progressed, so did the complex intrigue, sophisticated narrative and character growth.

Another feature of concern is subject Abrams' need to surround himself with people whom he knows well. He does not appear to seek out novel situations or stimuli but stays within his comfort zone. Once he develops an attachment with someone, he finds it difficult to let go. This tendency has its foundation in Abrams' unresolved psychosocial development and his family dysfunction. His feelings of anxiety and insecurity, as well as his difficulty with trust and intimacy, all serve as obstacles to the development of close personal relationships. However, once he has gotten over the hurdle of knowing someone well, he or she increases his self-esteem. Since subject Abrams' self-image is one of someone difficult to love, people who do care for him are reminders that he is lovable. Hence, he wants them close. Many of the actors on *Alias* (including star Jennifer Garner) are people he first met during his work on *Felicity*. Moreover, the fact that his best friend from kindergarten, Greg Grunberg, is on hand for every one of Abrams' projects is now part of the lore surrounding Abrams himself.

FAMILY CONSIDERATIONS – FATHER GIANTS

Gerald Abrams is a controlling and emotionally withholding father who looms larger than life. During subject Abrams' formative years, Gerald's vocation bled into his personal life as he sought to control family life as well as he did the TV and movie stories he produced. Moreover, the intense nature of his work resulted in his physical and emotional un-availability to his son. Young J. J.'s interest in the entertainment industry was an attempt to get his father to reward him with a hug or even a stately, "I'm proud of you, son!" However, subject Abrams came away from those encounters empty-handed. Consequently, he now projects his internal struggles to gain approval from his father onto his artistic creations. Many of the fictional characters he creates (from *Felicity's* Felicity and Ben to *Alias'* Sydney Bristow and Michael Vaughn and even some characters on his new series *Lost*) also search for the warmth, support and fatherly love that he craves. However, just like J. J., they are unlikely to get it because, in Abrams' universe, a father's love and approval is never freely given. Instead, if it is given at all, it is either unpredictable or conditional.

In *Alias*, two characters illustrate aspects of subject Abrams' father. While each one demonstrates different characteristics, both are power-ful and larger-than-life, just like he sees his own father. Arvin Sloane is the worst of the father figures, as he is controlling and manipulative. Sloane says that he loves Sydney and his biological daughter, Nadia, yet he forces them to place themselves in danger in order to accomplish his own goals. He injected Nadia with a painful drug that was killing her in order to access the Rambaldi prophecy, and he sent Sydney out in the field when she had been infected with an unknown virus. Thus, in Sloane, we see the strict father who, while perhaps stating his love, rarely gives of himself. It is this part of his father that subject Abrams despises, and he projects this feeling onto Nadia and Sydney. When Na-dia initially met Sloane, she said to him,

Every Sunday at the orphanage in San Telmo, they made us dress up in our finest clothes. They would have us stand in line for four hours waiting to be chosen by families. I wouldn't do it. I'd make myself filthy and always frown. I didn't want to be chosen, because I knew... I knew that somewhere my dad was still looking for me, and one day he'd come to take me away from that place. If I had known it was you I was waiting for, I would have cleaned up. ("Legacy," 3-21)

Similarly, Sydney states: "I don't know how much longer I can do this. Sit in these meetings with Sloane. Look at him as if I don't despise him, as if I don't want to leap across the table and use the skills I've learned against him" ("Doppelganger," 1-5).

While Jack Bristow is similarly emotionally withholding, through Jack, Abrams is offering redemption to his own father. Jack clearly loves Sydney. He tells other people about his love for her: "You asked me what I was afraid of. I can tell you, it's obvious. I'm afraid of losing my daughter" ("Dead Drop," 2-4). "I don't regret having married. I have Sydney because of our time together" ("Unveiled," 3-18). But he rarely expresses it to Sydney herself. Though his love for Sydney is evident in his body language and actions as he repeatedly protects her, Jack is uncomfortable with affection and, due to the hurt that he has experienced himself, does not allow others to get close. This closed aspect of Jack is a recurring theme in the show. When Sydney was asked if Jack raised her, she flatly denied it: "No. He hired a nanny" ("Q&A," 1-17). We also see Jack's withdrawn nature in an exchange between Sydney and one of her best friends.

WILL (reading from a book): "Laura, all my love forever and a day. Jack." That's not, like, your dad Jack, is it?
SYDNEY: Yeah.
WILL: Wow. That's uncharacteristically sweet of him.
SYDNEY: I know. He actually has a heart, which I'm learning little by little. ("Time Will Tell," 1-8)

In Jack, we see subject Abrams' need for his father to change, to become more than he ever was. If Jack Bristow can learn how to parent, then perhaps there is hope for Gerald Abrams as well.

Subject Abrams' complex role in the father-son relationship is represented, interestingly, through the characters of two women: Sydney and

Lauren. Both illustrate his longing for a positive father figure, as well as his anger that he didn't have one. Sydney's relationship with Jack is the most complex and, as such, is closest to the real relationship J. J. has with Gerald. She has a tortured relationship with her father. Jack gave her the tools she needs to survive and will literally go to the ends of the Earth to protect her, but he never truly gives her the affection and warmth she craves. Sydney's desire for his approval drives a lot of her behavior. She risked a great deal to break Jack out of solitary confinement yet is constantly heartbroken by what she believes is betrayal on his part. Time and time again, she expresses her disappointment to him: "Who are you to come to me and act like a father? If you want to help me, stay away from me" ("Truth Be Told," 1-1). "Every time I think I know just how awful you are, I learn something worse" ("Reckoning," 1-6). The end of the third season of the show depicted Sydney once again crying over something her father had done. However, despite this, she continues to have a relationship with Jack and crave his love. Thus, through Sydney, Abrams depicts his continuous struggle to win his father's approval, to get the fatherly hug that will let him know that he is a good person.

Lauren provides the most intense glimpse of subject Abrams' anger at his father for not giving him what he needed as a child. Lauren's anger toward her father's failings was so great that she had little problem with the idea of killing him. In this way, subject Abrams is sublimating his desire to hurt his own father (cleverly, he makes this desire acceptable through the medium of TV). However, even fictionally, J. J. realizes that killing his father is not what he wants—he desires love. Thus, despite the intensity of Lauren's negative feelings toward her father, she too is eager for her father's redemption. When her father demonstrated his love for her by suggesting that he take the blame for her traitorous activities, this one act was enough to keep her from killing him. This is particularly moving because you can see Abrams' hope for redeeming evidence of fatherly love. If Gerald showed love toward J. J. at great cost to himself, all of the pain he caused would be forgiven.

While his father withheld the love and affection he needed, there was a man in subject Abrams' life who did not—his grandfather. It was his grandfather who helped him develop his self-image and sublimate his internal conflicts through acceptable and lucrative work. Consequently, subject Abrams views his grandfather as his true father. This grandfather's larger-than-life influence is projected into the *Alias* universe, and the sadness subject Abrams still feels at the death of his grandfather can clearly be seen in the absent, ambiguous character of Michael Vaughn's father. At the time of this writing, all that is known of Vaughn's father is that he was a good man who died for the sins of others. His personality is not clearly defined, but his presence is, nevertheless, strongly felt. Thus, Vaughn's father is Abrams' attempt to work through his grief at the absence of his grandfather. Since Vaughn's father died when Vaughn was young, he never was able to truly know him. He lives his life with the knowledge that his father was courageous and heroic, but getting his tangible approval and affection is impossible. Like Vaughn, J. J. was unable to know his grandfather from anything other than a child's perspective and can no longer receive his nurturance. Thus, through Vaughn's father, subject Abrams struggles with the concept of a father who is caring and kind yet, like his own father, still emotionally absent.

Michael Vaughn's relationship with his father also illustrates the constant influence of the father, even in death. The father is always present, even when not physically available, and must be given continual respect. Thus, Vaughn still mourns his father's death and strives to emulate his dead father. Like Sydney, his desire to win Dad's approval provides the impetus for many of his decisions. It was Vaughn's father's watch that stopped when he first met Sydney (thus signaling that she could win his heart). He told her, "This watch belonged to my father. It's broken now, but it used to keep perfect time. And when he gave it to me, he said, 'You could set your heart by this watch.' It stopped October 1—the day we met" ("Passage, Part 1," 2-8). It was that same watch that, when fixed by Lauren, demonstrated that she did not truly understand him. Thus, through Vaughn, we see Abrams' belief that his grandfather is still guiding him through life's journey.

FAMILY CONSIDERATIONS - MOTHER BLAME

Like he does with his father, subject Abrams has an avoidant attachment to his mother, Carol. His mother's vocation of law professor, producer and writer kept her physically distant, and, when at home, she was emotionally distant as well. Thus, young J. J. learned not to express his need for affection because it typically would be rebuffed. This type of attachment style to his parents explains why he has difficulty trusting people and establishing intimate relationships and why, once someone shows him love and affection, he rarely lets them go. Subject Abrams is much angrier with his mother's failures as a parent than he is with his father's.

Although both parents have high-powered careers that took up a lot of family time, and both were withholding of affection, it is Carol who is blamed the most because she is the mother. Per societal values, subject Abrams expected his mother to be kind and nurturing, to sacrifice her time and plans for the sake of his sister and him. He did not have similar expectations for his father, so Gerald is not blamed so harshly for his failure to live up to the ideal.

Given that Carol was not the ideal mother subject Abrams expected to have, he was constantly unsure of her thoughts and feelings. When she did spend time with J. J., he could never be certain that she was there purely because she loved him or because she needed something for herself. She has never been comprehensible to him. As a result, subject Abrams' feelings toward his mother are wrapped in resentment and betrayal. As with his father, he desperately wants to believe in her love for him and seeks evidence that she, too, wants redemption for her past behavior.

This physical and emotional absence of his mother has so greatly affected subject Abrams that he punishes her again and again in his artistic creations. He is so angered by her failure to nurture him that mothers in his world are either nonexistent (*Lost*), weak (*Felicity*) or duplicitous (*Alias*). Almost every mother in *Alias* has betrayed someone close to her. In fact, Sydney's mother, Irina, seems to have set a record for the number of betrayals she made and was so remote a character that we were never certain about her true motivations. However, Irina's constant presence in the lives of both Sydney and Jack suggests that subject Abrams needs to believe that there is still some love in his mother somewhere. In one episode, Sydney told Irina, "I'm thinking of leaving the CIA. Which would mean giving up my clearance to see you." Instead of giving in to her desire to see her daughter, Irina did what was best for Sydney by saying,

> You're too forgiving, Sydney. Don't pretend I'm something I'm not. I've never been a real mother to you and...you don't owe me a second chance. If you make this decision about me, you're a fool. In fact, if you decide to stay, I won't agree to see you anymore. Take care of yourself. ("A Free Agent," 2-15)

Thus, as with Jack, we saw Irina demonstrating redeeming behavior. Subject Abrams has not given up on his mother just yet.

Moreover, as angry as he appears to be toward his mother, subject

Abrams always acknowledges the powerful nature of the mother figure. Just as Carol overshadowed his world, the mothers in *Alias* are women who are extremely powerful and full of influence. Irina is so powerful that her presence is constantly felt, and she always seemed to get what she wanted, even when she was in a position of weakness. As Jack stated, "No one wants a happy ending to this story more than I do, but I know this woman. I know her charms. I know her tricks. The way she presents herself, she disarms you. Some people have that talent. Compared to all of them, Irina Derevko is extraordinary" ("Dead Drop," 2-4). Irina even masterminded the theft of some Rambaldi artifacts while she was being held in a cell by the CIA. Similarly, at least two other *Alias* mothers—Olivia Reed and Elsa Kaplan—were revealed as enemy agents. Both women initially appeared meek and ineffectual but later showed themselves to be incredibly disciplined, persuasive and strong. For example, Olivia Reed appeared to be the long-suffering wife but ended up killing her husband and directing Lauren's treacherous activities.

GENDER IDENTITY CONFUSION

Subject Abrams exhibits a deeply conflictual relationship with women. On the one hand, he sees mothers as very powerful figures, and this belief extends to other women as well. Unlike many men who perceive female strength as threatening, he can let women shine. Most of the women in his world are complicated, smart and courageous with clearly defined personalities (e.g., Felicity, Sydney and now the stranded Kate on *Lost*). This is due to the powerful women—like his mother—who shaped his early life. However, on the other hand, many of the women in his world are cold, calculating and (especially if they are wives) treacherous.

This divided viewpoint on women stems primarily from subject Abrams' struggle with his own gender identity. On an intrapsychic level, he closely identifies with women. He has a kind disposition and yearns for affection, and, unlike most of his peers, his interests never extended to the physical realm (i.e., sports, games). As such, he never conformed to the norms of his peers and became an outcast. As subject Abrams himself stated, "Even as a kid, I was very aware of what was going on socially. It felt like the other kids, at least the boys, were much more interested in whatever they were doing and didn't care as much as I did about the social stuff." Thus, the female world is one in which he feels comfortable and that he wants to explore.

However, although he identifies closely with the world of women (i.e., people who do care about the social stuff), since he himself is not a woman, he cannot totally align with them. Moreover, as an adolescent boy with raging hormones, the feminine aspects of his personality started interfering with his romantic interests. Adolescent girls love to spend time with sensitive boys but rarely choose them as dates. Thus, he was always the "friend" but rarely the "boyfriend." This was especially challenging for subject Abrams given that he already had difficulties with trust and intimacy. Consequently, because of the pain of being different from both women and men, of being uncertain of his own gender identity, he began to dislike those aspects of himself that set him apart from his peers. He believes that it is the feminine aspects of his personality that betray him to the world of men. As a result, he projects his internal struggle of both loving and hating feminine qualities onto *Alias*.

Sydney Bristow is the "pure" woman who is powerful and good. Sydney represents the ideal: she is humble, courageous, kind and giving and maintains a firm sense of right and wrong. Sydney is the way a woman ought to be and, as such, represents the feminine world in which subject Abrams feels comfortable. However, she is the only *Alias* woman who embodies both strength and goodness. The other "good" women on *Alias* (i.e., Francie, Emily, Diane) are not physically strong and are quickly dispatched. In this way, subject Abrams acknowledges and celebrates his feminine side but, given his disdain for that which has caused him pain, weakens this feminine tendency and eradicates it as swiftly as possible.

There is additional evidence of subject Abrams' struggle with his gender identity. He is angry at the way in which his feminine qualities have caused rejection, the way they have betrayed him in love and friendship. Additionally, he is angry at women like his mother who fail to adequately inhabit the world to which he yearns to belong. His mother, a woman who could be completely feminine, has chosen not to be womanly enough. Consequently, subject Abrams feels major rage at women. However, he cannot totally accept this rage. The feminine qualities are a part of who he is and, at some level, have served him well. He also desperately seeks his mother's love and wants to be accepted by her. Hence, this rage is not acceptable for him, and, as such, he must guard against it.

Subject Abrams' solution to this dilemma is to sublimate those feelings of rage into *Alias* plotlines. He gets to act out his unacceptable feelings in an acceptable format. As a result, almost all of the wives in *Alias* (i.e., Irina, Emily, Lauren, Olivia Reed, Elsa Kaplan)—the women who are part of how the men see themselves—end up betraying their husbands. The aspects of the feminine world these men love the most, the ones they think they know, are incomprehensible to them. Through his portrayal of treacherous women, subject Abrams is finally getting his symbolic revenge on that which has caused him great pain. Perhaps the character of Michael Vaughn best described subject Abrams' feelings when Vaughn said to Lauren: "I am gonna erase you! I'm gonna remove any evidence you ever existed! You used me. You used my grief, my work, who I am. You took that from me—I'm taking it back!" ("Resurrection," 3-22).

ROMANTIC RELATIONSHIPS

As has been stated elsewhere in this report, subject Abrams has difficulty with trust and in developing intimate relationships. Thus, positive romantic entanglements are very challenging for him, and he views the concept of soulmates with suspicion. However, his artistic creations reflect the exact opposite viewpoint. All of his shows portray romantic relationships that are passionate and well-matched: *Felicity's* Felicity and Ben, *Alias'* Sydney and Vaughn, *Lost's* Kate and Jack. In *Alias*, Sydney and Vaughn were attracted from the start. Although Sydney loved Danny before she met Vaughn, only Vaughn could truly know who and what she was; only he could see into her heart. Similarly, Vaughn's serial dating evaporated once he met Sydney. Once Vaughn's dead father weighed in on their romance and endowed supernatural approval (via his watch), Vaughn was hooked permanently. As he told Sydney, "You need me to tell you what? That when you're on operations, I can't sleep at night? That when we're in debrief I have to force myself to remember what the hell we're supposed to be reviewing when all I wanna do is kiss you?" ("Phase One," 2-13).

The reason for the disparity between subject Abrams' personal cynicism about romance and the idealistic romantic viewpoint depicted on his shows has to do with his anxiety about intimacy. His belief in the difficulty and heartache of relationships causes him great anxiety because he does not want to be alone and desperately wants love and affection. In order to decrease the dissonance that these competing beliefs engender in him, he must guard against them through reaction formation. Thus, while his unconscious self does truly believe that relationships lead to pain, by displaying the opposite viewpoint to his conscious mind and the world at large, he can decrease his anxiety. Another way he bolsters his defense mechanism is through his religious beliefs. In Yiddish, there is a word, *bashert*, that means fate or destiny. While it can be used to describe other kinds of relationships, it most commonly refers to soulmates. However, having found your *bashert* doesn't equal bliss; people can ruin even the most perfect relationships. Consequently, "little" things like having to hide your romance for your own safety, being thought dead and another marriage partner can get in the way. Here again, subject Abrams projects onto Vaughn his own feelings about fate: "And the thing that makes me crazy every day is people that would kill us if we're seen together—the Alliance, SD-6, Sloane—are the very forces that brought you into my life to begin with. What kind of a sick joke is that?" ("Phase One," 2-13).

EXISTENTIAL BELIEFS

Unlike many other people, subject Abrams seeks to analyze and rationalize his inner self via his creative outlets. *Alias* deals with some profound existential issues, like good, evil and redemption. One of the consistent themes of the show is that good people do bad things while bad people do good things. As Jack once said to Sydney, "Then perhaps you'll finally understand the moral compromises you'll make when someone you love is in danger" ("Prelude," 3-7). Thus, through his *Alias* characters, subject Abrams poses interesting, complex questions (ones that are extremely relevant to those of us in the intelligence business): If your intentions are good yet you do bad things, does this make you evil? If your intentions are bad yet you do good things, does this have redemptive value? Abrams constantly vacillates between these issues as every character (with the possible exception of Sydney, the ideal woman) struggles with his or her darker nature.

     Clearly, subject Abrams wrestles with his own malevolent impulses. Like many people, he was taught that truly "good" people never have bad thoughts or deeds. Thus, evidence of selfishness, greed or wicked inclinations in people who otherwise seem good confuses him. As is true in many other parts of his life, the inherent contradictions lead to deep conflict within him, and he obsessively ruminates over issues of morality, fate, free will and evil. In trying to reconcile this struggle between good and evil and fate and free will, Abrams again projects his struggle into the *Alias* universe. *Alias* characters are rarely all good or all bad. Destiny provides the path to travel, while free will gives them the ability to choose how they will traverse it. Thus, Arvin Sloane murdered and maimed while sweetly loving Emily, and Michael Vaughn tortured a prisoner to get information that would lead to a positive outcome. Jack terrorized Will so that he would be allowed to live, and Lauren had no trouble executing Sark's father while wanting to spare her own. The cathartic outcomes in *Alias* mean that subject Abrams believes that he, too, has a path that he must travel but retains some faith in the power of his own decisions.

Abrams also is obsessed with the concept of redemption. In fact, redemption is a huge theme in *Alias*, thereby mirroring Abrams' strong desire to get what he wants from those he loves. If there is no redemption, then there can be no forgiveness or change. Consequently, while all of the characters in *Alias* seem to seek redemption in some way, particularly those who have more "evil" inclinations, subject Abrams is uncertain if it actually exists. He wants to see it; he needs to see it, but he isn't sure that people are willing to work to achieve it. That is why so many of the characters in *Alias* seem to hover on the edge of redemption only to go the other way. However uncertain his belief in redemption is, subject Abrams has a clear belief that we will all be held responsible for the choices we make. Based on the "what goes around comes around" perspective he was taught as a youth, he believes that payment is required one way or another. Thus, subject Abrams never expects to get a free ride for his mistakes and doesn't allow his *Alias* characters to get one either. This explains why Irina had to be separated from her children, Jack appears to rarely enjoy his life and Sloane had his finger cut off.

GENERAL CONCLUSIONS

Subject Abrams is a creative workaholic with Bipolar I Disorder and an adolescent mindset. His depression often looks like an extremely bad mood, while his mania is infectious and helpful to those around him. Those closest to him have learned to adjust to his moods and even enjoy the more prominent "up" swings. Abrams is loyal and deeply appreciative of talent and the simple things in life. Projects that he enjoys making usually will include passion, intrigue and a little bit of whimsy. His interpersonal relationships are reminiscent of the interactions he had with his family and friends while growing up. With parental figures, he is eager for approval yet gets angry at even the smallest slight. Trust is difficult for him, so those whom he already knows and likes are kept close. He constantly struggles with his gender identity and his darker impulses, although these struggles are kept at the more unconscious level.

However fun he is to be around, subject Abrams is constantly in search of meaning. Morality is important to him, and the battle between good and evil weighs heavily upon him. Consequently, he occasionally reads theology (*The Da Vinci Code*, with its religious overtones and tale of intrigue, holds real appeal for him) and discusses the existence of a higher power with close friends. Similarly, redemption is a concept close to his heart. Thus, when people do "bad" things, he looks closely for the reasons behind their actions. Whatever the rationale for "bad" behavior, he expects people to pay the price for their transgressions in some way!

RECOMMENDATIONS

At the present time, I see no urgency in the Abrams situation. However, the situation does warrant further monitoring and analysis. There is some concern with this disorder, as people exhibiting bipolar symptoms can be unpredictable. While subject Abrams appears to have a low severity of the disorder and is currently oriented to time, place and person (e.g., he knows the correct date, his whereabouts and his own identity), if severity increases, psychosis can result. If this happens, scenarios that are far-fetched often seem real in the subject's mind. Given this possible outcome, the *Alias* plotlines surrounding the Rambaldi prophecy bear further watching. Similarly, while *Alias*' tendency to parallel some aspects of comic books is currently harmless, an overidentification with comic book characters could be dangerous for the CIA, especially if the organization is cast as the villain. If at any point Abrams' bipolar disorder takes on psychotic features, the world of comic books is a likely place for his mind to inhabit.

With regard to his knowledge about the inner workings of the CIA, based on this analysis, I believe it is likely that he has someone on the inside giving him information about CIA operations. Although subject Abrams is highly intelligent and creative, I find little evidence that he can make such incredibly accurate guesses about the nature of our work and organization. Thus, it is my recommendation that we start hunting for a mole within our ranks. Based on my analysis of subject Abrams' personality, I believe that the person we are looking for is an older male agent or staff member with high-security clearance, one who has a "fatherly" air about him (we can overlook female agents, especially those who are "motherly"). This agent or staff member will embody strong masculine characteristics and be able to articulately discuss philosophical and theological issues and/or is good at spinning tales of adventure.

As mentioned previously, while subject Abrams should receive continued monitoring to ensure he is not a danger to the CIA, I do not regard him as a current threat to our operations. It is more important that we find the person who is undermining the security of our operations. However, I will continue to observe the situation and report any significant changes.

Misty K. Hook, Ph.D., is an assistant professor at Texas Woman's University and a licensed psychologist in clinical practice. She teaches courses in family psychology, the psychology of women, social psychology and the psychology of mothering, as well as supervising counselors in training. Misty is a lifelong fan of science fiction and mystery and cannot get enough of them. She enjoys spending time with her husband, reading, writing, watching quality television, swimming, biking and taking care of her young son. She has never been and is in no way affiliated with the CIA.

PAUL LEVINSON, Ph.D.

THE NIGHT THAT *ALIAS* REINVENTED ITSELF

I remember when I read the script for episode 2-13, "Phase One." I could not believe that J. J. and the writers were actually going to destroy the entire physical world of Alias—SD-6. What would happen to all that had been Alias up to that point? More importantly, what would happen to Marshall!?!?!? (Fortunately, he survived. Phew!) I have often marveled over these four years at how quickly the narrative evolves on this show. Alias does more in one year than most shows do in three or four. Incredibly risky, really. And in my opinion, something that has paid off.

SEPTEMBER 30, 2002, was not that night. But it was a nice Monday night in New York. I was walking with several colleagues to McNally Auditorium at Fordham University's Lincoln Center Campus, where we were to appear on a panel about *The Sopranos* that I had organized. The fourth season of the HBO series had premiered two weeks earlier and had attracted a record-breaking audience for television: for the first time in the history of the medium, a cable TV show had scored better in the Nielsen ratings than any of its competitors on free network TV.

The only thing bad about *The Sopranos*, I said to one of my colleagues—Lance Strate, who was to present a paper on *The Sopranos* and the state of New Jersey (cultural as well as physical)—was what to watch on TV on Sunday evenings when *The Sopranos* was not on. Lance looked at me and nodded sagely. "Watch *Alias*," was all he said.

I had vaguely heard of *Alias* then, which had just started its second season the night before. As it turned out, I didn't get to watch any of *Alias* until well into its third season, when my daughter (then seventeen) talked me into getting DVDs of the first two seasons (I'm sometimes a little slow to take a hint). Once I did, I was soon not only believing what Lance and my daughter had told me, but had come up with one way in which *Alias* was even better than *The Sopranos*, which might make it the best show in the history of television.

And this brings us to the subject of this essay. . . .

THE COMMON DENOMINATOR OF NETWORK TV

The prime commandment of network television has always been: "Thou shalt not offend!" The networks make their money from selling airtime to advertisers, who are happy to hand over big amounts of money for big numbers of viewers. The advertisers don't much care whether the viewer is thrilled with the programs he or she is watching, or merely interested—in fact, all the advertisers care about is whether the viewer is watching their commercials, preferably with at least one eye open.

The result is that television has long appealed to the lowest common denominator of public interest: shows that keep the largest number of people interested without turning anyone off and away. If a program keeps viewers on the coasts riveted, but sends Middle-Americans running from the screen, the inexorable arithmetic of advertising works against it. Better to have a show that is at least mildly interesting to the coasts and retains the heartland. The furor over Janet Jackson's breast on CBS during the Super Bowl halftime show in 2004 demonstrates just what can happen when this principle is violated even for a split second.

Now, a powerful corollary of "thou shalt not offend" on television has always been "thou shalt not confuse!" After all, a confused viewer can easily become an irritated viewer, a short distance from being no viewer at all. This is why daytime soap operas move at a glacial pace: you can miss at least a few weeks of programming and not lose much of the story. But all television drama steers clear of sudden, disrupting turns in events and characters. "Miss Ellie" was deemed so important to viewers of *Dallas*, for example, that Donna Reed was drafted to play her when Barbara Bel Geddes was sidelined by heart surgery—even though the two looked and sounded nothing alike.

Which makes the surprise reinvention of *Alias* right in the middle of its second season on ABC all the more remarkable and rewarding.

THE RUG THAT WAS PULLED OUT FROM UNDER

The original setup of *Alias*, which carried the show for a season and a half, was an elegant box within boxes. In the pilot, we were introduced to Sydney Bristow, a grad student working for the CIA. On this level, we in effect had a slightly older Felicity as secret agent. (J. J. Abrams conceived both *Felicity* and *Alias*. Jennifer Garner, who plays Sydney, also played a friend of Felicity.) But we soon learned that Sydney only thought she was working for the CIA. In reality, her SD-6 unit was a rogue operation, which used the CIA as a cover. Most of SD-6, including Sydney at this point, thought it was an entirely legal, if Black Ops, unit working for the good guys—which the CIA would deny all knowledge of, and which would kill anyone who revealed anything at all about its work. By the end of the pilot, Sydney's fiancé was killed by SD-6 because she told him that she worked for them. This led to her resigning, which put her own life in danger. The crisis was "resolved" when Sydney decided to stay on at SD-6 as a double CIA/SD-6 agent (that is, a good guy who works for the true CIA undercover as a bad guy who works for SD-6). Meanwhile, her mysterious father Jack revealed himself as another double CIA/SD-6 agent. Sydney was not happy about any of this, but working undercover nonetheless afforded her the best chance of avenging her fiancé's death by bringing down SD-6 and its allies—in contrast to her work at SD-6 up until this point, which she thought was for the good CIA but was really for evil SD-6.

That a plot of such complexity—look how long it just took me to summarize—was ever established on network TV indicates how far the medium had come since *Dallas*. The success of HBO on cable—which, as a premium subscription service, is free of the numbing yoke of advertising—was at least part of the reason that ABC was willing to be so daring. Indeed, *Alias* and *The Sopranos* were often in face-to-face competition at nine o'clock on Sunday nights.

The two shows have little else in common. *The Sopranos*, unlacerated by commercial interruption, tells its story in hour-long filmlike episodes; *Alias* decorates its commercial breaks with roller-coaster cliffhangers. Not burdened by the FCC's childish (and unconstitutional) provisions, *The Sopranos* gives us realistic nudity and language; the most we get from *Alias* in this regard are tight fits and an occasional "son-of-a-bitch." Although characters die with regularity on *The Sopranos*, the plot remains unrelentingly constant, and the persistent, singular complexity we experience is how such violent people can command something akin to admiration and even affection from us.

Although *Alias* has its emotional moments, especially in Sydney's relationship with her father, its supreme complexity is intellectual, and was especially so in the first season and a half. How could Sydney Bristow function as a good guy in an environment of bad guys who almost all thought they were good guys, and not give herself away to the head of SD-6, who in fact was a bad guy? She often went on missions with her partner, Dixon, an earnest good guy who did not know he was working in the service of bad guys. Sydney's job was often to confound the mission, or give the fruits of the mission to the good guys (the real CIA) right under the nose of Dixon—who, if he had any inkling of what Sydney was doing, would have assumed that Sydney was a traitor to her country. (In fact, he began to get just such an inkling.)

In the first year and a half, Sydney and her colleagues on both sides of the divide walked this tightrope in the face of ever more desperately complex situations. And then J. J. Abrams did something even more radical. He cut the tightrope. Right in the middle of the season. Right after the Super Bowl on ABC in January 2003, which meant right in front of a huge audience.

He didn't stop the series. He did something far more unprecedented: he changed its very premise.

THE NIGHT OF REINVENTION

The Super Bowl on television has long been about the closest the world regularly comes to being a global village. It vies with the Academy Awards for drawing the largest number of simultaneous viewers worldwide, and here in America it regularly doubles the number of Academy Award viewers (Super Bowl audiences are over 100 million in the U.S.; Academy Award TV audiences have been as low as 50 million). Coverage of American presidential election returns, to give another comparison, attract well under 100 million viewers on all stations combined, and of course far less on any single broadcast or cable network. When the Super Bowl is on TV, we are all seated in the same stadium, multimillions of us, watching the exact same action on the screen. Janet Jackson could not have picked a better occasion to attract attention with her exposed breast (in 2004). And *Alias* could not have found a better spot and time to reinvent itself (in 2003).

January 26, 2003: that was the night. The broadcast of the Super Bowl on ABC had drawn a record-breaking audience of 138.9 million viewers in the United States, according to National Football League statistics. More conservative Nielsen ratings estimated the number to be 88.6 million—still a record for a Nielsen-measured audience. *Alias* fans had been abuzz about the new episode that would air right after the game.

Victor Garber, who masterfully portrays Jack Bristow on the show, had promised that this episode would change things and help the ratings. (Viewers had averaged about 9.3 million per show for the second season of *Alias*, until this night.) ABC had decided to postpone an episode guest-starring Ethan Hawke until the February sweeps month in favor of this special *Alias* chapter. "It was a very conscious choice on the producer's part, and I think it will help," Garber was quoted as saying by Rick Porter (on tv.zap2it.com) eleven days before the broadcast.

There are certain unwritten rules on TV—certain specific principles in support of "thou shalt not confuse." Lead characters can be brought to the point of death as often as needed, but rarely killed (this used to be never, unless the series was ending or the actor or actress decided to leave). Institutions are even more robust and resistant to change.

Southfork (the Ewing ranch on *Dallas*) could be set on fire, but never burned to the ground or out of existence; Ewing Oil could be sold, but sooner or later it would wind up back in J. R.'s or at least Bobby's hands. Even *The Sopranos* could never survive Tony truly leaving the mob. If he did, that would mean we would be watching the series' finale.

According to the Nielsens, some 17.4 million Super Bowl viewers stayed tuned for *Alias*—twice the usual number of *Alias* watchers. "Phase One"—the aptly numbered episode thirteen of the second season—started out conventionally, if provocatively, enough. Sydney's "alias" was a scantily clad call girl on a private jetliner, tempting an ugly, powerful man in possession of some crucial data onboard the plane. Sydney bested the bad guy, got the data—but then apparently got shot. A tasty opener. But none of this had much to do with the real plot and purpose of this episode.

That pivotal story began with the revelation that Arvin Sloane, bad-guy head of SD-6, had gone missing and had been replaced by a new eloquent monster, one Anthony Geiger, portrayed by Rutger Hauer.

(One of the great strengths of *Alias* has been the high-octane star power attracted to the series for guest appearances. These have included not only Hauer but Quentin Tarantino, Amy Irving, Lena Olin, Angela Bassett and the aforementioned Ethan Hawke. See my comments below for more about Lena Olin's impact on the show.) Jack and Sydney had had a complicated relationship with Sloane—everything is complicated in *Alias*, one of its joys—and there was even a possibility that Sloane might have known that Jack and Sydney were double agents, but for his own reasons was allowing their deception to run its course. Sydney, Jack and viewers who had followed the series knew they could not expect such forbearance from Geiger. He presented something of a life-threatening problem.

And, in fact, Jack was soon unmasked by Geiger, who commenced torturing Jack for the truth. Sydney—who we learned had actually made good her escape from the sky (no real surprise, as even *Alias* cannot afford to kill off its lead character)—focused on rescuing her father. But only the real CIA could pry him loose from Geiger. Indeed, the CIA would need to field an all-out attack on SD-6 headquarters—but this would forever blow the CIA's game (also Jack's and Sydney's) of letting SD-6 think it was putting one over on the CIA. In other words, such an attack would blow the very premise of the series.

Well…television series have been no strangers to episodes and plots that put central characters in dire jeopardy and threaten to undermine the fundamental logic and setup of the series. But prior to this episode of *Alias*, the TV way of handling this would have been to bring the disruption *this* close to completion, to inflicting mortal damage on the plot, and then at the last moment ingeniously veer back and resolve the disruption in such a way that the status quo is maintained. (The very way that *Alias* had just resolved the opening tease with Sydney.) But the problem with this approach, of course, is that the ingenious twists were always predictable, since viewers knew there would be some kind of unexpected saving grace—and therefore the twist was not unexpected at all.

Alias tried a different tack this time. The real CIA indeed attacked SD-6. A fierce fight ensued. We expected SD-6 to somehow pull its survival, and the continuance of the complex terrain of the series, out of the fire. But the blaze was too strong. Geiger and SD-6 were destroyed. Sloane, the SD-6 mastermind, did survive. And in the last scene we learned that the destruction of SD-6 was exactly as he had planned. He—and the series—were moving on from "Phase One."

THE DIVIDENDS OF MUTATION?

Alias gained about a million viewers for the episodes that followed "Phase One." This was a limited improvement—*Alias* had reached that number (10 million viewers) at times during its first season. And in the third season, viewers often dropped below 8 million per show.

Alias' daring reinvention of itself was less than an unmitigated boon. What went wrong?

Part of the answer has to do with specific developments in the series, especially the availability of a particular actress, which has nothing to with the reinvention on the night of the Super Bowl. But part of *Alias*' problem after the reinvention flows from the direction of the reinvention, or where it pointed the series. Let's look at that part first.

Unfortunately for *Alias*, the very purpose of its reinvention was apparently to make itself less complex, simpler, presumably easier for the common denominator of television viewers to understand. In the interview with Rick Porter mentioned above, Victor Garber gave an indication of why the show reinvented itself: "I think it's a difficult show. It's not an easy show for people to follow." The difficulty he was talking about was SD-6—the complexity of two good double agents, Jack and Sydney, working undercover for a bad organization pretending to be good and consisting mostly of good agents who do not know they are working for someone bad. In other words, the very heart and soul and deepest intellectual jolt of the first season and a half. And the very heart and soul that "Phase One" blasted out of existence. Garber continued in his interview, "the Super Bowl episode is like starting over. It's almost like a pilot episode." Unhappily, the pilot was for a series which was less challenging and riveting of the mind.

Interestingly, all of the continuing characters, and most of their delicious conflicts and ambiguity, survived the revolution of "Phase One." But this ambiguity was personal, not structural or organizational, and therefore it was more commonplace than what it had been before. Sloane, for example, not only survived but was still calling the shots. Since we already suspected prior to "Phase One" that he knew something close to the truth about Jack and Sydney's loyalties, the tantalizing question kept arising: Why, then, did he allow them to continue to work for SD-6? Was Sloane perhaps in some way not just a villain, but a hero, too? This ambiguity continued and was further developed and exploited after the reinvention. But without the almost insanely complex infrastructure of

SD-6 to support it, Sloane became just another inscrutable, enigmatic character—almost a dime a dozen in spy stories.

Other characters were similarly deprived of their best conflicts. Dixon, Sydney's partner, was a good man who thought he was patriotically work-ing for the CIA in his work for SD-6. He was in fact no conscious double agent, but a decent person unwittingly doing bad work. Sydney knew this and had to struggle constantly with it. Dixon, for his part, started to suspect Sydney was not loyal to SD-6 (which, in Dixon's mind, meant Sydney could be a traitor to the U.S.A.), and was beginning to agonize about whether to bring this to Sloane's attention. Indeed, this counter-point came to the boil and played a central role in "Phase One": "You had your suspicions about me!" Sydney said to Dixon in one of the best mo-ments of the episode and the entire series. "You were right! I know this is insane, but you have to trust me now!...You have been working for the enemy you thought you were fighting." Thus Sydney convinced Dixon— just barely—to help her bring in the real CIA and bring down SD-6.

But once SD-6 was gone, what was left for Dixon? In place of a good man in an almost impossible situation, he became an embittered man who rightly feels he has been made a fool of for years. He was given other reasons in the series to loathe Sloane, but the upshot was we had a Hamlet of a character replaced by a conventional, by-the-book hater.

Marshall McLuhan not only coined the term "global village," but also noted that "the medium is the message." We might say that in fiction of this sort, the complex structure of the plot is the message. When that underlying structure was removed without warning from *Alias*, that was the most complex—and brilliantly satisfying—move of all. But without that undergirding, the characters of *Alias* have struggled to maintain their balance and even their reasons for being. With that fundamental rule of television—you can burn Southfork, but it has to be repaired or rebuilt—so courageously busted, the complex heroes and villains of *Alias* were left without a logical home.

OTHER MINUSES IN THE AFTERMATH

Other factors helped and hurt *Alias* in the aftermath of its reinvention on Super Bowl 2003 night. One factor in particular both dramatically helped and hurt *Alias*, and in the end shows the damage that another kind of transformation can wreak on a show—the unintentional loss of a character because the actress who plays her is no longer available.

Laura Bristow/Irina Derevko—Sydney's mother and Jack's wife—first appeared, in shadowy profile, at the end of the final episode of season one. Throughout most of the first season, everyone—including Sydney and presumably Jack—thought Irina was dead. But Sydney and Jack were beginning to suspect otherwise, and at the end of the last episode of that season we met Irina: her people captured Sydney, and she shot and wounded her daughter in an attempt to get her to talk.

In the first episode of the second season, Irina turned herself in to the CIA—to be close to their planning, to be close to her daughter, who knows? Lena Olin gave an incandescent, sterling performance as Irina in that episode, and indeed in every episode in which she appeared that season. She was beautiful, powerful, poised. Sparks flew every time she and Victor Garber were in the same room. Scenes between her and Jennifer Garner were superb. A two-part episode—"The Passage" (2-8 and 2-9)—took the "happy" family on a trip to India to prevent a war between that country and Pakistan over nuclear weapons. "The Passage" is generally regarded as one of the high points of the series, and I completely agree. The acting between Olin and Garber has seldom if ever been equaled on television.

Irina Derevko easily survived "Phase One"—she was not in that episode at all. In the stories that followed that evening of transformation, Irina's complex character and Olin's exquisite acting buoyed the show. Viewers had every reason to expect the same for the third season, whatever the twists and turns in the new, watered-down plot.

But this was not to be. For whatever reason, Lena Olin was not willing to play Irina Derevko in the third season of *Alias*. At first, Jack was obliged to resort to instant messaging to keep Irina in the story. This worked best once. *Alias* had few options. The *Dallas* "solution" of getting another actress to play the part had not worked well even in *Dallas* back in the 1980s. It would have been flatly ludicrous for *Alias*. A contrivance such as plastic surgery to change Irina's face would not have done it—a significant part of Lena Olin's power and presence is her voice. *Alias* eventually decided to bring Irina's sister Katya into the story, played by Isabella Rossellini. She is a fine actress, with more cinematic successes to her credit than Lena Olin. But she is not as scintillating at her present age as Olin is at hers. The volatile chemistry between Olin and Garber that literally lit up the second season was missing.

The moral of this part of the story of *Alias* is that not all transformations are equal. The loss of an electrifying character is very difficult to sustain. Perhaps if *Alias* had killed Irina off in a satisfying way, her absence would have been easier to take in the third season. But, even so, the shift from Irina to Katya—from Lena to Isabella—was a jump cut that left the viewer unsettled and dissatisfied.

HOPES FOR THE FUTURE: REINVENTION AS REINSTATEMENT

Genius is hard to maintain. Plots that flourish by reinventing themselves may be even more difficult. Live by the sword, die by the sword: once the cat of reinvention is out of the bag, viewers can come to expect it, and it can thus become boring. The weekly television series *V* tried a radical approach in the 1980s, after two successful miniseries which introduced the show and its characters. It killed off a central, seemingly crucial character every few weeks, something that seemed like a good idea at first. But pretty soon the series killed off not only many of its original characters, but itself.

Alias is not now in any danger of doing that. The fatigue it exhibited in its third season was not due to too many unexpected plot changes, but probably too few. Rather than building on the golden opportunity of Sydney's two-year amnesia that set the third season in motion, *Alias* essentially went in circles. With the exception of Sydney's sister, the third season ended up on pretty much the same terrain, with the same set of characters and conflicts, as the second season.

The fourth season of *Alias*, which began with a tip-top two-hour episode in January 2005, has tried something different: a reinvention that reinstates. Irina was once again dead, and this time in a more memorable way. That old SD-6 gang was back in business again with a new name and a few additions—with Sloane in charge and everything—except this time it *is* a bona fide CIA Black Ops squad, or so Sloane and Jack and the CIA director told Sydney.

There are some good possibilities here, ones that as of this writing have not yet come to fruition either way. Wouldn't it be something if Sloane was once again putting one over on the CIA—and Sydney and Dixon and their colleagues—and actually reconstituting something akin to the original SD-6, operating for his own evil ends, under the ingenious cover of being a reformed villain? Sydney is suitably suspicious. There is a welcome, nagging, ubiquitous tension afoot, missing since the night that the first SD-6 was apparently eradicated.

But a total reinstatement would bring the series back to square (or season) one, and what would be the point in that? The only way this reinstatement can jump-start the series is if there is enough new in it: back to launch, back to the strangely reassuring toothache of paradox, but with an engine significantly different from the original to lift the series to a higher orbit. The "meta-commentary" of the characters in the fourth season—they obviously know about SD-6 and comment on how good it feels to be back together again—was of course not in the first season, and is enjoyable, but won't be enough. Nor will Sydney's sister.

So *Alias* has a tough mission: restore the level of complexity of the first season and a half in a way that goes beyond it.

Whatever happens, nothing can ever erase the magic of those first twenty-two plus twelve episodes, and the brazen verve, the sheer nerve, of what happened in episode thirteen of season two. Win, lose or draw, from now on, that episode and everything that led up to it will remain one of the highest points of serialized fiction. It may well be that *Alias* will never recover from that magnificent destruction. Perhaps that is the price the series had to pay to achieve that moment.

It's up to J. J. Abrams and his brilliant collaborators. I'm betting we're still in for a few good surprises.

Paul Levinson's The Silk Code *won the 2000 Locus Award for Best First Novel. He has since published* Borrowed Tides *(2001),* The Consciousness Plague *(2002) and* The Pixel Eye *(2003). His science fiction and mystery short stories have been nominated for Nebula, Hugo, Edgar and Sturgeon awards. His eight nonfiction books, including* The Soft Edge *(1997),* Digital McLuhan *(1999),* Realspace *(2003) and* Cellphone *(2004), have been the subject of major articles in the* New York Times, Wired *and the* Christian Science Monitor, *and have been translated into eight languages. He appears on* The O'Reilly Factor, *the* CBS Evening News *and numerous national and international TV and radio programs. He is professor and chair of communication and media studies at Fordham University in New York City.*

ERIN DAILEY

A SPY IN THE HOUSE OF LOVE

*I have to admit, Erin's article made me smile. Not surprising, though,
as I am a longtime fan of Erin's. Where from, you ask? Well, I have
read her* Alias *recaps on Television Without Pity. Yes, it's true... I've
browsed the Internet to see what fans have to say. I'm human, people!
So, be nice, forum posters... you never know who's reading!*

—BY ERIN DAILEY, SPECIAL COLUMNIST TO MARTINI MAGAZINE —

YOU KNOW HOW IT IS. You're at some swanky art party at the Russian embassy, and you're just about to rig a miniature explosive device in the shape of a mushroom tartlet to blow the anti-American communications system sky high, when it happens. You meet HIM. The one. You know he's the one by the smolder in his eyes and the way his shoulders shift as he leaps for cover the second your bomb goes off. Too bad you have to run for the stealth jet parked on the roof before you can give him your number. Also too bad you're going to be deep undercover in a Siberian prison for the next three months. How can you get in contact with the man of your dreams? And if you even *can* make contact, how can you make sure he'll be yours forever? Especially considering your main occupation happens to require that you be a martial arts expert with the ability to change disguises faster than you can change your mind?

Face it. You're a spy. And your love life sucks because of it.

Well, you're not alone. According to Dr. Irene Derevski,[1] nine out of

---

[1] Names have been changed to protect the innocent. And when we say "innocent," we actually mean "us." And when we say "us," I mean "me." These people are scary.

ten female spies have difficulty maintaining a healthy and successful love life. "Being a spy is never easy," the good doctor[2] told us, "but being a spy in a relationship is next to impossible—even non-spy relationships are full of lies and deceit. Imagine: your whole life is a lie and you enter into a long-term commitment, perhaps even a marriage, with someone. That puts a tremendous amount of strain on both halves of the relationship. Especially if one of the people involved is actually trying to dupe the other person into believing that she's really in love with him when, in reality, she's actually just stealing secrets from him and basically making his life a living hell. Not that I would know anything about that. And if you try to prove otherwise, I'll kill you and everyone you know without breaking a sweat. Excuse me, I have to go…make a phone call."

Dr. Derevski has a point. Being a spy is difficult under any circumstances; being a spy in love can only heighten those difficulties. Especially if you're a woman and especially if you're not careful. No, we're not talking about condoms! (Although, really, do you want to get knocked up by that shady assassin from your past with the overbite? No, you don't. You really, really don't. So keep the condoms handy is what we're saying. A prepared spy girl is a non-pregnant non-dead spy girl.) We're talking about taking care with your words, your actions, your emotions. There's nothing that can end a spy love affair faster than saying, "Is that an AK-47 in your pocket or are you just happy to see me? Wait. IS that an AK-47? HANDS WHERE I CAN SEE 'EM! DROP THE WEAPON!" Or do you really think he's going to want to see you again after you step back and realize that all he's carrying is a box of long-stemmed roses and now you're going to have to have him "relocated" to a distant suburb of Des Moines because he can identify you as the woman who burst his testicles with her fist even though she's supposed to be a kindergarten teacher?

Relax. Help is here. We at *Martini Magazine* believe that every woman has a right to true and everlasting love, even if she has to wear a disguise and speak in an accent to get it. So we've developed some tips to not only help you get a man, but to help you keep him around for a long, long time. Or at least until you have jetted off to Kazakhstan in search of an ancient artifact that powers a machine invented by a long-dead (or is he?) prophet who may or may not be related to you. What? It could happen. And if and when it does, these pointers may just come in handy.

Keep them close, for emergencies. We've printed them on digestible paper, in case you have to get rid of them in a hurry.

---

[2] Derevski isn't actually a doctor, but one of her aliases is.

Lie.

What's that? You don't want to lie to your lover? Too bad. You're a spy, sweetie. Lying comes with the territory. And, as Dr. Derevski noted above, even the most stable and normal of relationships have their share of lies. So what if yours involve national security and the location of illegal arms? Lies are lies, and if you want to keep your man (and your relationship) in one piece, you won't tell him any more truth than is absolutely necessary.

"I learned this one the hard way," said Sandy Barstow, a former double agent for the Alliance-funded SD-6. "When I was working deep undercover inside SD-6, I made the mistake of telling my fiancé the truth about my spy life. I mean, I took precautions and told him in the shower with the water running in order to outsmart the bugs, of course, but that didn't help. Why? Because my fiancé got drunk and spilled everything he knew on an answering machine. ON AN ANSWERING MACHINE. It was a really sweet message, and he basically said he would support me in anything I did, even if it was being a spy, and it made me love him a little bit more than I ever thought possible, but if he'd just kept his mouth shut, maybe my sadistic troll of a boss wouldn't have slaughtered him and left him in a bathtub for me to find."

In short, what he doesn't know won't hurt him, and what he does know could get him (or you) killed. So watch what you say around the boy, okay? Nobody wants innocent blood on her hands. Or her carpet.

Distract him with sex.

Even on his worst days, any man worth his salt acts like a deer in headlights when it comes to sex. Bounced a check? Saucily suggest you skip dinner and take a hot bath together instead. Lost his season tickets? Rip off your shirt and cover your breasts with whipped cream and he'll forget about sports altogether. Crashed his car into an underpass during a high-speed chase that ended in an explosion near Garfield Park that required fifty undercover FBI officers to clean up and earned you a promotion to Super Spy? Unzip his fly with your teeth and he'll be offering you the keys to the new car he hasn't even purchased yet. Sex sells, baby, and what it does for the single spy is erase any potential problems from your boyfriend's pretty little head.

"I can attest to this wholeheartedly," remarked Moronen Rood, a former double agent working for the wrong side of the law, who also happened to be married to a really hot CIA agent for an undetermined amount of time. She was interviewed for this article shortly before her husband shot her dead, so her advice really should be taken with a grain of salt. And a margarita. "Whenever my rather goody-two-shoes husband started to ask too many questions, I'd just toss off my suit jacket and show him my absolutely fantastic breasts. Worked like a charm every time."

"I doubt that," sneered Sandy when told of Moronen's comment. "Her breasts wouldn't attract the attention of a love-starved prison inmate who's been in solitary confinement since 1972." It should be noted that Sandy was involved with Moronen's husband before Moronen came along.

Did Sandy ever use sex to distract her man? "Hell, no," responded Sandy. "I didn't have to. We were both spies. We trusted each other. Besides, if I did distract him with sex, he'd actually be distracted, you know, not searching frantically for the exits."

"That bitch!" hissed Moronen when told of Sandy's response. "Excuse me, I have to go...make a phone call."

Act dumb. (Deaf helps too.)

Acting dumb isn't just reserved for Laur—er, evil bitchy blondes. You can act dumb too. And don't worry about making your honey think you're less than bright. You know you're smart—acting dumb once in a while won't hurt you at all. Sometimes it can even help a situation. Questions like, "Hey, what happened to your eye?" or, "How'd you get that bruise in the shape of a combat boot on your back?" can easily be answered with a "Huh? What? Oh, that? You know how clumsy I am, sweetie. I just bump into things all the time. Now, gimme some sugar." When it comes to the more unexplainable questions (e.g., "What's with the Mister Softee truck being parked outside for three weeks? It's DECEMBER, for God's sake!" "Baby, why are you driving so fast? We're only five minutes late. WATCH OUT FOR THE LADY WITH THE STROLLER!"), just make sure you feign ignorance convincingly.

Faking a hearing problem can also help. For instance, any answer should begin with "Huh?" This one simple word makes him think you haven't heard him and gives you ample time to conjure up a properly stupid response. If you're still having problems coming up with a good answer, when he repeats his question, offer up "What was that? I didn't hear you." By the time he's delivered his question a third time, he'll either be so annoyed at having to repeat himself that he won't even bother asking you again, or you'll have had enough time to come up with, "Oh, I don't know who that guy with the gun was, baby. You know how I'm always meeting people and forgetting who they are! I'm terrible at names! You know that! Now, gimme some sugar."

Brainwash him while he sleeps.

This is especially helpful if you happen to be a clone as well as a spy, but can be just as effective for your average, everyday undercover girl. Frallison Duran Duran, a woman of many talents, once spent a significant amount of time living a truly double life: she was the clone of a non-spy, and she had to pretend to be that woman while carrying on a relationship with a man who used to be a non-spy but had recently embarked upon a semi-spy life. If you think that's confusing, think about how *she* felt.

"Here I was, shoved into the body of some woman who didn't even know the meaning of *kung fu,* and I somehow had to gather illicit intel from my roommate AND the dumbass guy I was supposed to be dating, all while acting like I loved him. It was totally ridiculous. For one thing, he was about two inches shorter than me, and for another, I was involved with a completely different—and much, much hotter—man at the time. It was extremely hard on me, you know? Not to mention the fact that I couldn't wear my dark eyeliner or smoke cigarettes unless it was a special occasion and I was in some distant warehouse somewhere. That really sucked."

Seeing as Frallison's "boyfriend" at the time, one Jonah Hotness, was doing some side work for the CIA, she was instructed by her superiors to hypnotize him while he slept in order to gain access to all of his valuable CIA intel. She also conveniently used the hypnosis to convince Jonah that they had had lots of hot and steamy sex. Looks like brainwashing your boyfriend can really come in handy whether or not you're a spy—especially when you have a "headache."

"Oh, sure," said Frallison, who's supposed to be dead but is really living in a cottage outside of Dinan, Brittany, "you can brainwash them to do anything. Think anything. Eat anything. It's fabulous. I once dated a guy who refused to take out the garbage. *Refused.* Listen. I don't *do* garbage, okay? I'm a SPY. So I whacked my boyfriend out with drugs, brainwashed him overnight, and from that point on, he actually *begged* to take out the garbage. Neat, huh?"

Brainwashing also worked for Moronen. After all, her husband-to-be had recently been heartbroken by the loss of his love, Sandy; getting him to fall in love with her so soon after Sandy's "death" would have been a monumental undertaking. So it's understandable that Moronen would use brainwashing to bring him over to her side. "*I beg your pardon,*" she said icily, when reached for comment. "I never brainwashed my husband. He loved me. He actually thought I was the sweetest thing ever. Little did he know...What? Oh, you found *The Spy's Guide to Brainwashing* in my desk drawer? How very interesting. It's not mine, unfortunately. To whom does it belong? I'm afraid I can't help you there. However, it could come in handy one day. Why don't I just...take it out of your hands?"

Don't tell your father or mother anything. Ever.

There comes a time in every woman's life when she feels she has no-where to turn but to her own parents. If you're a spy, however, please, whatever you do, FIND SOMEWHERE ELSE TO TURN TO. You may think your parents love you and adore you and would do anything for you, but you'd be wrong. Oh, sure, they may care for you, but the sec-ond you spill that you're not giving them the classified intel that they're asking for no matter how hard they beat you, they'll whip out a gun and shoot you in the shoulder faster than you can say, "Mom?" Simply put, your parents may love you, but your parents may also be working for the enemy.

If this is the case, then not only is your life in danger, but the lives of everyone around you are as well. Which is why it's very important that you never ever EVER let either of your parents know you're dating someone. Even if things aren't serious yet, you can't afford to have your domineering father, who may or may not have bred you to be a spy, knowing the identity of the guy with whom you're doing the horizontal mambo five times a week. And whatever you do, don't introduce him to your mother. The woman's capable of killing fifteen men before break-fast; God knows what she'd do to your boyfriend.

"I resent that," said Dr. Derevski. "I am a mother, and I was always very supportive of my daughter and her boyfriend. I think he's a lovely young man." When reminded that she may or may not have attempted to have said young man killed on several occasions, Dr. Derevski just scoffed. "Oh, please. How else could I have gotten him to prove his love for my daughter? Some boys just need a kick in the ass."

"Yeah, tell that to my first-grade boyfriend," said Sandy when in-formed of Dr. Derevski's statement. "She blindfolded him and made him pin the tail on a LIVE BULL because she said she had to be sure he was 'worthy' of my love. HE WAS SIX." Sandy looked mildly guilty. "Not that Dr. Derevski is my mother or anything. Is this being recorded? Is there someone behind that mirror? *WHAT'S YOUR REAL NAME?*"

Kill anyone who threatens to expose you.

"I would never kill anyone unless they tried to kill me first," said Sandy when presented with this tip.

"Oh, what bollocks," twitted Moronen when she heard this. "Of course she wouldn't TRY to kill someone—they all just conveniently fall on her knife or over a cliff. Isn't she just lucky that way? Look—killing people who threaten to expose you is one of the first rules of the spy world, okay? You can't risk exposure! Especially when you're a double agent! Killing your enemies is totally acceptable."

"Oh, this says the woman who once killed a guy in a parking garage just because she happened to HAVE A KNIFE ON HER," retorted Sandy. "She's shameless."

Okay, so we would never actually condone killing anyone in cold blood. That would be illegal, right? But if your cover is about to be blown, that could have a serious effect on your love life—not to mention your life in general. Being a spy is kind of like having an affair with a married man: your secret is in danger of being exposed at any given moment. You have to be on guard. Don't leave ticket stubs behind that could place you somewhere you shouldn't have been. Don't make phone calls from your house that you wouldn't want your boyfriend to hear. Don't let the credit card statements come to the house unless you want to run the risk of him absentmindedly picking it up and discovering that you purchased three small pontoon boats, a ticket to Sri Lanka and a case of ammo during the week you were supposed to be at a bank conference in Memphis.

Oh, and kill anyone who threatens to expose you. Just as a precaution.

Don't disappear for two years.

Just don't. Your boyfriend's loyal and loving, but he has the attention span of a fruit fly, and if you're gone longer than a month, trust us—his eye will start roving. Keep your "business trips" to a two-week maximum, and make sure you call him on a daily basis. If possible, leave little photographic reminders of yourself around the house, just in case he starts to forget what you look like. Most men think of women as shiny objects: when you're right there in front of them, they can't help but pay attention, but the second you disappear, they're liable to get distracted by any other shiny object that crosses their path. Keep that in mind the next time you get into a fight with your clone roommate and wind up crashing into a mirror and passing out, only to wake up in Hong Kong two years later with no memory of where you've been or what you did.

"Hey, it's not like I had a *choice*," snapped Sandy. "I found out later that I'd actually had to pretend to be an assassin for two years and then had my own memory erased. To make matters worse, someone faked my *death*. My boyfriend didn't have a wandering eye, okay? HE THOUGHT I WAS DEAD."

"I had a wandering eye," said Sandy's ex-boyfriend, Captain Frank Forehead, a member of the very CIA team Sandy worked for. "I did. I admit it. She was dead, yes, but the second she disappeared, I was on the lookout for the next spy girl. Hey, I'm a guy—we're just built that way."

So, if you want to keep your man, do yourself a favor—keep your disappearances to a minimum. Or, if you have to disappear for an extended period of time, make sure you contact him in the interim so he knows you're alive.

"Even if he has another girlfriend? Or a fiancée?" asked Sandy.

Even if he has another girlfriend and ESPECIALLY if he has a fiancée. What, she can compete with YOU? Super Spy Girl? We don't think so. Have more faith in your kick-assedness, girlfriend, and put your shiny objects right where he can see 'em.

Your boss is not your friend.

This probably goes without saying, but confiding personal information in one's employer probably isn't the best idea in any situation. But when the man you're working for is the kind of guy who sleeps with your own mother in order to create a half-sister whose sole job in life is to destroy you, you might want to think twice before telling him about your hot new fiancé. Some bosses can be trusted, sure, but they aren't working in the intelligence industry and they sure as hell aren't working for underground rogue agencies that go around seeking out dusty artifacts that may or may not bring about the destruction of the world.

It's also a fairly good idea not to sleep with your boss, especially when she's particularly naughty and there's a very good chance she's your mother. "I would never do that!" shrieked Sandy when posed with this potential scenario.

"But I would," calmly stated Jude Lawless in his crisp British tones. Jude used to work for "The Man," who turned out to be "The Woman," who it was long suspected might have given birth to Jude shortly after she gave birth to . . . Sandy herself. (Recent developments, however, have largely invalidated this possibility.)

"I don't care if my boss is my mother or my lover or both—she's not my friend and never will be," said Jude. "She'd just as soon kill me as kiss me, so I make sure to watch out for my own ass, no matter how hot she may be."

It must be noted for the record that, although we at *Martini Magazine* find this kind of behavior disgusting and inexcusable, if it were Jude Lawless engaging in the behavior, we might forgive him. Especially if he were wearing a black leather jacket and a red silk shirt. And if we were in his bedroom. And if he were pretending to be a bad, bad, VERY bad boy and wanted us to—ahem. Excuse us for a moment.

Make sure your friends aren't actually clones. Or fembots.

In the spy world, it's common knowledge that you should keep your friends close but keep your enemies closer. However, when you're actually keeping your enemies closer without your knowledge, things can get a little tricky. Primarily in the arena of your sex life (or lack thereof).

Case in point: When Sandy finally consummated her long-smoldering relationship with Captain Forehead, Frallison, the evil clone disguised as Sandy's roommate, was right there, closed-circuit video at the ready. It's all well and good to tape yourselves having sex, but do you really want your roommate doing it for you? Unless, of course, that's what turns you on. But in general, having a clone around the house is probably not the greatest idea.

Unfortunately, there currently is no surefire way to determine if your friends are who they say they are. But look out for telltale signs. Say she gives your boyfriend a tie for no reason. This is a sign because A) ties are stupid gifts in the first place, and B) your roommate shouldn't be buying your new boyfriend anything but a BEER once in a while, and even then it's dubious. Or perhaps she smiles to your face, but every once in a while, you turn away and turn back and it's like someone doused her smile with antifreeze. A smile that chameleonlike can only mean one thing—your roommate's a clone, honey. Or a fembot. Neither of them are good things.

"You could also perform the ice cream test," said Sandy. "I just spooned up some coffee ice cream and offered it up to her, and it disappeared into her mouth faster than my mother can kill a man. Too bad my *real* friend hated coffee ice cream. Heh. I got her that time."

"Of course," responded Frallison, "shortly thereafter I kicked her ass, and I even managed to show up months later *alive*."

"Wait," snapped Sandy. "You mean she's NOT dead? Again? Excuse me. I have to go . . . make a phone call."

Only have one-night stands. Forever.

It's not an ideal solution, but it certainly beats murdering people or having your loved ones killed by your boss. Who really needs a boyfriend when you're a spy anyway? You're always jetting off to one foreign land or another, you're constantly putting yourself in harm's way, your insurance plan doesn't cover "death and dismemberment," and the sad fact of the matter is you really, really, REALLY like sleeping alone. Having a boyfriend in your spy-life can only complicate matters, and let's face it—your life is complicated enough as it is. And hooking up for one-night stands is so easy when you're on the road. It's even easier when you're buff and hot and can do that bendy thing where you can lean backwards and touch your hands to your heels. Guys love that.

The next time you head off to Paris or Madagascar or Kathmandu or, God forbid, Poughkeepsie, just run back into that burning building, pick up the guy with the smoldering eyes and hot shoulders, drag him back to the safe house and do your thang. Then just knock him out with a swift kick to the head, pump him full of memory erasers and dump him at the nearest train station. You'll have had your evening of sex without strings, he'll wake up wondering why he feels so darn satisfied, and neither one of you will have to worry about the other person or the consequences of your night of lust ever again.

It's either that or dating only spies for the rest of your life. And you should know better than anyone: spies aren't really known for their stability, now are they?

Just ask your parents.

Television Without Pity columnist Erin Dailey didn't start watching Alias *because it was her job; she has actually electively tuned in every week since the premiere, wondering what crazy wigs Sydney would sport next and trying to estimate just how long it would take for Vaughn to make his move. And then she was hired to recap it. And it was good. And then she got to interview Bradley Cooper. And it was supergood. And kind of hot. And you can quote her on that.*

In addition to covering Alias *for* Television Without Pity *(www. televisionwithoutpity.com), Erin has also contributed to* This Is Not Over *(www.thisisnotover.com),* Shebytches *(www.shebytches.com) and* Metroblogging Chicago *(chicago.metblogs.com/). Her print ventures have included* Red Streak *and* The Underground Guide to Chicago. *She lives and breathes in the great city of Chicago. You can catch up with her life ramblings at www.redhead-papers.com and her travel ramblings (and photos) at erindailey.typepad.com/journeygirl.*

AMY BERNER

THE GREAT AND POWERFUL ME

Meet Milo Rambaldi: prophet, seeker, soothsayer, architect, scientist and great cook (not sure about that last one...just an educated guess). Most of all, though, he's the source of one of the key components of Alias, *the major player in the overall narrative—the central story arc. So I like him. He's helped the writers continue to scribe, which allows the show stay on the air, which, in turn, helps me pay my mortgage.*

CONGRATULATIONS, PILGRIM. You have unearthed this manuscript, which shall enlighten you regarding the workings of my superior mind. Of course, I knew that you would succeed in this undertaking. I am Milo Giacomo Rambaldi. I know everything. I must confess that my enormous intellect and tremendous amounts of talent in more disciplines than you could conceive is sometimes a burden. Omniscience can be a difficult cross to bear. But innate superiority is not a burden so easily relinquished.

For example, I already know that one whose star rose to prominence in the mid-twentieth century by nefarious means will use the name "Nostravinci" in reference to me. I must tell you that I am already quite insulted. Leonardo da Vinci is a younger colleague of mine, and his supposed brilliance is only the result of his craven eavesdropping of my own private conversations. He is, in the term that will be used over five centuries hence, a "wanna-be." As far the one who will be called Nostradamus, I foresaw not only his coming, but also how he stumbled across a few of my more minor prophecies and a corrupted version of a certain formula that revealed a few basic concepts of cell regeneration. Any accolades given to these two individuals are truly due to me.

But do I receive the accolades from the world's population that I so richly deserve? No. Not currently, and not at the time of your reading. This sad fact is the fault of Claudio Vespertini, who, by unfortunate coincidence, shares a similar name with the order of monks who raised me. May his soul rot inside a mutilated corpse upon his eventual demise, which I continue to pray (despite knowing the precise date) is soon, as his advice to my benefactor, who is now Pope Alexander VI, is sadly lacking in wisdom. I was once his most trusted adviser! I was his architect, and my designs deserve to become legendary. I revealed some of my most remarkable prophecies to him. That cursed Cardinal Vespertini mistook my brilliance for insanity. Idiot.

Vespertini fears that I may cause a revolution with my scientific breakthroughs and skills as a seer. He called me "heretic," simply because I believe that science is the path to knowing God. How is this heretical, except to the simpleminded who cannot conceive such glory? It is ridiculous. Me, the trusted adviser of a man who rose from the ranks of Cardinals to the holy office of Pope, a heretic? It is all due to jealousy, I tell you! All men are jealous of me when they glimpse how much better I am than anybody else. Damn that Vespertini to the seven hells for excommunicating me and, worse, for destroying my treasured workshop and erasing my name from the annals of history. I deserve to be honored!

And now they have made the misguided and shortsighted decision to sentence me to death. It is only by my own ingenious means that I have hidden my most important works so that they will not be forgotten. My inventions and manuscripts will be scattered to the four corners of the Earth. It is unavoidable at this juncture. However, I have ensured that, over time, there will be those few who shall possess the knowledge of my superiority and will safeguard my creations. There will be those who will guard my works, and there will be others who set my works in motion at the appropriate points in history. The mists of time part before me, and I see what is to come.

No doubt this is why you have sought out what you read today. Your knowledge is superior to that of the ignorant masses, pilgrim. You have sought out this manuscript. You know of some of my peerless technological innovations and my foresight regarding future events. I shall now reveal to you and you alone my thought processes regarding some of my works. I trust that you feel suitably grateful for this opportunity.

I am somewhat disappointed that my engineering and technological creations are beyond the understanding of my contemporaries. They are mystified. They believe that I am a lunatic. I pity their lack of intelligence. My inventions would have revolutionized our society. For example, a device for communication over distances without a physical connection? It would have been marvelous! But I fear that this, the fifteenth century, was not prepared for my wandering the halls of the workshop complex with the prototype of this device, repeating the all-important question, "Canst thou hear me now?"

And what about a small three-terminal amplifying device that shall transmit energy in order to form the basis for communications devices and sound transport over great distances? I see no complexity in this. I created these plans on one rainy morning while half asleep, but this "transistor" will not see the light of day for five centuries. This shall occur when a scientist in a laboratory titled similar to a ringing instrument happens across a small fragment of my plans.

I present another example: a language that will be readable by devices that we create. I do not understand why this confuses my fellows. It is simple mathematics. To use a term that the slowest of humans can comprehend, a device is either working or not working. Even the laughably simple printing press falls under this. Using a one and a zero to represent such elementary concepts is an obvious choice; any child could understand such a thing.

The needs of my creations do sometimes transcend the natural materials that I have available to me. Unlike those who shall whine and complain incessantly about the "destruction of ecosystems" centuries hence, I am of the opinion that the invention of nonbiodegradable materials is not against God's Will, but rather the best use of what we have available to us. I do admit that my tests prove that such materials will indeed be unable to decompose into the Earth, and although I foresee that they shall one day fill our lands as eternal rubbish, such are the ways of science. If I want to create a part of a window with such a substance, then I shall. Because I can.

I am aware that my devices could look somewhat ostentatious to the uninitiated. To them I say: no, they certainly are not. A battery that shall be called a Mueller Device, whose centerpiece is a gigantic floating red ball of liquid dangerous to those foolish enough to interfere with it, is not extravagant. It is perfectly normal and natural. In addition, you should never underestimate the effectiveness of impressing others with sheer size. Also, when this device is used in conjunction with the extract of a certain orchid, a substance that can affect behavior when added to simple water, the device becomes a powerful tool for anyone willing to wield it in his or her quest for peace. You see, I envision the possibility of peace in the world, although some would dispute my means.

Indeed, I do have many interests. I am an artist, architect, inventor, engineer and prophet, and I throw a mean bocce ball. But, as you are no doubt aware, I do have a few stronger passions that have contributed to my oeuvre more than others, and one of those is the concept of eternal life. I do not refer to the eternal life of the spirit, but instead extending the life of the body in which the soul resides, and have therefore studied self-sustaining cell regeneration in great detail. I have even created medications that can heal those who are grievously wounded and near death. Ingenious, no? What could prove my dominance more than mastery over the human form and time itself? After all, time is an immutable force, and all of our bodies are susceptible to its ravages. My colleague Giovanni Donato, a skilled clockmaker and one of the few men of my time with some small ability (however feeble compared to my own), understood the nature of time all too well. I trust that my dealings with him have made him understand this all the more. I shared much with him in exchange for his clock-making assistance. What, you say, if I am as great and adroit as I claim, why couldn't I have made the clock myself? Of course I could have. I can do anything. It was simply an occasion in which delegation was warranted, as I will be unable to complete the entire task myself.

You see, I had much to concern myself with when Vespertini began his rampage against me. There were a great many plans that I needed to set in motion in a short amount of time. Some of the methods implemented by myself and by those who will follow may seem extreme to you, pilgrim, but I assure you that such methods are necessary. Besides, it's not like the methods are really all that excessive. The creation of catacombs in Siberia is no great challenge, although I regret that the small chemical pouches that instantly create heat will not be successfully produced by society for centuries. Traversing the oceans in order to reach the southern continent of the new world that has only just "officially" been discovered is simplicity itself, and it is surely as effective a location to hide my works from Rome's eyes as the coldest wastelands.

I have hidden much of my work within my artwork and devices. What could be a more appropriate vessel for my brilliance than my own works? As an additional safeguard, I have encoded much of the work that shall lie in wait over the centuries. Do you think I fear that it will fall into hands other than those for which it was meant? Of course not. Have you not been paying attention? I only know that greater difficulty is required in order ensure their safekeeping until then. It was nothing, really. I can encode a mathematical formula into a music box melody in my sleep. Can't you?

My writings are thus hidden, encoded or a combination thereof. One can never be too careful. For a code, I just whipped up in an afternoon an Italian/Demotic hybrid that contains a few selected symbols which shall be used more widely in other circumstances many years from now. That is all. The paper that I used in my notebooks is unique to me alone, and you will know my works by this material. In addition, there is a symbol by which my works can be recognized, one that you will know if you are reading this. Think of it as my eye gazing upon you.

My manuscripts, the necessary objects and the information which is required to read my words, and the components of my devices shall be distributed across the planet as yet another measure to ensure all shall be as it must. They are of many shapes and sizes, such as cubes and hearts and keys, and the number of my objects available will seem to never end. Each of these items must be collected at the proper time and brought to where it shall prove illuminating or useful. I have named this collection strategy a "scavenger hunt." It's going to be big. Years from now, people will play scaled-down versions of this concept at parties.

There will be those who think me paranoid for going to such lengths. They do not understand that everyone is out to get me and will be for centuries to come. If each and every person you met planned to either destroy you or steal the fruits of your brilliance, you would do no differently than I.

You see, many would want to use my devices. I do not blame them for their desire. As an example, I have designed and created a device that is able to destroy living creatures while leaving all inanimate objects and structures intact. Why? Let's just say that I did so because I can. This particular device would be a boon to any organization that is in pursuit of power. It would make it unstoppable. Such is the case with much of my work—it is all far too valuable to leave it just laying around. I'm that good.

Much of what you have discovered has similar characteristics, such as my use of the number 47. I know that you wonder unceasingly about that. What is its significance? What does this number mean? I hope that it is not news to you that 47 is the fifteenth prime number. It is the atomic number of silver, as well as the number of miracles that Jesus performed according to the New Testament. I have also had a vision of it appearing often in multiple series of dramatic presentations set in the sky many centuries hence, involving distant travels where no one has gone before. All of this information is irrelevant. Perhaps. My link to the number 47 shall be revealed in time if circumstances warrant.

Now, I shall share a few thoughts—although considering the time in which you shall be reading these words, I may not reveal overmuch—regarding The Chosen One. She alone will battle.... Wait, sorry, wrong prophecy. I refer, of course, to the woman on the page with which you will by now have been made familiar. I shall refresh your memory with the words that accompany her portrait:

The woman here depicted will possess unseen marks. Signs that she will be the one to bring forth my works, bind them with fury; a burning anger. Unless prevented, at vulgar cost, this woman will render the greatest power unto utter desolation. This woman, without pretense, will have had her effect, never having seen the beauty of my sky behind Mount Subasio. Perhaps a single glance would have quelled her fire.

This woman is one I know well, though she shall not live until centuries from now. She haunts my dreams. Her face dances before me. Her fire shall not be quelled.

She shall live an overly complex life, one that most human beings could not possibly sustain and keep their sanity intact. For a time, she shall conceal her true calling behind a mask of money-changing. She shall be known for her chameleonlike qualities. She shall also attempt to combine her vocation with time spent pursuing higher learning, and endeavor to maintain personal relationships amidst all else that surrounds her. Family members will disappear and reappear in her life, friends shall suffer from her various involvements, and her life path will at times become jagged. And yet, through the many complications, her head shall not whirl upon her neck, despite a myriad of revelations and betrayals.

She shall play a major role in the revelation of my greatness, or perhaps I should state that she shall play major roles. She has many tasks to complete according to what I have foretold. Her familial bond to The Passenger, the one who shall deliver my words, shall be deep. More I shall not say at this time.

As you might have heard by now, you shall know The Chosen One by the following signs: her platelet levels, her DNA sequencing and the size of her heart. And you shall know The Passenger by DNA as well. Yes, I hear you scoff, but I do know these terms even now, although the chirurgeon next door looks at me funny when I mention these topics. If you also believe that some of these words are gibberish, then this manuscript has been discovered earlier than anticipated, it is not yet the twenty-first century, and you, sir reader who is not one of the pilgrims for whom it was meant, will no doubt die a painful, hideous death for your desecration of this document.

But if you are indeed a pilgrim who pays homage to my magnificence, then, from my seat here many centuries before you, I can hear your thoughts. Your mind remains full of questions. You yearn for more. You wish to ask me, "Yes, but what is your master plan? Why go to such lengths? What exactly is the point of all this?"

Foolish one. You are not yet worthy of such knowledge. My endgame will be known in due course.

You think that I toy with you? That I give you answers only to leave you with more questions? Perhaps, but every man must have a hobby. I will tease the world with hints of powerful weapons and control of both body and psyche, hints that serve only to inspire both the initiated and madmen (and, I must add, madwomen) to take extreme measures in their quest for world domination. Smaller minds will attempt to bring forth my works. I laugh even now at their paltry efforts.

This should be no great shock to you, as I have predicted that this is done to the masses in your current society on a regular basis. You should be quite used to this kind of treatment. For example, in your time, I foresee that a certain imaginative mind shall do the same, and he shall create a string of dramatic performances regarding those who do covert works in the beginning years of the twenty-first century. It shall be projected into homes of the people first on the evening of each week's seventh day, and then, due to a cursed collection of overexcitable family caretakers, on its third and then fourth, the light and sound of which will be transported by an entity owned by a mouse which is reminiscent of the alphabet.

So sayeth me, the great and powerful Milo Rambaldi.

Amy Berner has a not-so-slight obsession with quality genre television. Using what spare time her "day job" and her cats let her have, Amy pops up all over the place with reviews, essays and short stories. Amy was also a contributing author to BenBella's Five Seasons of Angel *and* The Anthology at the End of the Universe. *She is a regular columnist for DarkWorlds (www.darkworlds.com) and lives in San Diego, California.*

BRITTA COLEMAN

THE *ALIAS* GUIDE TO PARENTING

In terms of family dynamics, the Bristows certainly have their share of dysfunctions. Throw in Aunt Katya and the recently discovered Aunt Elena, and Nadia and Sloane, and it's enough to make any therapist's head spin. (Much different from the cast's energy on the set of Alias, *which truly is like a family atmosphere.) But, as Britta Coleman reminds us, that doesn't mean there isn't anything worthwhile to take away from their relationships.*

SOME FANS WATCH *Alias* for the show's stunning plot twists and international conspiracies. Others relish the campy soap aspect of Sydney's world—the rubber masks, funky gadgets and odds-defying rescues. And some, to be quite honest, are in it for the leather pants.

As for me, I'm all about the family values. As a parenting columnist, fiction author and overworked mother of two, I look for life lessons wherever I can. From the first episode, when Jack Bristow handed Sydney the product-placement Nokia phone and inducted his daughter into her new life as a double agent, well, it had me at hello.

Who's got time to read Spock when there are perfectly applicable examples from television's most intelligent, dysfunctional and far-flung family?

I wouldn't go so far as to say that everything I know about raising kids I learned on *Alias*. But I will confess the things I've seen in my favorite hour of television make me feel better about my little world.

Here's what the parenting gurus behind *Alias* have taught me thus far.

1. WHEN IT COMES TO FAMILIES, THERE'S NO SUCH THING AS NORMAL.

From broken marriages to parenting snafus, from misguided children to double-crossing adults, the clan on *Alias* isn't really all that different from the average American household. Honestly, when was the last time you met someone with an ordinary family?

The show's cast represents a full spectrum of parental authorities. There's control-freak and ever faithful daddy Jack, the shadowy I-might-be-your-biological-father-yet-I'm-your-mortal-enemy Sloane and the world's sexiest Ubermom, Irina Derevko. The fact that this triumvirate dates back thirty-plus years, with secret affairs and DNA mysteries, only makes for better viewing. Not to mention a few extra pages in the parenting manual.

Toss in one long-lost half-sister, vixen aunt Katya Derevko (the only woman alive besides Irina to bring stolid Jack to his knees) and the whirling vortex that is superspy Sydney Bristow, and you've got the seedlings for one tangled family tree.

The characters on *Alias* may speak more languages than my family does. They may know how to detonate a bomb in under three seconds and look great in blue wigs and dog collars. Still, the key dynamics of working together, of learning to love and trust one another, really aren't all that different from what happens in my home or yours.

While none of the key players maintain what CIA psychiatrist Dr. Judy Barnett might consider a normal family life, they're all trying in their own ways. Nobody ever said raising kids was easy.

2. IT TAKES A VILLAGE.

Alias has taught me that no matter how many mistakes I make during my kids' childhood, because of other, smarter adults, they still have a decent shot at meaningful lives.

Sydney survived the tragic death of her mother (so she thought) and a truly strange childhood (Project Christmas, anyone? *Wait a minute, you're not Santa!*), and now juggles a dual role of partner/child to an emotionally absent, sometimes deadly scary father.

Enter Arvin Sloane, the yin to Jack Bristow's yang. As Sydney's adopted father figure, and possible sperm donor to an adulterous Irina, Arvin breaches the emotional distance between Jack and Sydney. He cheats, he steals, he lies, he kills, but at his best, Arvin displays all the paternal characteristics Jack lacks.

Where Jack is reserved and aloof, Sloane is verbose, freely complimenting Sydney on her character and performance. No matter how intense the outward conflict in their relationship became, Arvin continued to profess his admiration for Sydney, the woman he believed for most of her life might be his biological daughter.

Even his attempts to kill her convey a sense of pride and adoration. In fact, some might say his murder attempts are the highest compliment: he considers his pseudo-daughter a worthy adversary.

Children, I've learned, thrive under this kind of affirmation. While the "you're so intelligent I have no choice but to eliminate you" tactic may not win any parenting awards, you can't deny it's an ego booster.

Arvin's gentle wife Emily also helped fill the gap left by the assumed-dead Irina, serving as a surrogate mother and nurturer. When Sydney learned the truth about Arvin's role at SD-6, she was able to separate her love for her adopted mother from her opinion of Sloane's treacherous activities. Sydney went on to perform a beautiful eulogy at Emily's funeral, even while secretly planning Arvin's total ruin.

Does growing up in a dysfunctional home make a better CIA agent? Perhaps not. But it doesn't appear to hurt, either.

3. HEALTHY RELATIONSHIPS REQUIRE A CERTAIN AMOUNT OF TOUGH LOVE.

Families must fight fair, with respect, and, except under extreme duress, refrain from cutting off one another's fingers.

Children look to parental figures to establish their own parameters for relationships. How we as parents behave in love and war creates a trickle-down effect, and influences our kids whether we're aware of it or not.

Sloane's unconditional love for Emily transcended his terrorist activities, and even his loyalty to the Alliance. He longed for a trusted leadership position within the group, but when poison came to wine, he was unable to murder his beloved wife. This type of prioritizing (family first, work second) establishes healthy boundaries and sets a positive example for future generations.

The best partnerships are based on a certain amount of sacrifice (as when Arvin cut Emily's finger to attest to her fake death); each partner must be willing to give a little of himself or herself for the greater good. Children can learn from this type of selflessness.

Care should be taken in how parents deal with each other in less than ideal situations as well. If the parties are separated, whether through death or divorce, respect must be shown at all times. That means no name calling, no talking trash of the other partner, no "your mother was responsible for the deaths of countless CIA agents."

We all have our weak moments, and honest anger is acceptable. When Jack Bristow reveals zingers about Irina, we can sympathize. Who among us hasn't carried the burden of the duplicitous, double-agent ex?

In spite of past history, when Irina came back into the picture, she and Jack had an undeniable chemistry. Sparks flew because A) he wanted to kill her, and B) his attraction to her infuriated him. The barbs they threw at one another were part flirtation, part deadly animosity.

This type of mixed behavior can be confusing to children, but Jack's willingness, even eagerness, to put Irina in prison for her global misconduct in spite of his attraction reinforced the notion of tough love to an observant and impressionable Sydney.

4. PARENTS WITH CONTROL ISSUES RISK LOSING THE VERY CHILDREN THEY SEEK TO PROTECT.

(Or, in the immortal words of Sting—another undervalued authority on life—"If you love somebody, set them free.")

Although our favorite *Alias* moments often happen when Jack Bristow's anger leads him to violence, his spiral into the Terminator when Sydney's in trouble may not be the best parenting tactic. Jack has bailed his daughter out of numerous situations, from saving her from a lobotomy to paying off a firing squad, but sometimes Sydney needs to feel the consequences of her own actions.

Perhaps Jack operates from guilt over exposing Sydney to Project Christmas when she was a child, verifiably recruiting her in the Kool-Aid years as a future intelligence agent. What would have happened if, instead of tests and brainwashing, Jack had given Sydney an Easy-Bake Oven, a soccer ball or a Sit'n' Spin? We'll never know. But a lifetime of overcompensating won't make up for earlier mistakes, and in fact might make things worse.

When the parent acts as savior, it teaches children they don't have the skills or intelligence to work out their own problems. Both Jack and Sydney are most successful when he allows her to embrace her own adulthood instead of swooping in with a helicopter or special ops squad every time she needs rescuing.

Parenting requires a certain amount of protecting, and there's nothing wrong with shielding one's child from potentially hazardous situations or people. But again, balance is important. In various episodes, Jack has overreached in his fight to keep Sydney from Irina, Sloane and Vaughn. Her resentment was apparent, and his interference implied distrust. The truth of the matter is his daughter is a grown woman and must make choices for herself.

Jack's overprotection can be translated as not accepting Sydney's choices. Whether in his daughter's selection of men or her decisions during CIA missions, Jack needs to let go and allow Sydney to work her magic. Otherwise, he risks losing her altogether.

This is one of the reasons why Sydney's relationships with Irina and Sloane are, in their own unique way, as strong as the bond she has with her father. Irina and Sloane excel at the watch-and-cheer, freeing Sydney to take risks and make mistakes, and ultimately become her own person.

5. WHY BE A SOCCER MOM IF YOU CAN BE AN ÜBERMOM?

(How Irina Derevko may be the best mother since June Cleaver.)

In their first meeting in twenty-five years, Irina Derevko declared she should have killed Sydney when she was born, and went on to shoot her in the shoulder.

This is a vivid example of tough love, from a woman who soars where Jack stumbles.

Not only does Irina maintain a mind-boggling figure and break through over-forty stereotypes, this Übermom is smart, sexy and unafraid. She radiates confidence in herself, and in her daughter.

Children need positive images of their parents, in spite of past histories and whether or not that parent has fired an automatic weapon at them. Irina may have pulled the trigger on Sydney but, as she later revealed, it was in her daughter's best interests.

The two women have much more in common than Sydney would like to admit. Like Irina, Sydney uses her sex and intelligence to get what she wants, be it a computer disk or statistics from a malleable informant. She traps, she connives, and she looks great in a black jumpsuit. Men fall like flattened flies in her wake, and she doesn't look back.

Irina's done an excellent job of modeling the multifaceted responsibilities of the modern woman. Still, she must work harder to share her own imperfections with her perfectionist daughter (treason and murder notwithstanding).

Irina displays strong leadership in the way she continually tests Sydney, challenging her in battles of wit and intrigue. Good parents believe in their children's abilities, and pride in her daughter is something Irina possesses in spades. Also, she refuses to explain her motivations and behavior, which, in my book, counts as a good thing. I don't like going around explaining myself, either.

Though her mystical urgings that "Truth takes time" bring little immediate comfort to a daughter searching for identity and reality, Irina sets a high standard for her daughter to follow. She shows her faith in Sydney's cognitive abilities by letting her grapple with the truth for herself.

Never was this more fully displayed than in the uncovered Rambaldi drawing, with the mysterious prophecies regarding a dangerous person who would "render the greatest power unto utter desolation." The image on the scroll was undeniably Sydney's, but research allowed it could be Irina. Sydney was left to wonder whether it was indeed her or whether it was her mother. The eternal question being: am I my mother's daughter?

That's a question Sydney must answer for herself, and we sense that Irina is watching by the sidelines with that knowing smile and a toss of her hair.

6. BLENDED FAMILIES TAKE MORE WORK.

(Or, My Two Dads, from Sydney's point of view.)

Arvin's possible parentage of Sydney inflamed jealousy in Jack, and he wrestled with himself both as a man and as a father. The truth is, even if Jack Bristow had not ultimately been revealed as Sydney's biological father, it wouldn't have made him any less important as an enduring presence in her life—just as Arvin is permanently tied to Sydney's family tree, whether she likes it or not. Even disregarding Arvin's longstanding association with the Bristow family, the discovery of Arvin and Irina's daughter, Sydney's half-sister Nadia, has linked the Bristows and the Sloanes for future generations.

Although Nadia shares many traits with Sydney (a career in intelligence, a distorted childhood and the ability to look knockdown gorgeous in any given situation), it's clear that in the early stages of their relationship Sydney acted as the savior, the parent, swooping in to make things right. But with such similar personalities, we can see the coming collision of superspy sibling rivalry. Will Sloane play favorites? How will Jack handle this addition to their cozy preestablished clan? A new person always notches up the tension, and those getting-to-know-you kinks can be tough to smooth out.

We don't know if this blended situation will work, especially with mama Irina only recently re-entering the picture. But now that she has, simply imagine the Thanksgiving dinners!

Family counseling can ease the transition, but only if participants provide full disclosure. (And what are the chances of that?) Sessions with psychiatrist Dr. Judy Barnett helped on an individual basis, but intensive family counseling with all parties (Jack, Irina, Arvin, Sydney, Nadia and Katya) would certainly be beneficial. Of course, since Arvin and Dr. Barnett slept together, that might make things awkward.

7. THE FAMILY THAT PLAYS TOGETHER STAYS TOGETHER.

Take, for example, the classic Bristow outing when Jack, Irina and Sydney disguised themselves as a loving family en route to Kashmir. They conversed, they laughed, they played their roles to perfection, all the while clearly enjoying their combined talents at subterfuge, and making the mission a success.

It proved the old cliché—right up until Irina took advantage of the disarmed security necklace and (temporarily) disappeared, anyway. Still, uniting against opposing forces brings out the best in a family. As Sydney said, some families play miniature golf, some hunt for nuclear warheads.

Sydney's ongoing missions where she and her father work together on equal footing help establish the trust and communication that seems strained between them in other, more casual situations. They're stronger fighting side by side than they are when they're alone. It may up the tension factor, having to save your dad at gunpoint, but high stakes make for high emotional payoffs.

And when Jack was forced to rely on his unreliable ex for information and help regarding Sydney, his and Irina's mutual desire to protect their daughter superceded past transgressions and hurts. A little forgiveness and a little trust go a long way in family bonding.

Family fun time took on new meaning when Sydney infiltrated the labor camp in Chechnya to rescue The Passenger. What she found was her sister strapped to a bed, apparently catatonic. Heredity didn't cheat Sydney's half-sister of the winning-against-all-odds gene, and Nadia soon rose to the challenge of fighting for freedom.

Together, they battled their way out, in a flurry of strength and beauty. These two might have missed childhood Monopoly tournaments and playing hopscotch at the park, but due to their common interest in kicking international booty, their relationship is sure to thrive.

8. IT'S NEVER TOO LATE TO START OVER.

Just as Arvin leapt (needle in hand) at the idea of building a relationship with his long-lost daughter Nadia, families should always be ready to forgive if not forget. Parents can learn from the type of unconditional acceptance displayed by one of the show's darkest characters.

New beginnings are possible. Perhaps Arvin's enthusiasm helped Sydney overcome her own doubts and willingly travel through a labor camp in Chechnya (in a completely unflattering outfit) in order to save her sister, not knowing what would meet her at the other end.

Although Irina and Jack might not qualify as perfect parents, they share a love for Sydney that transcends their own agendas. Thankfully, Jack's cynicism has yet to taint Sydney's outlook on life, and Irina's selfishness ("I'm leaving my family to become 'The Man' and run a worldwide underground organization") is still incomprehensible to a daughter who sacrifices for others, day after day.

Can healing and forgiveness occur in the extended Bristow clan? Or will these imperfect parents end up warping Sydney beyond redemption? So far all evidence points to the contrary.

Jack enrolled Sydney in Project Christmas. Irina has a less than stellar track record as a mother, what with all the shooting, stabbing and punching. Adopted dad Arvin's dabbling on the dark side wasn't such a great example. Yet the combined influence of this grab bag of adults has somehow resulted in the resilient, self-possessed woman we know and love. Sydney has managed to rise above her upbringing and become a brilliant young woman with a pureness of heart undamaged by the misdeeds of her parents. Really, it's something of a miracle.

It gives hope to a regular, flawed parent like me.

But, still, I find myself wondering: how will these examples ultimately affect Sydney? If she decides to one day have children of her own, what kind of mother will she be?

Perhaps an involved type, who wants to watch over and know every facet, like Arvin. Maybe she'll be a tender listener and encourager like Emily. She could exhibit the traits of an overprotective, alpha type, like Jack, functioning with unquestioned loyalty and devotion.

Or would she operate as a daring, elusive, hands-off parent like Irina, possessing pride and confidence in her child's abilities while pursuing her own goals?

The question is is Sydney her parents' daughter?

We can't know. After all, truth takes time.

Britta Coleman writes the column "Practically Parenting" and is the author of Potter Springs, *a novel from Warner Books (June 2005). She lives in Fort Worth, Texas, with her husband, two children and a fussy Chihuahua.*

MARY LAVOIE

ALIAS ALICE
THE WORLDS OF J. J. ABRAMS AND LEWIS CARROLL

I never considered the numerous parallels between Alias *and* Alice in Wonderland, *but there are certainly plenty of them, from Sydney's Alice costume early in season one to the syringe labeled "Inject Me" in the copy of* Through the Looking Glass *Vaughn used to get information about his father in season four. A word to the wise: ingesting mind-altering substances is not suggested prior to reading this piece, as possible brain implosion might result. Seriously.*

"I DECLARE IT'S MARKED OUT just like a large chess-board!" Alice said at last. "There ought to be some men moving about somewhere—and so there are!" she added in a tone of delight, and her heart began to beat quick with excitement as she went on. "It's a great huge game of chess that's being played—all over the world—if this is the world at all, you know. Oh, what fun it is! How I wish I was one of them! I wouldn't mind being a Pawn, if only I might join—though of course I should like to be a Queen, best."

She glanced rather shyly at the real Queen as she said this, but her companion only smiled pleasantly, and said, "That's easily managed. You can be the White Queen's Pawn, if you like, as Lily's too young to play; and you're in the Second Square to begin with: when you get to the Eighth Square you'll be a Queen—" (*Looking-Glass*, 207)[1]

SLOANE (to Jack): I thought Rambaldi's work was that window to the past. Today, I am one move away from proving to you that it is so much more than that. And this time, Sydney won't be a pawn in our venture. ("Second Double," 2-21)

What does a modern television hybrid of the spy drama and the glossy soap—*Alias*—have in common with a Victorian-era children's nonsense book and its sequel—Lewis Carroll's *Alice's Adventures in Wonderland* (*Wonderland*) and *Through the Looking-Glass and What Alice Found There* (*Looking-Glass*)? Perhaps more than you might at first imagine. Both center on assertive heroines who have led rather lonely childhoods. Both involve a secret, exclusive world of sorts—one, a world of spies where one can never be entirely certain of the validity of the data in hand or the fidelity of one's companion; the other, an imaginary world where ordinary rules don't apply. Both worlds are cut off from and invisible to the ordinary world we know.

DOWN THE RABBIT HOLE...

Those who view *Alias* regularly cannot have failed to notice the writers' fondness for throwing occasional references to Carroll's works in their scripts. As early as "Doppelganger" (1-5), Sydney dressed as Alice for her and Francie's Halloween party. In "Snowman" (1-19), Sydney's code name was "White Rabbit." In addition to the pawn reference from "Second Double," chess references can be found scattered throughout *Alias*, notably in "Breaking Point" (3-8). The most obvious Carroll reference was the revelation in "Reunion" (3-3) that Sydney's mother, Irina, gave her a first-edition *Wonderland* on her fifth birthday.

However, the most compelling reference unwound in "The Telling" (2-22), in which Sydney fell through a mirror (a looking glass) during the climactic fight, after which she awoke to a world apparently turned upside down. Her code phrase when she called in to Kendall was even "Confirmation Looking Glass."

---

[1] Carroll, Lewis. *The Annotated Alice*. New York: Bramhall House, 1960. All quotations come from this volume.

Further Carroll references can be found embedded within continuing aspects of the series, such as the name of Vaughn's girlfriend during the first two seasons, Alice. A more subtle possible reference is the fact that Allison Doren has a similar sound to that of "Alice in Wonderland."

All these references invite us to take a closer look at *Alias* with our copies of *Wonderland* and *Looking-Glass* in hand, to see how each work can help us increase our understanding and enjoyment of the other.

GOO GOO G'JOOB

When Alice meets Tweedledum and Tweedledee, she attempts to get directions from them, but instead gets poetry (*Looking-Glass*, 233–237). "The Walrus and the Carpenter" appears to simply be a nonsense poem, but it contains an interesting question of passion versus reason.

In the poem, the Walrus and the Carpenter plot together to lead the oysters out of their bed to devour them. At first, they behave as though they are the oysters' friends and want to take them for a walk. When the oysters learn what is to be their fate ("Now if you're ready Oysters dear, / We can begin to feed"), they object:

> "But not on us!" the Oysters cried,
>   Turning a little blue,
> "After such a kindness, that would be
>   A dismal thing to do!"

The Carpenter seems completely callous:

> The Carpenter said nothing but
>   "The butter's spread too thick."

Meanwhile, the Walrus appears to be upset by the oysters' fate:

> "It seems a shame," the Walrus said,
>   "To play them such a trick,
> After we've brought them out so far,
>   And made them trot so quick!"

Alice immediately responds, "I like the Walrus best...because you see he was a *little* sorry for the poor oysters."

Tweedledee points out, "He ate more than the Carpenter, though.... You see he held his handkerchief in front so that the Carpenter couldn't count how many he took: contrariwise."

This causes Alice to change her mind: "That was mean! Then I like the Carpenter best—if he didn't eat so many as the Walrus."

Tweedledum points out that, "He ate as many as he could get."

Alice responds from a completely emotional viewpoint; she sympathizes with the oysters. First, she decides she likes the Walrus better because the Walrus appears to have sympathy for the oysters as well. However, Tweedledee's logical argument—that this didn't stop the walrus from devouring more oysters than the Carpenter—causes Alice's opinion to shift. But the Carpenter isn't a much more sympathetic character, for, as Tweedledum points out, he ate as many oysters as he possibly could. All this logic leaves the sympathetic Alice confused as to which character to find more likable.

Alice and the twins discussing the Walrus and the Carpenter might as well be Sydney and her father discussing the relative merits of Irina and Sloane. Like Alice, Sydney bases her value judgements largely on emotional assessments, while Jack has learned to drain emotions from the equation and look at situations more dispassionately: as he told Sydney in "Almost Thirty Years" (1-22), "while I might look at scenarios more strategically than emotionally, you could learn something from my experience." Before season four, both Irina and Sloane were pleased to lead others down the garden path only to betray them in the end. Sure, Irina says she's sorry, but it didn't keep her from carrying through the betrayal, did it? Sloane has occasionally expressed some remorse for his actions (as evidenced by his response to Conrad in "Countdown" (2-20) that his search for Rambaldi "[f]rustrated me? You mean that meaningless quest that you sent me on thirty years ago that made me abandon the CIA and betray everyone I ever loved?"), but he is more likely to behave as he did in "A Higher Echelon" (2-11), when he cut his losses on the abducted Marshall. As Jack described it: "It was as if someone had overcooked his steak."

As we watch Sydney learn facts about both her parents, we see her own affections swing back and forth, just as Alice's do (although thus far they have not so readily swung back to Sloane).

One question we might ask is does the Walrus truly feel sympathy for his victims, or is he simply expressing sympathy while actually feeling no more sympathy than the Carpenter? If the second case is true, the Walrus truly is a hypocrite (professing feelings he does not hold).

However, there is the possibility that he does feel sympathy, but that it simply does not stop him from devouring those that he simultaneously weeps for. What kind of creature, then, is he? Does it even matter how the Walrus feels? The end result does not change.

In fact, the case has been made2 that Carroll is saying that for all that mankind may *give lip service* to moral sympathy, it continues to *behave* in a cruel manner. This has been Jack's point to Sydney regarding her mother: judge her by her actions. In "Salvation" (2-6) he pointed out, "Before she surrendered to the CIA, Irina deliberately ordered Sark to expose some of her own operatives to the virus in order to study it. Ask yourself if that's a person worth saving." (Despite Irina's earlier betrayals—which await explanation—she ultimately brought down her sister Elena at the conclusion of season four.)

PLAYING THE GAME

"I don't think they play at all fairly," Alice began, in rather a complaining tone, ". . . and they don't seem to have any rules in particular...." (*Wonderland*, 113)

". . . why, what *are* those creatures, making honey down there? They can't be bees—nobody ever saw bees a mile off, you know—" and for some time she stood silent, watching one of them that was bustling about among the flowers, poking its proboscis into them, "just as if it was a regular bee," thought Alice.

However, this was anything but a regular bee: in fact it was an elephant—as Alice soon found out, though the idea quite took her breath away at first. "And what enormous flowers they must be!" was her next idea. "Something like cottages with the roofs taken off, and stalks put to them—and what quantities of honey they must make! I think I'll go down and—no, I won't go *just* yet," she went on, checking herself just as she was beginning to run down the hill and trying to find some excuse for turning shy so suddenly. (*Looking-Glass*, 215–216)

---

2 Mark Jackson, http://www.victorianweb.org/authors/bronte/cbronte/73walrusmj.html

Carroll's worlds might be nonsense, but that doesn't mean that they're entirely devoid of rules. Although rules in *Wonderland* appear to be arbitrary, Alice's progress through this world is strictly one-way; she cannot retrace her steps. In *Looking-Glass*, they seem to be a combination of reversal, in keeping with a mirror-world, and the rules of chess. In chess, the pawn can only move forward as well. What about in Sydney's world?

In *Looking-Glass*, when Alice attempts to walk toward the hill, she finds herself approaching the house. Later, when she wants to approach the Red Queen, she decides to try heading in the opposite direction and finds that this, in fact, succeeds.

The *Alias* corollary to this, of course, is that a direct assault rarely succeeds in achieving the objective. In season two, when Jack set up Irina Derevko to remove her from influencing the CIA and (more importantly) Sydney, his attack failed. However, he then moved in the opposite direction of his goal, removing Irina from Sydney's sphere by assisting her in attaining her goals and eventual escape—as well as saving Sydney the pain of a personal betrayal by taking it upon himself. (Note that Jack's behavior has been interpreted in other ways.)

Alice, as a pawn, must move only forward, one square at a time. Therefore, when she sees the fascinating elephantine bees, she must find some excuse for continuing her path rather than following her impulse to investigate them. Similarly, Sydney seems at times to be led in certain directions, and her viewpoint is limited because she asks few questions about the larger ramifications of her missions. She is sent after Rambaldi artifacts and she turns them over, rarely wondering where they go afterwards or what they are being used for. Irina casts large plans and sends herself around the globe, queenlike, while Sloane mostly sits tight as a king, sending minions to do his bidding. But Sydney is still following orders, generally confining her viewpoint to those things that directly affect her—her job and her friends.

BEAUTY AS THE BEAST

"Never mind!" Alice said in a soothing tone, and, stooping down to the daisies, who were just beginning again, she whispered, "if you don't hold your tongues, I'll pick you!" (*Looking-Glass*, 202)

[A] Canary called out in a trembling voice, to its children, "Come away, my dears! It's high time you were all in bed!" On various pretexts they all moved off, and Alice was soon left alone. (*Wonderland*, 53)

Nina Auerbach states that "[t]here is no equivocation in Carroll's first Alice book: the dainty child carries the threatening kingdom of Wonderland within her," and describes her as "that 'fabulous monster,' the Victorian child."[3] Indeed, many critics note that the majority of Wonderland's denizens appear frightened of Alice.

In *Alias*, that Sydney might be a "monster" of sorts is vaguely hinted. However, these themes are not well developed as of this writing. Project Christmas conjures up a picture of a sort of spy-producing factory, and Sydney's accusations indicate that she considers it in many ways monstrous: "You took away my choices in life. You programmed me to be a spy. I will never forgive you for this" ("The Indicator," 2-5). (Note that this "monstrous" protocol apparently protected her from the Covenant's brainwashing protocol in "Full Disclosure" (3-11).) The SAB 47 project (that we know even less about) that Sydney discovered in "Resurrection" (3-22) suggested a similar program designed specifically with Sydney in mind, but "Authorized Personnel Only" (4-1) recast the meaning of that document.

No matter how we interpret these programs or Jack Bristow's motives for being involved in them, however, questions regarding the CIA's plans for Sydney remain. The simple fact that Sydney was entered as an unknowing subject into at least two secret projects conjures up visions of psychological manipulations and horror-like scenarios.

Rambaldi's page 47 prophecy regarding Sydney also suggests the possibility of a monstrous future for her: "Unless prevented, at vulgar cost, this woman will render the greatest power unto utter desolation" ("The Prophecy," 1-16). If one interprets "the greatest power" to be the U.S., as Kendall did, Sydney might be considered a monster indeed. (Note that Kendall might have had ulterior motives for his actions.)

Further, there are even vaguer hints that there might have been some sort of intervention in Sydney's conception. This possibility is brought up by the existence of a Rambaldi box marked "Irina," the original contents of which are unknown. (It is unlikely that it held the Di Regno

[3] "Alice and Wonderland: A Curious Child." *Modern Critical Views: Lewis Carroll*. Ed. Harold Bloom. New York: Chelsea House Publishers, 1987. 32.

heart, as that was within Mr. Di Regno before Arvin Sloane began his Rambaldi quest; it must have been Sloane who put the Di Regno heart into the "Irina" box because he was the last person in possession of the heart and *Il Dire* before turning them over to the U.S. government.) However, because so little is known about this item, any conclusions at this juncture would be pure speculation.

IDENTITY AND TRANSFORMATION

"Dear, dear! How queer everything is today! And yesterday things went on just as usual. I wonder if I've been changed in the night? Let me think: *was* I the same when I got up this morning? I almost think I can remember feeling a little different. But if I'm not the same, the next question is, 'Who in the world am I?' Ah, *that's* the great puzzle!" And she began thinking over all the children she knew that were of the same age as herself, to see if she could have been changed for any of them. (*Wonderland*, 37)

So they walked on together through the wood, Alice with her arms clasped lovingly round the soft neck of the Fawn, till they came out into another open field, and here the Fawn gave a sudden bound into the air, and shook itself free from Alice's arm. "I'm a Fawn!" it cried out in a voice of delight. "And, dear me! you're a human child!" A sudden look of alarm came into its beautiful brown eyes, and in another moment it had darted away at full speed. (*Looking-Glass*, 227)

"They're putting down their names," the Gryphon whispered in reply, "for fear they should forget them before the end of the trial." (*Wonderland*, 144)

SYDNEY: I don't know who I am anymore! ("A Broken Heart," 1-4)

Throughout *Looking-Glass*, and particularly *Wonderland*, references to loss and transformation of identity are rife. Alice begins by wondering who she is, then suspects she might have turned into an acquaintance named Mabel—in which case she decides not to come back out of the rabbit hole until she turns into someone she wants to be. A miniature Alice encounters the Caterpillar, leading to the following exchange:

"Who are *You?*" said the Caterpillar.

This was not an encouraging opening for a conversation. Alice replied, rather shyly, "I—I hardly know, Sir, just at present—at least I know who I *was* when I got up this morning, but I think I must have been changing several times since then." (*Wonderland*, 67)

The Caterpillar supplies Alice with pieces of his mushroom, which lead her to an odd physical transformation (of both size and shape), inducing a further identity crisis. After encountering Alice's head on a long stalk of a neck above the trees, a pigeon accuses her of being a serpent, which Alice denies:

"Well! What are you?" said the Pigeon. "I can see you're trying to invent something!"

"I—I'm a little girl," said Alice, rather doubtfully, as she remembered the number of changes she had gone through, that day. (*Wonderland*, 76)

In *Alias*, changes of identity and pretending to be something you're not are tools of the trade. Of the newly tiny Alice, Carroll writes,

[T]his curious child was very fond of pretending to be two people. "But it's no use now," thought poor Alice, "to pretend to be two people! Why, there's hardly enough of me left to make *one* respectable person!" (*Wonderland*, 33)

But, as an undercover agent, Sydney is used to pretending to be two people. The problem with this is, when one leads a double life, how does one know what one's "real" life is? Almost from the moment that we meet Sydney, she is constantly forced to question and reevaluate her conceptions about herself, her family, her friends and her position in life. In the first episode ("Truth Be Told") she learned that she is not who she thought she was, a CIA agent working for the good of her country, but an agent working for a division of the Alliance of Twelve, a renegade intelligence group that she thought she was working against. Further, she discovered that her father was not at all the boring aerospace salesman that she thought he was, but a spy himself—and not for SD-6 as he said at first, but undercover for the CIA at SD-6.

In this way, she was forced to question her own identity, which itself was already more fluid by virtue of the constant role-playing her work required of her. Then her father was transformed from the man she thought he was—one she meant to cut out of her life—to another man entirely—one forced into her life by their common circumstances, a man she didn't know. Was it any wonder that she questioned who she was?

It was easy for her to think that this man—her father—from whom she had been estranged, might have been the mysterious assassin responsible for the deaths of many CIA agents twenty years previous. However, she was shocked to find her beloved, deceased mother transformed from college professor and loving mother to ruthless KGB assassin and spy who married as part of her assignment.

In *Wonderland*, the Cheshire Cat vanishes with at least as much ease as Irina Derevko. And, as Carroll tells us of Alice's thoughts on the Cat, "It looked good-natured...still, it had *very* long claws and a great many teeth, so she felt that it ought to be treated with respect" (*Wonderland*, 87–88). Similarly, Irina had her own variety of claws and teeth, which she had been known to use without compunction. Both Irina and the Cheshire Cat have proven difficult to execute. Irina appeared to place her neck beneath the blade in "Salvation," but Sydney was easily influenced to stay the executioner's blow. By the same token, the Cheshire Cat eludes beheading by causing its body to vanish, leaving itself with nothing to remove its head from. Even after her apparent death, Irina has remained as elusive as the Cheshire Cat. It took time for knowledge of her death to surface, and after the news broke, many fans immediately began speculating on how she might have survived—speculation that eventually proved correct.

After discovering the disturbing truth about her mother, Sydney secured from a manuscript written by Rambaldi a blank page containing a hidden drawing that could only be revealed by a special fluid ("The Prophecy"). This drawing, along with its accompanying text, the aforementioned prophecy, revealed Sydney as a potential threat. Again, Sydney had to question who she was in light of this finger pointed from centuries past.

In the second season, she found that she couldn't even believe what her own eyes told her when her very best friend Francie was replaced by an exact genetic double, a feat made possible by the credulity-stretching process called Project Helix ("Phase One," 2-13). But this was nothing compared to the shock that came (seemingly) shortly thereafter, when she awoke to find that it was two years later, Vaughn was married, and Sloane had somehow pulled off a presto-change-o trick of transforming

himself from criminal to philanthropist while her own father had somehow been changed from respected CIA agent to imprisoned enemy of
the state ("The Two," 3-1).

But her biggest questions were about herself. As soon as she returned
to the CIA and obtained her father's freedom, he showed her a video
that apparently showed her assassinating a Russian diplomat ("The
Two"). Sydney had to ask herself if she had been transformed into a
terrorist assassin—another personality entirely, someone by the name
of Julia Thorne. She later learned from Kendall in "Full Disclosure" that
Julia Thorne actually worked undercover for the CIA and in fact faked
Lazarey's murder. However, this revelation was one more example of
how Sydney must continuously reevaluate who she really is and how
her traversal through this treacherous domain has transformed her.

If we follow the chess metaphor of *Looking-Glass* and *Alias* to its
logical conclusion, we find Alice and Sydney transforming from pawn
to queen. This metaphor suggests that, sooner or later, Sydney must
assume a role of enlarged perspective and power—she should begin to
take control of the chessboard and become a player in her own right.

WHOSE DREAM IS IT?

"Well, it's no use *your* talking about waking him," said Tweedledum, "when you're only one of the things in his dream. You know
very well you're not real." (*Looking-Glass*, 239)

In *Wonderland*, it would seem that—as much as Alice seems at the
mercy of the denizens of her imaginary world—that world is, after all,
her creation, and she is capable of ending the illusion and leaving the
world at any time. In *Wonderland*, she breaks the spell by asserting that
the Queen and her court are "nothing but a pack of cards!" (161). Less
satisfyingly, in *Looking-Glass*, she ends her adventures by pulling the ta-
blecloth out from under the feast (a sort of tip-the-chessboard solution)
and shaking the Red Queen, who turns into her little black kitten.

Yet, in *Looking-Glass*, Tweedledum insists that the sleeping Red King
has literally dreamed up the world, and everything in it, including Alice,
is part of his dream and would vanish the moment he awakened. Alice is
affected enough by this incident that she has to ask about it after everything is over: "*Was* it the Red King, Kitty? You were his wife, my dear, so
you ought to know" (344).

Who's in control of the action in *Alias*? Certainly it has its share of plotters, Sloane and Irina being obvious master long-term manipulators. And we can't count out Jack, whose actions are, if anything, even subtler than Irina or Sloane (his long-term plans surface long after he takes action). Further, Kendall, the FBI outsider who always seems to have a hand in CIA business—especially when it has to do with Sydney and Rambaldi—can't be excluded from consideration. Ah, but isn't Rambaldi an even longer-term strategist, whose schemes have spanned centuries? He left prophecies and sprinkled his inventions and manuscripts across the globe like a trail of bread crumbs. He left an organization behind entrusted with the mandate of protecting his legacy... but for what purpose? If it was only about keeping his inventions from the wrong hands, why not simply entrust his followers with destroying them? At the end of season three we seemed to be looking toward a "resurrection," but we must wait to see Rambaldi's true endgame revealed.

And then there's Sydney herself. As The Chosen One, the one who might "render the greatest power unto utter desolation," Sydney is hardly without power. Jack might proclaim himself her protector, but more and more (and with Jack's assistance), Sydney is coming into her own.

In season three, Sydney discovered that she was pretty much on her own, undercover in the Covenant as Julia Thorne, and eventually learned that her amnesia resulted from her own efforts to erase her memory. It was Sloane who put Sydney back on the trail to what really happened during her missing two years by giving her the key to Julia Thorne's apartment.

Ah, but was it Sloane or Sydney who set Sydney on the trail to the box containing the vial of Rambaldi's tissue? Sure, Sydney seemed to want to hide the box, but why take it from a vault that requires seven keys turned in exact sequence (where it's been secure for centuries) to an easily breached vault in a hotel? If the idea was to keep this object from falling into the wrong hands, why not simply destroy it? (DNA is easily degraded.)

Not only that, but Sydney left herself clues (such as the name of the hotel, *Verlustzeit*) that would easily lead her back to the box. The trail that Sydney followed to the box was partly given to her by Sloane, but Sydney was the one with original access to most of the items in that trail. The key to Julia's apartment was sent to Sloane in an envelope addressed by Sydney's hand and written in a code that only Jack and Irina knew (and possibly Sydney, if she had encountered Irina during her missing years, which is likely considering that both Irina and the

Covenant have strong KGB ties). Sydney had access to Lazarey's hand (which she herself severed when they recovered the box together). It's even possible that she implanted the memory of Will to follow to Lazarey, because there was no compelling personal reason for her to connect Will and Lazarey through the name St. Aidan.

So, did Sydney, on the run from the Covenant, ditch the box and have her memory erased lest they catch her before she could escape to the CIA? But if she could afford the risk of stopping for a memory-erasure procedure, she could probably have given the Covenant the slip for extraction—with box in hand. Further, the extreme step of memory erasure in this case is rather on the level of amputation as a cure for a head cold. Sydney is loyal, but she also strongly considered leaving the CIA. She would need strong *personal* reasons for taking extreme measures.

In *Looking-Glass*, the White Queen poses a riddle to Alice including these lines:

Which is the easiest to do,
Un-dish-cover the fish, or dishcover the riddle? (333)

The riddle has a straight answer, but it also poses a question about knowledge in general (dishcover/discover). The question is, is it easier to know something (discover a secret), or forget something you know ("undiscover" something)? Of course, the answer is that once you know the answer to the riddle, it is almost impossible to forget it. The tantalizing possibility is that Sydney might have found herself in possession of knowledge she couldn't live with and found a way to un-discover it. However, neither the Rambaldi box nor Sydney's circumstances fit the description of something "too horrible to remember." This suggests information as yet unrevealed.

Perhaps, then, it might be that Sydney took complete control of matters as Julia Thorne and knew exactly what she was doing when she entered into the nightmare of season three. Ironically, we saw Sydney feeling powerless and out of control. If this potential storyline were pursued, it would serve as an example of how Sydney is growing into her possible future incarnation.

Sydney has seen herself in two ways: as a pawn, pushed by forces beyond her control (Project Christmas and the like), and as an independent agent (the woman who chooses her own destiny). However, she cannot control her destiny as long as she continues to underestimate herself and look no further than capturing the next bad guy. If Sydney has the ability to bring down the "greatest power," could she not be in control of the *Alias* world—or potentially so? Beyond being a potential "queen," does Sydney, like Alice, have the capacity to dissolve the very illusions so carefully constructed by the powers that be—the illusions that form the basis of the world she inhabits?

Mary Lavoie works undercover as a technical writer in Provo, Utah, where she lives with her husband, Robert, and cat, Inx.

LEE FRATANTUONO, Ph.D.

CLASSICAL MYTHOLOGY, PRIME-TIME TELEVISION
SYDNEY BRISTOW AND THE QUEST FOR FEMALE IDENTITY

*I think it was the philosopher Schiller who said that there are only
seven basic human stories (or myths) that have all been recycled and
told in different ways over the years. Alias has some really strong
and apparent classical mythology overtones. Ours happens to center
around a woman who "suffers on a nearly constant basis because of
her life-threatening occupation." The classic "man (or in this modern
setting, woman... you go girl) against the world" scenario is taken to
the next level—a modern day woman dealing with newfound social
pressures and a spiritual and individual journey of what it means to be
a woman in today's society. Ach, what am I rambling on about... it's a
show about a girl in wigs who kicks with a very sexy-in-his-own-way
tech geek in tow. Run, Sydney, run!!!*

ALIAS CAN BE STUDIED in any number of profitable ways: spy series, action-adventure series, series about a powerful female character who battles external and internal demons while trying to
achieve a greater good. For a classicist, a person whose business it is to
study Greco-Roman antiquity, one of the particularly interesting facets
of academic life is to study what the Germans would call the *Nachleben*
of a story: its "afterlife." In other words, the pursuit of themes across
time and place, the pursuit of mythological or other archetypes, can
help lead to a deeper understanding of a particular work of art. In the

case of *Alias*, there is little evidence that the creators and writers have any aspect of classical antiquity in their minds as they produce episode after episode, plot twist after plot twist. But, as is so often the case with quality works in either television or film, elements of the classics lie behind the basic story of *Alias*: the tale of one woman and her search for identity. This essay has the difficult task of considering a show that is still alive and well; at the time of this writing, what will happen after February of 2005 remains unknown. Predictions are a dangerous game, but I will stick my neck out on this one: I suspect *Alias* will end badly for Sydney Bristow. Most searches for female identity in classical mythology end with the untimely demise of the woman. *Alias* is the first post-9/11 depiction of this ancient quest on television, and it would be perfectly in keeping with our uncertain times for *Alias* not to have the quintessential "happy ending" television has time and again offered its audiences, even after the most harrowing of journeys.

I am going to start my examination of *Alias*, though, about a decade before it aired, with a different television show, and one that today is barely remembered (undeservedly so). In the fall of 1990, a new series debuted in syndication: *She-Wolf of London*. A graduate student, Randi Wallace, began her master's in mythology at an English university. There, under the eye of Professor Ian Matheson, Randi learned about mythology the hard way: in the first episode, she was attacked by a werewolf and transformed into one. Week by week, Randi and Ian would try to find a cure for her malady while encountering the supernatural. *She-Wolf* was witty, engaging, creative—and a commercial flop.

She-Wolf aired at the end of a particularly strong period in horror/science fiction anthology series: from 1985 to 1990, show after show appeared both on major networks and syndication venues: *The Twilight Zone, Amazing Stories, Friday the 13th*. Some of these shows featured new stories and casts every week, while others—Micki and Ryan on *Friday*, and Randi and Ian on *She-Wolf*—had a recurring cast and overarching story that framed each week's adventure. Randi and Ian may not have lasted long, but series like theirs laid the foundation for shows such as *Buffy the Vampire Slayer* and even *The X-Files*, the two reigning genre hits of the 1990s.

In some way, all of these shows reflected the late-twentieth-century American culture that produced them. Before 1990–1991 and the end of the Cold War, there was fear of total nuclear annihilation. After 1991, especially with the rise of troubles in the Middle East, the Balkans and the general explosion of "little problems" that had been simmering more or less silently during the days of global conflict between the U.S. and the U.S.S.R., American culture settled into a period of uncertainty, of millennium jitters—and then came September 11, when our worst fears seemed to be materializing in an unforeseen and deadly way. The nervous world of the nineties and beyond faced a horror never contemplated during the Cold War: instead of four thousand Soviet nukes, now there were unknown quantities of possible nukes circulating among rogue terrorists, not to mention biological and chemical hazards, and planes flying into buildings. No wonder the television of the last fifteen years or so has been so nerve-wracked.[1]

Alias, coincidentally, debuted on September 30, 2001. The show is not easy to classify. Calling it a "spy show" hardly seems a sufficiently just response to the show's range of genres. On the other hand, it isn't what one would term a "supernatural" series in the way *Buffy* and *Angel* were supernatural. But it isn't a straight spy show either. In a way, it blends the genres of *Buffy* and *X-Files*, borrowing freely from each model what it needs to create its own new territory in a post-9/11 world. *Alias* was conceived and cast, and started production before the disaster of the Twin Towers—in other words, *Alias* was a product of the same vague sense of angst and ennui that had been reflected in many similar shows since the end of the Cold War. But it was barely able to get through its first season without existing in a world where terrible fears were beginning to come true. In a very real sense, *Alias* does what Chris Carter's *Millennium* avoided: it tackles the problems of a world that didn't end at the stroke of midnight in the year 2000, but that is still full of fear and apprehension. There is a constantly brooding, nervous quality to *Alias'* episodes: each one is fraught with the same tensions that afflict its heroine. One of the show's successes is its ability to convey the worries Sydney suffers on a nearly constant basis because of her life-threatening occupation.

Shows about Randi Wallace, Dana Scully, Buffy Summers—and, now, Sydney Bristow—are, at their most basic level, about the transformations of their lead female characters. That transformation is the move from a state of self-ignorance to a state of self-knowledge. The woman

---

[1] So-called "dark shows" were not terribly common during the Cold War. A spate of them appeared during the early, hottest days of the Cold War (*The Twilight Zone*, *The Outer Limits*, *Thriller*), but what made such airings as *The Day After* (1983) so shocking was the unusual starkness of the "entertainment." The eighties were the decade of the mega-comedies, not dramas. Significantly, some critics have more recently spoken of the death of comedy on television. I would link this to the rise of reality television: when real life becomes too frightening, the ultimate catharsis television can provide is harmless "reality."

who ends the journey is radically different from the one who started it. Each series is a reflection on the changes in the development of a woman who, to differing degrees and with different intentions and outcomes, tries to master her own universe. Where *Alias* breaks significant new ground is in its depiction of Sydney's relationships with the men in her life: family, friends, coworkers, romantic interests. In this, *Alias* does more than just traverse paths of female characterization unexplored by television. *Alias* borrows, however unconsciously, from some very old stories indeed. In effect, *Alias* offers a fresh examination of the ancient problems of female identity, grounded in our post-9/11 world.

Since women in ancient Greek and Roman society were far more restricted in their social and economic opportunities than women are today in modern America, it might seem that societies like ancient Greece and Rome, so far removed from early-twenty-first-century America, would have little to offer us on a topic such as female identity. But the literature of the ancients contains a far more serious and in-depth appraisal of the female pursuit of self-knowledge than anything television has depicted previous to the last fifteen years or so, and many of the same issues examined in poetic splendor by the ancients remain alive and well today.

While most people are familiar with Amazon lore, the truly terrifying women of antiquity were not necessarily Amazons (who lived in organized society, however matriarchal, and in the myths had contact with men and at times lived at peace with their neighbors, male or not), but rather those few women who operated outside of almost *any* societal system. These women were often followers of Artemis/Diana, goddess of the wilderness and the hunt, and eschewed the company of men. Occasionally, such women did cross over into the "normal" society that operated so close and yet so far from them, and, in every case, such women spelled death and disaster for the *men* they encountered—and sometimes doom for *themselves*. Sydney has already cheated death on numerous occasions in *Alias*. It remains quite uncertain—perhaps more so than in any other show in television history—whether the character will outlast the series. After all, a real search for identity is fraught with extreme, indeed life-threatening, dangers. In classical antiquity, where death was a fact of daily life, mythological stories often ended badly—especially for female characters in search of self-discovery in a man's world. *Alias* taps into that ancient model at a point in modern history when even the safety of its American audience has been called vividly into question.

Alias began with Sydney Bristow inadvertently causing the death of her fiancé Danny, a death that could have been avoided had she either not entered into a serious, premarital relationship with Danny, or kept her SD-6 connections a secret, as she had been warned they needed to remain. In a sense, Sydney forgot the title of her own series: the central "problem" of the show is not her getting married, but her letting *one* alias get confused with *another*. Sydney Bristow, sort of quiet and shy graduate student and wife-to-be, shares space with Sydney Bristow, central figure in a global conspiracy that may be tied in with Renaissance prophecy.[2] Like Camilla, the huntress who leads her father's people into battle against a Trojan invasion in Virgil's *The Aeneid* and who dies as a result of confusing the world of hunting with that of warfare,[3] Sydney failed to grasp the incompatibility of her two roles. The process of learning what one is and is not, and what one can and cannot do, often punishes missteps with dire consequences.

Camilla is not the only woman in mythology whose quest for self-knowledge ends badly: Medea, the witch-lover of Jason (of golden fleece fame), whose rage led her to murder the princess Jason chose over her, the princess' father and even Medea's own children; Phaedra, the wife of Theseus and lover of her stepson Hippolytus, who, when her relationship with Hippolytus was found out, committed suicide as the result of the scandal; Electra, the daughter of Agamemnon, whose brother Orestes murdered their mother to avenge their father's killing and who spent years in captivity before her brother saved her; Antigone, who risked death by daring to bury the body of her traitorous brother and was ultimately destroyed for it. Sydney's mistake, and the price she paid, was only the latest incident in an ancient pattern.

Sydney Bristow, on one level, is defined by the men in her life: she has partners, contacts, bosses, a father, a dead lover, a would-be lover, the usually anonymous torturers who frequently have her at their mercy in some cliff-hanging moment. But, through it all, Sydney not only herself survives, but manages—however inadvertently—to cause the death or suffering of many around her. Her occupation effectively precludes her

---

[2] After Chris Carter's alien black oil and Super Soldier *X-Files* mythology, later series writers have had a much easier time with credulity and plausibility issues.

[3] Camilla's death comes about when she is distracted by the golden robes of a eunuch priest she happens to see on horseback. Camilla is uncertain what to do when she sees the eunuch: does she want to kill him and offer his rich raiment as a thanksgiving offering to her patron goddess, Diana, or does she want to wear the gold herself, as a *huntress*? Virgil makes explicit the serious confusion in Camilla's mind: huntresses do not wear golden robes, and Camilla's momentary pause over the clothing, and the use she should put them to, gives her killer enough time to strike.

from any serious, long-term romantic relationship—when she removed Danny's engagement ring, we realized that she was moving from being married to death to being married to no one, and that both relationships are essentially the same. Sydney principally removed the ring to give her friend Francie the courage to remove the ring of her cheating boyfriend. Danny, in effect, cheated Sydney out of a chance at a normal, happy life: he failed to catch the plane that would have whisked him away to safety in the Far East. Weighing on Sydney is the reality that, lucky as she is to save herself, she can never guarantee the safety of a lover, a husband—or, most profoundly, a child. Danny's death was followed by Noah Hicks': a former lover of Sydney's, he, too, paid with his life for his involvement with her. Her relationship with Vaughn, we suspect, was the reason for the Covenant's interest in him: if she had not loved him, and he her, Lauren would not have been ordered to seduce him, and both he and Sydney would have been spared the torment they suffered during much of season three.

As in much of classical mythology, Sydney's destiny, it seems, was chosen for her: "Project Christmas" decided if children would grow up to be suitable spies, and trained them accordingly. In *The Aeneid*, Camilla's father is forced to cross a raging river while escaping from his pursuing fellow citizens. Arriving at the torrent, he prays to the huntress goddess Diana that she protect his baby daughter. Diana agrees to save Camilla, but the price is the dedication of Camilla's life to the goddess' service. Jack Bristow told his daughter that he did not intend for her to live any sort of double life in espionage, but the excuse is unsatisfactory: what exactly did he think would happen once he exposed his daughter to early Project Christmas training?

Sydney's mother was an agent for the KGB, but what is significant about the character for *Alias* is her absence from Sydney's formative years. Like many of her sisters from antiquity, Sydney Bristow grew up without a mother. In some sense, the result was not surprising: Sydney developed more of what could stereotypically be called her "masculine side." More important, though, is the possibility that such women yearn more than most for a "normal" home life, for their own maternity. This is the blow that we see repeatedly delivered to Sydney as time goes by: she is denied not only the chance at satisfaction in a romantic relationship, but also denied motherhood, from the consequences that follow Danny's offhand remark about future pregnancy that spurs Sydney's decision to tell him about her double life to the Covenant's removal of at least some of her eggs, and possibly her ovaries themselves.

If Sydney cannot define herself through relationships either with lovers or children, and has even been denied the normal ties to a mother—not to mention the complications of trying to form a relationship with a father as involved in espionage as she is—then what is left, principally, is career. For Sydney the problem is also identical to the troubled women of antiquity: the life of a spy, especially one working in as intricate a web of deception as Sydney's, provides little or no security. In a sense Sydney is a perfect heroine for a post-9/11 world: she has no resting place, no permanent ties to anything that are not at risk of fraying or even severing, no *home*. And without home, there is no lasting identity. Sydney's work makes Mulder and Scully's oft-ridiculed, seemingly endless travel budget appear trivial: she is constantly in motion, always just back from or just off to travel abroad. Further, the subtle undertone is that even the act of traveling so often in a world held hostage to terrorism is dangerous: Sydney cannot even rest on the plane, as it were.

Another significant area of attention on *Alias* is the strange, almost ghoulish aesthetic pleasure the show takes in showing its heroine in various positions of life-threatening jeopardy, especially threatened torture. The ancients, similarly, often have strangely erotic death tableaux for young females: Camilla's death in Virgil's *Aeneid* is one, and the much-depicted death of the Amazon Penthesilea is another.[4] Dido, the would-be lover of Aeneas, and even Cleopatra, the historical threat to the Roman Empire and lover of Mark Antony, also receive elaborate death scenes in surviving classical literature. The ancient poetic sources expend lavish detail on all of these deaths, describing them, in effect, as perversions of the natural rites of marriage and motherhood that these women *should* be enjoying.

Why this interest in the woman-in-peril motif? On the one hand, the traditionally defined role of woman in society as wife and mother, and, by extension, as object of male protectiveness, creates a definite heightening of dramatic emotion when women are endangered. But there is a darker side as well: *Alias*, no differently than the ancient Greek and Roman poets, bluntly captures the sexual draw of the female in peril. The fact that Sydney Bristow belongs to no one man allows both these as-

---

[4] Penthesilea comes to Troy late in the war against the Greeks, and is killed by Achilles. Achilles is said to have fallen in love with the young heroine as she was dying; the scene was illustrated frequently on Greek vase paintings (including a famous one by the so-called "Penthesilea Painter"). Achilles is mocked by one of his fellow Greeks for his infatuation with the dead young woman, and in anger Achilles retaliates by killing him on the spot. After his own death, Achilles' ghost is appeased by cutting the throat of another young woman, Polyxena, as a "marriage sacrifice" on his grave.

pects to appeal to all the male members of the audience. Further, since Sydney's ultimate safety is almost guaranteed, there is also an element of danger for her captors and torturers: we know that they will pay, probably with their lives, for their acts of violence against Sydney. Before dying, her Covenant torturer told Sydney with admiration that she was his favorite subject because she never "broke" under torture. Sydney's romantic isolation allows her to function in these tableaux as object of perverse lust, and because of this, the sexual dimension of her life is also a departure from the norm and another challenge in her attempts to discover her own identity.

For Sydney, difficulty in finding her identity forms the traditional "cliff-hanger" at the end of every season. In the spring of 2002, Sydney's mother was revealed as alive (and behind the very organization Sydney had been working against). In the spring of 2003, Sydney discovered that she had, effectively, lost two years. In the spring of 2004, her mother's death and her father's involvement in it, as well as the degree to which her father had been controlling events surrounding her life, were brought to light. Just before Sydney discovered the proof of her father's conspiratorial influence in her life, Covenant member Lauren taunted her that she still did not know the truth about herself (and, of course, we the voyeuristic audience learn everything at the same time as Sydney, and so are taunted after three years that we do not yet know this woman either). Their exchange took place only moments before Vaughn saved his beloved Sydney by shooting Lauren and sending her down a mine shaft, but the truth, it seemed, hurt almost as much as bullets.

Significantly, when Sydney woke up and saw her closest friend and recent (at least to her) lover Vaughn after what she would soon discover had been a two-year hiatus, he was wearing a wedding ring: once again, we were reminded of what Sydney does not have thanks to her line of work. The wedding ring is a recurring motif in *Alias*. Vaughn can have one, despite being in the same occupation as Sydney, precisely because he is a man. Women, it seems, can be spies, but there are inequalities in the workplace. These inequalities aren't over who can perform the most dangerous missions, but about who can carry on multiple identities at the same time: women, *Alias* seems to be saying, are capable of the most perilous work, but no man would knowingly allow his exclusive lover, the potential or actual mother of his children, to do so. Vaughn might well have ended up married to Sydney had it not been for her extended disappearance; in the end her disappearance may well have saved his life. Interestingly, Vaughn's wife Lauren died at his hand, another instance of a woman's attempt to mix aliases—in Lauren's case, her cover as Michael Vaughn's wife and her responsibilities as Covenant agent—sealing her doom.

It is no surprise, actually, that Sydney has problems with identity and time. From the first season, with the introduction of the complex Milo Rambaldi story line, the idea was raised that Sydney is herself somehow *timeless*: a figure whose future existence was prophesied during the Renaissance. Sydney scaled a mountain to avoid being the woman of Rambaldi's prophecy, but the overarching story line remained intact: what does Pope Alexander VI's architect, executed in the early sixteenth century for "heresy," have to do with the shy graduate student/master spy? From beyond the grave, another male manages to wield control over Sydney—whose ascent of a mountain peak in northern Italy to escape him represented yet another conquest for the show's heroine. Sydney became a literal "Mountaineer" (as reflected in her changed CIA call sign); she became likewise a "Phoenix" (her APO call sign), both metaphorically and literally in her return from the dead. The phoenix was a bird that committed self-immolation, only to rise reborn from the ashes of its suicide. It is likely that Sydney is destined for further acts of self-destruction; like so many women of classical antiquity, she probably should not have embarked on her journey of self-discovery, *if* the preservation of her life was a higher goal than self-awareness.[5] But, like her mythological predecessors, Sydney has made her choice: whatever the physical risk, she will discover who she is.

As I said at the beginning of this essay, I would not be at all surprised if the show breaks one of the few remaining taboos of prime-time television and kills off its star. The main reason this has rarely, if ever, been done in television is that it precludes any conventional sort of sequel; the secondary reason is the desire to avoid serious fan backlash. But devotees of *Alias* want to know more about Sydney Bristow. Even if that quest ends in Sydney's death, *Alias* will have offered another chapter in the ongoing attempts of Western civilization to describe the female search for identity. This theme now spans from ancient Greece to Wednesday nights in 2005 America as *Alias* offers another story of one woman's journey to self-understanding.

---

[5] Sydney Bristow's character bears comparison, in the world of film, to Ripley in the *Alien* films; I suspect Sigourney Weaver's character was an influence on the creators of *Alias*, who, I further wonder, may have appreciated the neat balance of *Alien-Alias* and *Sigourney-Sydney*.

Lee Fratantuono, Ph.D. holds degrees in classical languages and literatures from Holy Cross, Boston College and Fordham University. He has published on Virgil and other Latin poets. At present he serves as a professor in the classics department and as director of academic counseling at the University of Dallas, where he teaches courses in mythology, Latin and Greek literature and classical archaeology. In August of 2005 he will be moving to Ohio Wesleyan University, where he will be teaching myth, legend and folklore in their Humanities-Classics program.

JULIE E. CZERNEDA

OVER SUDS
(IN WHICH EXPERTS DISCUSS THE RELEVANCE OF HOMELY DETAILS TO THE APPEAL OF A CERTAIN FEMALE SPY) (WITH OCCASIONAL INTERRUPTION BY AN UNCLE)

*Over the years, I've noticed that Alias really strikes a chord with wom-
en of all ages. I've had many encounters on the street with mother-
daughter pairs, and the show seems to have created a strong bond
between them. (Who knew Sydney and Irina were such good role
models?) I've come to the conclusion that Alias works because it is
empowering for women, while not threatening for the fellas. That said,
my grandmother still has no idea what is going on in the show. (Sorry,
Grandma—I love you. . . .)*

*T*HE KITCHEN WAITS, *countertops groaning beneath the remnants
of the afternoon theme party with thirteen little friends too excited
to clean their plates, but not too excited to sample every course; the
obligatory survival tea for their parents; the family birthday supper for the
lucky youngest (who missed most of it playing with her new toys and then
falling asleep); and the final semi-exhausted round of wine and cheese on
the back deck for those not in bed by seven.*

*The door cracks open, a beam of light falling on the towers of dirty plates
and stacked pans, the forests of food-encrusted utensils and the seemingly
endless array of glassware. With spots.*

The door slams closed.

The kitchen waits.

A moment later, the door opens again, wider this time, and two women stride through, the first hitting the light switch to reveal the total carnage that lies within. By the way both put their hands on their respective hips and glare at the mess, they are related. By the difference in years, and jean style, one is old enough to be the other's mother.

And is.

"What happened to using paper plates!?" the daughter wails. *Let's call her Abby.*

The mother—*let's call her Abby's mom*—shrugs and heads for the upward heave of porcelain where the sink should be. "We did. It would have been worse if we hadn't." She pauses. "Remind me next time not to sit outside while the kids clear the table."

Abby shakes her head. "I'll wash." She sees the appalling state of the sink and begins fading back toward the door. "On second thought, Mom, why don't I dry? Call me when you're—"

"I want to watch *Alias* too, you know." Her mom grins at her. "You can start scraping the leftovers."

Abby sighs and walks around, attempting to find something to pull free that won't precipitate a massive dish slide. "It's on in an hour," she fusses. "We'll never finish in time."

"We will." Her mom conjures a way into the sink and suds begin to rise.

After a few minutes, they've established a routine. Abby organizes the loads coming to the sink, drying those on the rack while others sit in rinse water. Her mother washes, humming to herself as if this is fun. Abby endures the humming for another few minutes before blurting out: "How can you possibly be enjoying this?"

Her mother gives her a surprised look. "I don't think *enjoying's* the word. Dishes are part of life. Everyone does them."

"Not everyone." Abby stops a cold hot dog's flight to freedom, makes a face at the slimy feel of it. "Sydney," she proclaims, "doesn't do dishes."

"Yes, she does," her mom says comfortably. "It's why we both like the show so much."

Abby attempts to wrap her head around this while avoiding the business end of knives someone has stuffed into an empty juice pitcher. "Nope. I'm pretty sure dirty dishes have nothing to do with why *I* watch the show." There's abundant implication about her mother's sanity, or lack thereof, in her tone.

"Really." Her mother drains the sink and refills it, tipping in a variety of glasses. She pauses to let the hot soapy water work on dried chocolate milk, rubbing her thumbnail pensively over what is likely gum. "Okay. Think of all the shows we've both watched with characters like Sydney."

Abby grimaces. "Including your old tapes?"

"Including my tapes. You know the type. Secret identity, saving the world, kick-butt women." Her mother holds up a soapy hand. "Other than Buffy. Spies. Thought of some?"

"Sure."

"Pass me more glasses, please. Thanks. So why are such shows so popular?"

"Because guys like watching beautiful women," Abby snorts. "*Wonder Woman*? Bathing suit, boots and whip! Emma Peel? You told me her name came from 'Man Appeal.' *Charlie's Angels*? More of the same. Sex. Sex. Sex. With cool cars," she adds, dropping a handful of purple tumblers into the sink. "It's a formula that works."

"Really." Her mom chuckles. "Then why do you like them?"

The door opens. A cheery male voice announces: "Found some more!" as the man—let's call him Uncle Gordon—delivers a tray of assorted dishes. With a horrified look at those already stacked, he beats a hasty retreat, but says over one shoulder: "'Mrs. Peel. We're Needed!'"

"I don't like the old ones," Abby protests, trying to find room for the new arrivals. "Well, okay. Uncle's right. *The Avengers* is the exception. Emma's too cool."

"Can you dry this? Great. So why do you like the new ones better?"

"Why?" Abby covers her puzzlement by clattering dishes. "I dunno. They're just better."

"I see the advantage of those years of higher education," her mom teases.

Abby grins, rising to the challenge. "All right. Shows like *Alias* and *Nikita* have contemporary settings. I can relate to the characters, the situations they face."

"You care."

"Who doesn't? Not to mention these shows are more realistic. Wonder Woman's costume? Who in their right mind would fight in that? Ouch!"

Her mom lifts a stack of dishes into the sink, swishing water around gently. "I concede the point. Unrealistic women always drove me nuts. And the first female spies shown on TV lived such completely different lives from us—if they had any—I couldn't form a bond with them."

The door opens again. This time, Uncle Gordon is carrying a large bowl of melon rinds. "Bond?" he echoes. "Now there's a guy who knows how to show a female spy a good time." Abby takes the bowl and shoos him back out the door. He protests: "We can hear you in the other room, you know."

"Bond movies aside. Producers had to pay attention," Abby says. "Women are a huge audience—not to forget the number of us who now work in television and film. They weren't going to stand for bimbos much longer."

"So you're saying *Alias* owes its allure to a more realistic portrayal of Sydney Bristow as a woman."

"As a person," corrects Abby. "Yes, I'd say that. She might have fabulous abilities, but she could be someone I'd meet on campus. Makes me care about what happens to her."

"She's like you."

"I suppose." Abby hangs her saturated towel over a chair back and hunts for a new one.

"In the drawer," her mom suggests. "Why is Sydney like you?"

"You have to ask?" Abby snaps her fresh dish towel at her mom's hip, just missing. "She's brilliant, beautiful and brave—just like your favorite daughter!"

Her mom nods at the full rack of dishes. "While I must agree, I somehow doubt what makes Sydney a great spy is what makes her like you." She holds up a palmful of suds. "Like I said. I think it's about washing dishes."

"Really." Abby scrunches up her forehead. "You do. I don't see it."

"Think about it. We see her kitchen all the time. We've watched Sydney prepare food. She eats with friends and clears away the dishes. We've even seen her with a dish towel in hand! Just like any of us. That's pretty honest television." Her mom holds up a clean glass. "In the past, we were led to believe famous female spies didn't know what a sink was, let alone how to soak a pot. When Emma Peel finished a glass of champagne, someone would whisk it away."

The door opens. Uncle Gordon pokes his head in to check on their progress, being the type of houseguest who knows better than to raid the fridge while the Big Clean is underway. Seeing he's premature, he offers his two cents as he retreats: "I bet Steed did his own dishes."

"He seems the type," Abby's mom agrees. "Not trusting with the china."

"Okay." Abby nods. "I'll concede it was rare to find a female spy dipping her fingers into floating food grease. But why should they? It's hardly the image."

"What about Amanda King?"

"Hence the tapes." Abby rolls her eyes. "*Scarecrow and Mrs. King.* Definitely the first female spy to be shown not only doing dishes, but"—gives a theatrical gasp while clasping hands and towel over her bosom—"vacuuming. Laundry! Getting her car repaired!!"

"She even paid bills," her mom adds calmly. "Pushed the envelope of connecting with your audience into pretty scary territory. The show was ahead of its time."

Abby again worries about her mom's grip on life. "She was a house-wife!"

"With dishes."

"You can say that again. Every episode started in the kitchen, with dishes someplace in the picture. Honestly."

"So does life around here," her mom points out. "But let's think about that. What could be more intimate and revealing than a person's kitch-en? Oh, the bedroom's a fine and splendid thing, but face it—the real you comes out when the dishes are stuck together and shoulder-high and the pots rimmed with days-old starch—much like the condition of your sink."

"Don't get me started on my roommates," Abby shudders. "I just know by the time I head back to campus our sink will be filled with its usual cold, congealing mass—with things hiding in the depths ready to take my hand off. I swear to you, Mom. It's like a new form of life down there."

Her mom reaches for the next pile of plates while Abby salvages candleholders from the remains of the cake. "So who did Emma Peel's dishes?"

"Hmm. I did see a kitchen in one of her apartments. That wild modu-lar one with the curves. I'd love that place. That style's back in, you know. Reminds me. Can I borrow your shoes again? The ones from the seventies?"

"Go ahead. Good thing I didn't toss them."

"You know, I don't think Emma had a kitchen later in the show. Guess she started eating out. Handy." Abby tugs at her mom's hair. "As for your Amanda King—if I remember correctly, whenever she had to save the country, her mom did the dishes! I like that plan."

"Think Irina ever did Sydney's dishes?" her mom sniffed. "Not likely."

Abby wraps both arms around her mom's waist in a quick, sudden hug.

"Oof! What's that for?"

"You know"—Abby goes for more dishes—"If there's anything I find disturbing on *Alias*, it's the whole mom-daughter subplot."

"It's only a TV show."

"Still. Makes me glad we're boring, that's all."

Her mom raises her eyebrow at Abby. "Boring, are we?"

"It's not a bad thing," Abby confesses, somewhat embarrassed. "We trust each other. You don't have deep dark secrets or motivations I'll discover too late. I know who you are."

Her mom flicks suds at her. "Not to mention I've done your dishes."

The door opens and a hand appears, waving a set of greasy barbeque utensils. "I love a woman with secrets!" As the door closes, Abby puts the utensils into the sink to soak.

"Sydney," Abby decides, "does her own. And she picks good room-mates—well, most of the time—better than mine, anyway. I'm sure they do their share." She pauses. "Although if I had her schedule, I'd own a dishwasher."

The hint is not lost. "We do own a dishwasher," her mom reminds her. "It just isn't working at the moment. Good thing you came home this weekend."

"I have great timing."

"I thought so. You see... dirty dishes are about people. How they live."

"You're getting awfully deep for a woman with a pink sponge in her hands."

"Am I?" Her mom turns and leans her back against the counter's edge. She gestures with the sponge. "The places that surround us, that make us who we are, come with faces, missing or otherwise. Faces mean dishes. I think there's a very real reason why writers who give us modern female spies, like Sydney and Amanda, have their characters get their hands wet. Dishes imply home. Home implies... so very many things. Safety, privacy, trust—"

"That special drawer where you stuff all my embarrassing mementoes from high school," Abby volunteers.

Her mom ignores this. "Home is where 'you' are. Your real self. Just think of *La Femme Nikita*. The main character only dared show her personality within the walls of her own apartment. Even then it was a risk, but it was important for the show itself. If the character can't logically tell us who she is, then how are we to know if she's like us? Through—"

"Dishes," Abby obliges.

"Dishes mean a home, a home the viewer believes in. Having a home gives a character relevance, a sense of self to which viewers respond." Her mom turns back to the sink, her fingers running lightly over the faucet. "A home, however, is something to risk."

"I see where you're going," Abby says thoughtfully. "We protect our homes, however small or grand. Lock doors. Check windows."

Her mom nods. "That's why we instantly knew anyone uninvited at Amanda King's front door was a threat."

The kitchen door opens. Uncle Gordon peers in. "You're not done yet?" Before either woman can reply, he offers: "Amanda's back door was something else again. What was that dashing spy of hers called? Scarecrow? Always sneaking around her yard, you know."

"If you help dry, Gordie, you can join the whole conversation," invites Abby's mom.

The door closes very quickly.

"I'll never forget when Sydney found Sloane in her apartment," Abby shudders. "Talk about creepy."

"Home's supposed to be safe," her mom agrees. "That entire business with Sydney's roommate, Francine, being replaced by an evil double? It worked because we all can imagine how vulnerable we'd be to someone inside our home. It—well, the expression 'hits home' means exactly that."

"We invite those we trust inside," Abby counters. "Sydney thought Francine was her friend. She had a right to be trusting."

"Making it the ultimate betrayal."

They work in silence for a moment. By this point, the kitchen has clear counter space. The table has reappeared. The first sink loads have been dried and put into cupboards. There's only a mixing bowl and serving platters yet to do, as well as the dreaded roasting pan.

"At least it isn't always that way," Abby says at last. "You know the deal with the drawer. Wow."

"The drawer? Oh." Her mom leans over the sink, smiling to herself. "Vaughn."

Abby tugs her mom's hair again. "Don't tell me you didn't think that was a 'wow' moment. We watched it together, remember?" Gives a happy sigh. "So romantic."

Her mom laughs. "I'll take your word for it."

"What stronger commitment do you want?" Abby picks up the rest of the dirty dishes and brings them to the sink, then starts to wipe those in the rack. "Did we ever see Irina in Sydney's home? Other than as a face in family photos?"

"I don't think so. No. Her dad, yes."

Abby rubs a plate for several seconds, deep in thought. Then: "Which means she couldn't have done dishes. With Sydney." She shakes her head. "I don't believe it."

"Believe what?"

"This dishes thing of yours actually makes sense."

Her mom keeps a straight face. "How so?"

"You do dishes with people you trust enough to invite into your home. Or who belong there. If they didn't do dishes? There was never a moment we could trust Irina; because there was never a moment we truly believed Sydney trusted her."

"It's a great show," her mom states with satisfaction. "Because they've made Sydney into a real person as well as a spy. It would still be fun to watch if they didn't, but . . ." She lets her voice trail away.

Abby finishes: "We—people who do dishes—wouldn't care."

"Exactly."

The counters are cleared and gleaming. The last sullen suds are rinsed down the drain. The rack sits with its final load of pan and utensils. Abby and her mom look up at the clock at the same time.

"Ten minutes to go," Abby announces. "You've put on the answering machine?"

Her mom heads for the fridge. "Not yet. I have to grab some munchies for your uncle and the rest first."

"Oh no," Abby wails. "More dishes!!"

"Real life's like that," her mom observes contentedly. "Don't worry. It'll be your uncle's turn."

Biologist turned award-winning author/editor, Julie E. Czerneda has nine novels with DAW Books, presently working on Regeneration, *the conclusion to her acclaimed Species Imperative trilogy. She has edited themed sf anthologies for DAW, as well as Fitzhenry & Whiteside's* Tales from the Wonder Zone *and* Realms of Wonder *series. In her spare time, she promotes the use of sf to develop scientific literacy, consults for Science News for Kids, canoes, flies rockets and loves to chat about exceptional TV with her family, even over dishes. Go to www.czerneda.com for more.*

SUSAN M. GARRETT

YOU'VE COME A LONG WAY, BABY:
A FORTY-YEAR LEAP FOR THE SPYGIRL
FROM THE SWINGIN' SIXTIES TO THE NAUGHTY OUGHTIES

I've always said Alias is steeped in classic sixties and seventies espionage thrillers like The Conversation, All the Presidents Men *and* The Avengers. *So it doesn't surprise me that Susan M. Garret has decided to trace the lineage between sixties spygirls and our very own Ms. Sydney Bristow. Now all we need is the Q to Marshall timeline....*

THEY WERE MORE THAN FLASH AND DAZZLE, those slinky sixties spygirls who could deliver karate kicks in go-go boots without turning a hair or breaking a heel. Women like Emma Peel (*The Avengers*), Agent 99 (*Get Smart*) and—yes, heaven help us—even April Dancer (*The Girl from U.N.C.L.E.*) could be counted upon to offer their lives, their fortunes, their sacred honor and their non-waterproof mascara to protect the forces of freedom, goodness and niceness from evil, power-mad individuals and organizations. They're Sydney Bristow's predecessors on the small screen—independent and self-reliant, with a sense of duty toward justice and honor.

So what happened? How could the virtual descendent of those sexy female superspies from the nuclear age and nuclear families, as gifted, intelligent and resourceful as her forebears, find herself in a world where she is everything to everyone and yet lost, searching for a personal identity?

Let's face it: the Cold War was a hot place for spygirls. It was Us against Them—depending on which side of the Iron Curtain your safe house was located—and there was no real question as to who was wearing the white hats. Whether fighting mad geniuses, KAOS, THRUSH or the KGB, a spygirl could usually unmask the bad guys (hint... they had *accents*) just before the last act faded to commercial. There was no question that a spygirl could trust her boss, or her partner or her family—if she had any—because a sixties spygirl wasn't about trust.

A sixties spygirl was about *empowerment*.

By the mid-sixties, bras were burning and women were entering the workplace in ever-increasing numbers, demanding equal pay for equal work. A woman's place was no longer just the home, as women like Peggy Fleming, Cathy Rigby and Billie Jean King proved that women had the stamina to compete and win A-list sporting events. Why shouldn't women have the right to fight for the red, white and blue, albeit covertly? They were every bit as clever, as educated, as competent and as resourceful as their male counterparts... and they carried purses, which could hold all sorts of high-tech goodies to help them with their missions. They were flashy fashionistas who could play chess with a grand master, knock the gun from the hand of an armed thug with a single high kick and still have enough energy to dance away the night in the hippest nightspot in the city.

But they also often had male partners in espionage. The partner of a sixties spygirl was her professional equal, someone who respected her abilities and talent and still appreciated exactly how sharp she looked in the latest Carnaby Street fashions. He was her friend, her comrade in shared experience, possibly a potential lover or future mate; her partner became the logical outgrowth of her familial affection. Except for the obligatory episode where the partner or the spygirl was suspected of being a double agent—there would be an awkward scene about good guys and bad guys, but everything worked out in the end, and the episode always ended up on the top ten list of fan favorites—there was no doubt that she was loyal to her partner, her country/organization and her friends, usually in that order.

A sixties spygirl was as likely to rescue her partner as to be rescued by him (with the notable exception of April Dancer, whose partner, Mark Slade, had to rescue her from *marriage* on more than one occasion), but she was his equal in every way. In fact, for spygirls to be accepted as competent in their chosen professions, a spygirl had to be not only qualified but *overqualified* to enter the male-dominated field of espionage.

Mrs. Emma Peel, talented amateur, assisted John Steed in *The Avengers* in his intelligence inquiries, which often proved to have Cold War overtones. Although the Russian dossier on Steed exhibited a respect for his abilities ("Dangerous—Handle with Care"), the dossier on Mrs. Peel was even more telling ("Very Dangerous—Do Not Handle At All").[1] Mrs. Peel was Steed's equal in flair and fashion, as well as strength and endurance, and may even have been his intellectual superior. She had multiple degrees in a number of subjects, was the chairman of Knight Industries (a legacy from her father), and her wardrobe was always an expression of her personal identity, seldom a disguise. To misquote a popular phase, "She was who she was"; Mrs. Peel never questioned her own identity.

Another icon of the period, Agent 99 from *Get Smart*, had an even more impressive pedigree—although she had thought her father was a greeting card salesman, her mother told her, quite cheerfully:

99's Mother: Oh, didn't you know, dear? Your father was a spy.[2]

That her mother believed her daughter to be a greeting card saleswoman when her spy-husband used the same dodge isn't at all surprising—it *was* the age of *Batman* and the secret identity. Perhaps more difficult to accept is that someone as intelligent, competent and fashionable as Agent 99 would fall in love with a bumbling, although well-meaning, egotist like Maxwell Smart, but she appeared to have fallen for Max from their first meeting. It was Max's stubborn refusal to recognize the possibility of a romantic relationship between them (he thought of her only as a fellow agent) that led Agent 99 to quit CONTROL and become engaged to a wealthy playboy...who, of course, turned out to be a KAOS agent.[3] It was the only time in the series that Agent 99's personal life ever caused her to question her choice of profession. Even with the sexual revolution in full swing, a small-screen spygirl with the love 'em and leave 'em attitude of a James Bond would have been unacceptable to Middle America. Just as Mrs. Peel remained hip and yet socially acceptable (a widow in a friendly and committed, if casual, relationship with John Steed), Agent 99 returned to her job...and to Max.

Entire forests have been denuded in recounting exactly what went wrong with *The Girl from U.N.C.L.E.*; suffice it to say that our inter-

---

[1] "The Correct Way to Kill," *The Avengers*
[2] "Snoopy Smart vs. The Red Baron," *Get Smart*
[3] "99 Loses Control," *Get Smart*

est lies with the concept of the character, particularly in the pilot, and her relationship to her partner. At the age of twenty-four, April Dancer, played initially by the soft-spoken Miss America, Mary Ann Mobley, was supposed to be U.N.C.L.E.'s first female agent. Her partner, Mark Slade, was an avuncular forty in the pilot, giving the relationship paternal overtones. With April Dancer recast as the vivacious Stefanie Powers, the character of Mark was changed from an older agent nearing retirement to a young agent in tune with mod fashion, including turtlenecks and jaunty caps. The relationship between the two agents ranged from brother/sister camaraderie to a mild flirtation, and neither the spy nor spygirl seemed interested in anything more permanent. Although April Dancer could hardly be called competent, the character was a true spygirl, seeking empowerment and independence by working in a male-dominated field.

Fast-forward to just past the edge of the millennium and we find Sydney Bristow—a professional spygirl worthy of her predecessors—in a whole new world. The Cold War has faded with the dissolution of the Berlin Wall, leaving the United States as the world's sole superpower, with thousands of lesser political and economic competitors and interests nipping at its heels. As in the past, men and women compelled by a sense of patriotism and duty have dedicated their lives to pursuing the protection of American ideals.

Sydney is a graduate student who thinks she's been recruited as a spy for the CIA. She's also the child of a dysfunctional family with above-average (possibly genius level) intelligence, stamina and physical ability. She can fight, she can think, and she can wear Prada with the best of them. But unlike her spygirl predecessors of four decades before, she doesn't need empowerment—she already has the respect of her peers, both friend and foe. She's a woman who finds success in a traditionally male role by becoming an "alias"—unlike the spygirls of the sixties, her power lies not in a firm sense of personal identity but in her ability to become anyone, anywhere, anytime. The question "Who are you?" becomes irrelevant on a personal level; Sydney Bristow is defined entirely by her profession, whether as an agent of SD-6 or the CIA.

As the modern spygirl, personifying the goals of self-realization and self-actualization sought by her sixties predecessors, Sydney has succeeded professionally as a woman in a man's world—but is still unfulfilled, desperately searching for herself. She has gained the prize of professional recognition and acceptance as a spygirl, but at the cost of meaningful personal relationships and a core identity.

A sixties spygirl could build her place in the world and in society on a strong foundation established by her family relationships—Sydney is denied that option, and that causes her to question every personal decision she makes. When she pursued a graduate degree, she wondered if she did so only to keep alive the memory of her dead mother, a professor of literature. Her emotional abandonment by her father, Jack Bristow, after the death of his wife and her unmasking as a KGB agent, led Sydney to question every relationship she initiates, especially since her career, at least initially, required every personal relationship to be based on lies.

Her fiancé, Danny, was murdered by SD-6 because Sydney broke one of the rules: anyone who discovers the truth about an agent's identity is to be terminated. Sydney's revelations to Danny about her chosen profession were doubly tragic in that Sydney's reason for telling Danny the truth was entirely selfish: she needed someone she didn't have to lie to. Afraid of yet another abandonment resulting from secrets, Sydney brought Danny into her confidence in an attempt to build an identity that didn't revolve completely around her profession and which didn't rely on her family history. Instead, she was directly responsible for his death—her career destroyed her chances for a successful romantic relationship.

Oddly enough, it was Sydney's choice of a career as a spy that brought her father back into her life. Sydney grew closer to her father when she discovered that he, too, was a double agent, but her trust in him fluctuated from minute to minute—she suspected him of having murdered her lover, of having been a KGB agent and of having framed an innocent man to set her free. Each new revelation threatened to destroy the tentative state of détente they had established, and yet Sydney kept returning to her father out of a sense of desperation. Whatever else he might be, Jack Bristow was still her father. But her work, and her dedication to it, continually contaminated and threatened to destroy her family relationships.

Sydney and her father reached an understanding, only to have that blown apart by the revelation that Sydney's mother, Irina Derevko/Laura Bristow, might be alive. Sydney placed her own life, as well as the lives of her friends and the renewed relationship with her father, in jeopardy as she blindly pursued clues that might lead her to her mother. Her monomania was due to a selfish quest for personal validation and a driving need to confront the woman who had assumed an almost mythic standing in her life as a foundation for her personal identity. The kind of uncertainty and identity instability Sydney faced in dealing with her mother would never have touched the sixties spygirl's psyche. Parents were trustworthy; and even if they weren't, the spygirl's sense of identity was strong enough to withstand a betrayal or two. Sydney's constant shifting between identities doesn't allow her to maintain the same sort of strong base.

A sixties spygirl would often rely on her partner to fulfill the role of confidante, safe object of flirtation, extended family member and even potential mate—they functioned as a mainstay for the spygirl's sense of self. For the first season and a half, Sydney's SD-6 partner, Marcus Dixon, was a happily married man, dedicated to duty, who erroneously believed that SD-6 was a Black Ops section of the CIA and that he was faithfully serving his country. He was also a constant reminder to Sydney of what she couldn't have: a happy family life and the inner confidence that her actions were serving some good in the world. Again, Sydney found herself in a moral quandary; telling Dixon the truth would make it easier for her to pursue her responsibilities as a double agent and provide her with a certain amount of safety, both in terms of her work and her identity, but believing her would destroy his world and *his* sense of identity. Her relationship with Dixon is professional—she was well aware that to move it into the personal realm as an honest friendship based on truth instead of lies could mean the destruction of the relationship and possibly the death of Dixon and his family.

Michael Vaughn, as Sydney's CIA handler, also served as her partner on covert missions, offering the friendly comfort of someone with shared experience and the potential for romance. But the CIA had rules about handlers romancing double agents—although the outcome from infringement would have been less draconian than SD-6's penalties, at the very least Vaughn would have been removed as Sydney's handler (as well as from her daily life), and could have been demoted, fired or imprisoned. Vaughn was yet another professional relationship with the potential for becoming a personal relationship that was threatened by Sydney's spygirl identity; by providing Sydney an emotional safe harbor or pursuing her romantically, Vaughn would have endangered his life and his career.

At the beginning of many episodes of *The Avengers*, we would see Mrs. Peel painting, sculpting, returning from a luncheon or charity event—she had a life beyond her career. Like any sixties spygirl, Sydney *does* have the option of a private life between missions...time permitting. There, too, she sought normalcy with Francie and Will, but her proximity exposed them to the world of espionage and led both of her friends into perilous and eventually tragic situations. Her friends, just like her family, partners and coworkers, were endangered by Sydney's very presence, making them a risky thing on which to base her sense of self.

Sydney's quest for successful personal relationships is constantly undermined by her professional success. Although her espionage identity is solid, the foundation for her personal identity is based on shifting sands of familial distrust, abandonment and paranoia. She is the embodiment of the intelligent, competent woman who has made a man's world respect and accept her—at the cost of everything that could bring her solace and contentment. In Sydney, the spygirl achieves the sixties ideal of empowerment, but at the cost of personal identity and personal relationships outside of the workplace.

You've certainly come a long way, baby. And just as surely as that pro-empowerment, smoking establishment chant of the sixties led to lung cancer in tens of thousands of women, the irony of professional self-empowerment for women can also been seen in the current fate of the spygirl, a post-millennium icon in the form of Sydney Bristow, who has gained success in a male-dominated profession only to lose her soul to the cancer of loneliness.

*Susan M. Garrett is a lifelong television addict with a fascination for bizarre television trivia. Okay, so who else knows that Jaime Sommers and Jim Rockford had the same telephone number but different area codes? A long history of writing fan fiction resulted in the assignment of a TV tie-in novel—*Forever Knight: Intimations of Mortality *was published by Boulevard Books, a division of Berkeley/Penguin/Putnam, in 1997.*

LEIGH ADAMS WRIGHT

ONLY OURSELVES TO BLAME

Trust is a key component in the relationships between the men and women of Alias. It's an ever-wavering one, though. From Lauren and Vaughn to Syd and Sloane to even Syd and Jack, trust—or the lack thereof—has fueled many a story line. At this point, after reading so many scripts in which characters backstab and lie to each other, I still don't know if I trust the writers not to kill off poor little Marshall. I know, I know...never gonna happen, right? Hey—on this show, you never know!

ALIAS IS ALL ABOUT DECEIT, both on the macro-level—family betrayals and professional double crosses—and on the micro. Every mission Sydney Bristow completes employs more subterfuge than the average person engages in during his or her entire adult life. (Or at least more than I do in mine.) She sneaks, she lies, she bats her considerably effective eyelashes. It's par for the course for the average spy, male or female.

But there's a difference in the ways men and women on *Alias* perform their espionage duties. Vaughn never has to flirt with the door guy; Dixon may have to wear dreads once in a while, but he's always fully clothed. It's only Sydney and her fellow female agents who end up parading around half naked and charming their way past high-tech security systems into top-secret labs.

Sure, it's not the only tactic Sydney uses in her fight for truth, justice and the American way, but feminine wiles are a favorite weapon in the *Alias* female spy's arsenal.

Just take a look at all the fake relationships we've been presented with, at all the somehow (despite rigorous agency training) hapless men and the women who pretended to love them: Jack and Irina, Christian Slater and that blonde chick, Will and "Francie," Vaughn and Lauren, Senator and Olivia Reed. (You have to wonder what they're teaching those KGB girls, and their Covenant heirs.) It happened so often, one would think the audience would have started to get bored—but we didn't. It was just as delicious a shock every single time another enemy spy wife was revealed. It was just as engaging, just as horrifying and just as satisfying to watch.

So why does this story line resonate? Why did learning Irina and Lauren's true affiliations surprise us in the specific but feel familiar—make a certain kind of sense—in a general way? Especially in Lauren's case, the response wasn't so much "I can't believe it!" as it was "I knew it! I knew she was evil!"

Part of this was the difficult position the character was put in. She was, in many ways, Sydney's replacement: a pretty, vulnerable but ultimately capable young woman with father issues in love with Michael Vaughn.[1] But part of it was also our cultural distrust of women, a distrust that, at least in prime-time television, is rarely disappointed.

THE FEMALE OF THE SPECIES

JACK BRISTOW: There were times—moments—when I became curious: How had she occupied her morning? What were her plans when I was out of town? Usually she told me, but occasionally she'd stop what she was doing, walk over and offer me a kiss. A spontaneous gesture. But on one occasion it struck me: this impulsive kiss, what if it was an evasion? Camouflaging the truth in an expression of love? ("Unveiled," 3-18)

---

[1] The events of season three were a slow reversal of their positions: allegedly dead Sydney began as Julia, a blonde Covenant assassin, and ended the season in Vaughn's arms; Lauren began there, and concluded both her life and the season as a blonde Covenant assassin who could have been Julia's double. Everything Sydney faked as Julia, however, Lauren did for real. This reciprocal aspect of Sydney and Lauren's relationship to one another was highlighted by the parallel discoveries we made about each as the season progressed: it was the same episode in which Sydney's murder of Andrian Lazarey was revealed to be a fraud that the viewer learned Lauren's true identity...through the very crime—ending Lazarey's life—of which Sydney was just absolved. With Lauren's death at the season's end, the story line was resolved, and Sydney was able to truly begin to regain the life she had lost.

Women in our culture are considered fundamentally untrustworthy. From Eve on down, the female of the species has been repeatedly cast in the role of seducer, of temptress, whether her tempting is done intentionally or not. The bad woman, the woman who uses her femininity for her own purposes and who every woman therefore has the potential to become, is a danger to unwary men everywhere, and the consequences of a man being so unwise as to trust her is a myth of horror that repeats itself over and over, warning us of what can happen should a man be caught off guard.

The enemy spy wife is exactly this sort of woman; her story is exactly this sort of story.

But let's back up a moment and consider: what is it about women that makes them so dangerous, both in the cultural imagination and the espionage world of *Alias*? The answer is the thing which to this day remains the most salient perceived difference between men and women, the thing at which women are supposed to be preternaturally adept and men to be complete lummoxes: the expression of emotion.

It is the clever application of emotion that is at the heart of Sydney's best ploys, whether desire (as with the Russian scientist in the season four opener), fear (when she was caught coming up the stairs in Taiwan in the series pilot) or grief (the technique she used to convince Will—at least temporarily—to stop investigating Danny's death).

A woman need not be employing these emotions with the intent to manipulate: the expression of emotion in itself is read as manipulative. When Alice's father died early in season two, just as Sydney and Vaughn finally appeared ready to act on their mutual attraction, it was hard not to blame Vaughn's former girlfriend for her grief—Vaughn's choice to be with her while she mourned her father's death somehow felt like her fault. The manipulative potential of the situation was highlighted and reinforced in season three when Lauren agreed to kill her father in order to effect a reconciliation with Vaughn—again, just as he and Sydney were ready to move their relationship forward.

It was emotion and its persuasive power that Lauren used to learn the location of The Passenger when Sark's torture of the kidnapped Vaughn failed. Her words, the apparent depth of her regret, recontextualized her actions in a way that both assuaged Vaughn's pride—she may have married him for the Covenant, but she did in fact love him—and made her rescue of him from Sark's custody make sense. And despite everything Vaughn now knew about Lauren, both he and we still wanted to believe her. Thankfully, the second time she used the tactic, in the abandoned warehouse where Vaughn had her trussed up in "Resurrection" (3-22), her tearful recriminations failed to move him. (Of course, they did distract him long enough for Katya Derevko to put a knife in his back.)

It's hard to blame him, though, for nearly being fooled. Because when the men of *Alias* show emotion, they invariably *really mean it*. Women's heartfelt declarations quite sensibly invoke suspicion—and how could they not, considering the number of cutaways designed to reveal female loved ones' true emotions? Think of the shots of "Francie" embracing Sydney, and the way the camera held the extra few seconds necessary to show the cold expression Allison's smile became once Sydney could no longer see it. But when Jack's eyes glimmer with unshed tears of love for his daughter, we can trust that no matter how ill-advised his subsequent actions may be, and no matter what the fallout, the emotion is sincere. He loves Sydney. He thinks he is doing what's best for her. Sloane's a cool, slippery bastard in the office, but his anger and sorrow at Emily's illness, and his love for her—as well as his affection for Sydney—was genuine. We should have known immediately that the Agent Lennox in CIA custody was not Project Helix doctor Markovic: his grief over his murdered fiancée was too honest, and too raw ("Double Agent," 2-14).

Why? Because when men on *Alias* show emotion in front of others, it's because they have lost control: of the situation, and of themselves. When women show emotion, they're *exerting* control.

Good girl Sydney has the decency to break down only at home alone in her bubble bath; she uses tears in public only for the good of her country. In the office she is often rash, volatile—but never what one would call "emotional." Compare her strict self-containment, and her father's, to Irina Derevko's exquisitely-tuned emotionality during her time in CIA custody. It was easy to tell who the bad guy was, no matter how much we may have wanted it to be otherwise. Irina may have cared about her husband and daughter, but she was also using them. It's harder to be wary of Irina's trembling professions of devotion toward Sydney than of Jack's steely glare—but while we knew how Jack felt, Irina's true emotions (and thus her motivations) remained a mystery. Because Jack shows his feelings so rarely, any emotional expression is understood as being against his will—and therefore undeniably *true*. The very ease with which Irina communicated her love made her, and it, worthy of suspicion.

IT'S ABOUT POWER

In general, male power in *Alias* is associated with lack of emotion, especially in situations where weaker men would break down. It indicates control: the ability to keep one's vulnerabilities concealed. The few times we've seen Jack, arguably the most powerful man in *Alias*, in the field, his aliases have usually been expressionless men in sharp suits: his Mr. Werner in "Repercussions" (3-5), for instance, whose eyes remained placid even as Simon Walker went on at lewd length about Sydney-as-Julia's ingenuity in bed. Jack's advantage is always, first and foremost, his inscrutability, as well as the knowledge that inscrutability often hides.

But male power in *Alias* lies not only in a man's ability to appear unruffled and unmoved, but in his ability to command respect. Jack's reputation in this sense is earned, but such reputations can just as easily be borrowed—as in the case of most missions where male spies serve as point rather than backup.

It's often the professional position of their alias (whether the CIA's and SD-6's one-offs, or the long-term variety the young but eminently capable—and notably imperturbable—"Mr. Sark" employs) that carries them through the mission. When Dixon masqueraded as a Jamaican diplomat in order to steal K-Directorate go-between Brandon Dahlgren's ring in Las Vegas ("The Coup," 1-14), his success was due in large part to the powerful, well-respected alias SD-6 had arranged. Of course, a good poker face and having Sydney around to spy on his opponent's cards didn't hurt either.

Spying among men is actually very much like a game of poker, with all the players on equal footing (if with unequal amounts of chips and experience) and well aware of their opponents' strategy: to win by amassing the most valuable resources and thwarting other players' attempts to do the same. Every man at the table is both capable of lying about the cards he holds, and expected to do so. The challenge is separating the truth from the fiction.

While the female spies on *Alias* are certainly capable of playing professionals—Sydney is a scientist as often as she is a call girl—their lies are not simply factual. Their lies are emotional, and not just by omission. They lie not only with their words, but with their bodies—their sexuality and their tears—as well. Female spies don't just lie about their cards. They lie about the rules of the game; they lie about their ability to play.

THE GUN IN THE SOCK DRAWER

All of this goes a long way toward explaining why women can be so successful in the field in situations where men might not be—using the perception of weakness where their male equivalents would rely on strength, and thereby tricking their way into thieves' houses (as Sydney did in "The Awful Truth," 4-3) and other otherwise unattainable spaces. Men will allow women, especially emotional—and thus erratic and incompetent—ones, places they would never allow another man. But it leaves a lot to be desired in explaining the apparent success and longevity of the marriages we've seen on *Alias*.

Marriage in general is a risky business. When you combine marriage with espionage, intimacy becomes that much more treacherous a landscape to traverse—and, when it comes to keeping secrets from their spouses, one where women have the upper hand.

Part of the reason may very well be heightened emotional intelligence—an intelligence which, biologically based or not, is cultivated by little girls simply because society expects it of them. But there's more to it than that. There's something men do—or rather, *don't* do—that keeps them in the dark about their wives' true allegiances. And that thing is really *see* the women they claim to love.

Men and women have a history of seeing each other as "men" or as "women"—as stereotypes—rather than as people. The opposite sex has long been billed as a mystery, their actions, their motivations, alien and unfathomable. Even modern attempts at understanding each other—think *Men are from Mars, Women are from Venus*—separate us through metaphor as much as they bring us together via understanding. We learn catchy terms like "caves" and "rubber bands," but we come away even more assured of our innate and insurmountable differences. Eventually, we stop trying, and the other person becomes defined chiefly by how we interact with them: what they do for us, what role they play in our lives. Especially in marriage—in the relationship in which you'd think a man and a woman would know each other best—these roles, the result of a multiple-century buildup of gendered expectation, tend to overshadow our individuality; it's easy to view our partner as a function of what they *do* rather than who they *are*. Provider and homemaker. Husband and wife.

So that means the playing field is pretty even, right? Women don't know their husbands any better than men know their wives.

Not so much.

There is a very important factor here that assists women in deceiving and assists men in being deceived, and that, surprisingly enough, is the rise of feminism.

One of the consequences of the embrace of feminism in the female population has been a broadening of women's worlds, and of their expectations for both themselves and others. Feminism is all about freeing people, both male *and* female, from the stereotypes that limit them; it's about teaching people how to *break out* of those roles that the bifurcation of the household unit had a strong, guiding hand in creating. And in learning to see other possibilities for their lives, in choosing lifestyles outside the box of gendered expectation by joining the workforce, being the provider, wearing the proverbial pants, women have also gained the benefit of better understanding their husbands' lives.

It hasn't worked the same way for men; while it's become commonplace for both husband and wife to work, it's still rare to find the man staying home to take care of the kids. That men have been slower to embrace the domestic sphere, and feminism as a whole, makes sense: women were eager to join the professional world of men, and leave behind housework and childcare, in part because earning a wage was so valued, and keeping a house so *de*valued. But while women have usually ended up doing both (the famous female "double shift"), men have not. Men may accept women as their professional equals, but we're all still a long way from accepting keeping house as a viable life choice. And because of that, men's understanding of their wives' daily lives is extremely limited.

The end result is a significant blind spot—and it's this very blind spot that gets the men of *Alias* in trouble. For the vast majority of men, home is place of peace, where at the end of a long, hard day fighting corporate battles and besting other men in the pursuit of professional advancement or foreign artifacts, a man can let his guard down and be taken care of. That's what home (and, for a significant period of recent history, one's wife) was *for*. No matter what happened between the hours of nine and five (or whatever hours the CIA works these days), they could always count on the safety of home. And not just the home itself, but the agreement of its sanctity. Home was sacred—and therefore uniquely vulnerable, particularly from within.

Not so for women. For women, home had always been a place of work, a place where one did not shed one's obligations at the door, but rather picked up a whole set of new ones. The wife participated in creating the illusion of sanctity, of safety, of peace—but she did not feel it. The home was her domain: her husband was often as not a visitor, a guest in his own house. Historically, he may have paid for the food and furnishings, but she was the one who put the food in the pantry, who hung the curtains, who folded his laundry. In a situation like this it's easy for a woman to keep from her husband the signs of her deception: the mysterious errands, the gun in the sock drawer, the bug on the bedside table.

What the enemy spy wife does, essentially, is violate the sanctity of the home. By revealing the marriage as a façade, she alters her husband's conception of the world and, perhaps more importantly, makes him look like a fool. The enemy spy wife, in short, cuckolds her husband. She is, in this way, precisely like an adulterous wife: the betrayal is political rather than sexual, but its impact is the same. It's not a coincidence that both Irina and Lauren were shown to have had or be having extramarital affairs—the sexual betrayal is a powerful parallel to their patriotic unfaithfulness. The spy wife is revealed to be loyal to neither her husband nor her supposed country.

But let's look closer—let's look at a few of *Alias*' most double-crossed males and the women who, by ripping away their illusions of domesticity, ruined their lives.

MICHAEL VAUGHN, BOY SCOUT: THE DANGERS OF CHIVALRY

Vaughn's a great guy. He obviously respects his female coworkers' professional abilities. But he's also old-fashioned. He constantly tried to protect a very capable Sydney, and not just in the it's-his-job way. The angriest we saw him in the first half of season three was when Jack put Lauren in danger: Lauren, who did work very hard at making herself look as helpless as possible, but who in the end turned out to be running the North American cell of the Covenant behind his back—*in her spare time.*

His efforts to protect her made it that much easier for Lauren to do her work. His choice to stay with her after her father's death was born out of this desire—something Lauren and Sark were counting on. And his need to defend his wife against Sydney's suspicions made admitting to his own that much harder.

Vaughn, notably, is not domestic; his character is defined by his work. By the end of season two, neither we nor Sydney had ever seen his apartment, despite all the time they spent cooking, sleeping and having frequent and enthusiastic trysts in hers. In season three, we never saw him in his living space without Lauren, at least not until he was finally clued in to his wife's duplicity by Sydney—his ex-lover and our heroine, yes, but more importantly, another female spy. In this scene in "Unveiled," alone on-screen in his bedroom for the very first time as he searched for evidence of his wife's betrayal, it was almost as if he was rediscovering the space in which he lived. Nothing in it—not his marriage, not his wife, not even her suitcase—was what he'd thought. Not safe. Not an escape.

Home, for Michael Vaughn, was a foreign space, mediated and made accessible by female presence. Weiss' revelation that Vaughn burned down the home he'd shared with Lauren at the beginning of season four was hardly surprising—the space was never really his to begin with.

THE EDUCATION OF JONATHAN BRISTOW

Before Irina's betrayal, Jack was, I imagine, much the same as Vaughn: his manipulative if always well-intentioned paternalism toward Sydney, his treatment of her as his daughter first and her own woman second, indicates an inability to carry the clear, unsentimental vision he exercises in his professional life into his personal one. He has trouble seeing her external to his relationship to her. Another clue to who Jack used to be lies in Sydney's recollections of Laura Bristow. She appears in Sydney's memories as a variation on the domestic goddess: a wonderful mother, a loving wife. This wouldn't have been the case if Jack had not responded to such a woman; Irina, in creating Laura for Jack to fall in love with, wouldn't have crafted her as such otherwise. We suspect that Laura, despite her work as a Russian literature professor, took care of both Sydney and the majority of the household duties. Honestly, can you imagine Jack Bristow dusting?

After he learned of Irina's betrayal, Jack withdrew from the domestic sphere—and from Sydney—altogether. Would he have been able to do so had he been more involved before? And wouldn't he have discovered his wife's true loyalties if he had been? "What I do regret [about my relationship with Irina] is, once I saw signs of her duplicity, once I sensed her betrayal, I chose to ignore it," Jack told Vaughn in "Unveiled." If he'd paid attention, perhaps he would have noticed who his wife really was—not just what she did and was for *him*. The enemy spy wife's secret life is an apt metaphor for the modern woman's reality: dangerous, subversive and characterized by a simmering frustration. There was always more to Irina's life, to *her*, than Jack chose to see; her job may have been to fool him, but he didn't have to make it quite so easy.

One of Jack's most appealing qualities is, in a way, his very distrust of Irina: she is possibly the only person he does not believe he can outmaneuver, the only person who has successfully played him for a fool. And he respects her for it. He doesn't like it, or her (as much as he is still drawn to her), and he certainly doesn't approve of her actions. But he does respect them, in the sense of acknowledging their power, and hers. She is his equal, or better, and that is why their dynamic is so...well, *dynamic*. He may have taken her for granted before, but now he makes it his priority to watch her—I imagine it's almost a kind of revenge for Irina, for all the time he spent before not really seeing her at all.

WILL TIPPIN, AND SUBJECTS SUITABLE FOR INVESTIGATION

In contrast to Vaughn and Jack, Will was associated from the beginning with hearth and home—he, together with Francie, was the very definition of home for Sydney (her "safe place," but also the place she felt the need to guard her secrets most difficult and most necessary). He was also feminized in comparison to the other male regulars—he was more transparent regarding his feelings, *Alias'* version of the damsel in distress. When he jammed the syringe into Dr. Lee's neck in "Almost Thirty Years" (1-22), we cheered in a way we did not when Sydney fought her way out of his clutches in the pilot: we expect that kind of thing from our heroine, whereas Will's success was an out-and-out triumph.

Will's investigation of Danny's death managed to unearth the existence of SD-6, but not the fact that Sydney, with whom he practically lived, was involved—at least until she fought her way through Khasinau's men in Paris to rescue him. He spent the whole first season being smarter and more observant than the average civilian, but only regarding his work. He was still vulnerable to being taken advantage of in his emotional life, and Allison was able to use that.

He was, however, the only one of our ill-fated men to discover his lover's duplicity on his own—incidentally, in the home. Perhaps being suspected of being the second clone was what brought the intersection between his personal and professional lives into focus; it was with these new eyes that his search of Sydney and Francie's bathroom turned up

Allison's supply of Provacillium. In more than just the folder Allison found on the living room side table, Will had finally brought his work *home*.

LOVE THY ENEMY: ARVIN SLOANE AND JULIAN SARK

Romantic and professional betrayal isn't limited to the good guys. Emily would have been Sloane's downfall if she hadn't changed her mind at the last possible moment, revealing the CIA wire taped beneath her blouse. (And even so, Sloane paid for his trust with her death.) Sark certainly wasn't expecting Lauren's betrayal when she took the Covenant cell leaders' bracelets to Cole behind his back—though, considering the duplicitous nature of her Covenant assignment, he really should have.

Sark, incidentally, may be the closest thing to a male feminist[2] *Alias* can boast. Sark treats female opponents the same way he does male ones—usually with a bullet to whatever body part seems most expedient. He also doesn't like to work alone; his instinct is to form partnerships, and to form them (largely) with women: Irina, Allison, Lauren. Not to mention his unabashed praise of Sydney's abilities and his attempts to convince her to work with him.

And where his affections lie, there also lie his true allegiances. Despite his claim of "flexible" loyalties, his faithfulness to Irina during her CIA incarceration and the extent of the damage Vaughn had to inflict in order to extract Lauren's location from him indicate otherwise.

As admirable as this might be (if you can call anything about Sark admirable), it's a dangerous thing in the emotional landscape of *Alias*, where only one thing remains constant: you can't trust women. Even after they became sexually involved, Lauren (we suspect) would have turned on him in an instant had circumstances favored it; she was certainly quick to assume *he* had turned on *her* when Bomani ordered her death. Irina gave him up to Sydney and the CIA without a second thought. Even Allison betrayed him in her attachment to Will—and very well may have betrayed him literally had the assignment continued, eventually coming to consider her feelings for her mark more important than her professional loyalties.

In our world, these relationships likely would have gone differently. In our world, the average Jane on the street will tell you that, in roman-

---

[2] Or more accurately, a *postfeminist*—a member of the first generation to really benefit from feminism's advances, and therefore prone to taking his or her enlightened view of women for granted.

tic relationships, it's women whose intentions are honest and trustworthy, and men who are frequently duplicitous snakes. There's obviously an important disconnect here between our world and the world of the show. The question is what that disconnect is, and what it tells us about ourselves.

A CAVEAT, OR WHY *ALIAS* WORKS

The *Alias* universe is not our own. It's fiction. But as fiction—and as fiction that *works*—it exists in a complex, often delicate, dialogue with our own. Reality is inverted, fragmented, reflected back to us in ways that tell us both about who and what we are and, more crucially, who and what we *want*. *Alias* is a fantasy in the deepest, most meaningful way, one that is satisfying to both men *and* women—and in the end, creates a story that brings us closer together rather than driving us further apart.

The basic premise of *Alias* is, of course, appealing to women: its heroine is a strong, attractive, *capable* young woman who kicks ass and takes names, excels at her work and, despite the dramatically requisite gauntlet she and Vaughn are forced to fight their way through to get to one another, is undeniably loved. But what also appeals, on a much more visceral level, is the pervasiveness of female betrayal.

Being an enemy spy is bad. Sleeping with somebody for information is immoral, and really, really mean. But the very fact that these women *can* do these things, that they are strong enough, clever enough, ruthless enough, to do them, is very, very appealing—they are as empowering in their way as Sydney is in hers.

Even more than that, *Alias* is a revenge fantasy. This impulse finds a fairly acceptable outlet in the missions in which Sydney, appearing to put herself at her male mark's mercy, turns the tables on him ("What," Sydney memorably demanded in "Phase One" (2-13), razor-thin wire wrapped tightly around Alliance agent Giles Macor's neck, "was wrong with the black one?"). But it's even more darkly and appealingly played out in Lauren's merciless use of Vaughn, in Irina's brutal exploitation of Jack's need of her. These men in particular may not have deserved it, but men *in general* did. It's the female viewer's revenge for every man who pretended to love her and violated her trust. The female spy uses men's weaknesses against them. And some part of it feels *good*.

So what here is appealing to men? Certainly it's not the betrayal itself.

While domination and power play may be appealing to some, the typical male fear of cuckoldry is too deeply ingrained for this to be the crux of the appeal. And it's possible that you can attribute the male viewership largely to Sydney's outfits, but I think it's more than that. The fear of being betrayed—a chief component, if not the main one, of the fear of intimacy—is exacerbated by *Alias'* plotlines...but it's also soothed by them. With the possible exception of Irina, whose status as the heroine's mother affords her significantly more complexity, these women are portrayed as out-and-out *evil*. And the punishment for their betrayal? Death. In fact, the enemy spy wife's likelihood of living is directly proportionate to the regret she expresses for her actions. Elsa Caplan (the blonde chick married to Christian Slater) kept her life and regained the husband and son who meant so much to her only because her guilt was keen enough to make her confess—and commit treason against her country, all for the sake of the man she was *supposed* to simply use, not love. And if that's not enough, the male viewer always has Sydney to look to—Sydney, who is held up as the paragon of everything womanhood can be: she's emotional, and she's powerful, but she's also honest, and good, and looks hot in black leather. What more could a viewer of either sex want?

WHAT'S TO COME

The brilliance of *Alias* is its projection of the interpersonal onto the complexities of global espionage: every relationship pitfall becomes a matter of national security. Marrying the wrong woman puts others' lives at risk. Putting your trust in a pretty face could mean losing your own. In a landscape this fraught with possible missteps, a spy must guard against not only her opponents, but her loved ones—and herself, as Sydney's missing time as Julia Thorne attests.

As Sydney and Vaughn continue to negotiate the difficult terrain of the international spy's love affair, with its two-year disappearances, classified investigations, cliff-hanger revelations and whatever else the staff of *Alias* can manage to come up with, they will have to take care. Probably neither of them will turn out to be a true enemy—*probably*—but neither are they insulated against the relational slings and arrows that their ever-changing lives, loyalties and aliases are heir to. But with Sydney older, wiser and aware of Vaughn's secrets, and Vaughn's eyes opened to his own self-deceptions, I have faith that, whatever happens, their relationship will show the way toward a better paradigm of male-female relations: one based on sincerity, emotional honesty and genuine respect.

If Leigh Adams Wright told you who she really was, she'd have to kill you. Leigh would like to thank Antonio at the Dallas Starbucks on Lower Greenville for covering her essay-inspiring peppermint hot chocolate when she left her check card in her other pants. She didn't bat her eyelashes once. She swears.

See more of Leigh's work in Finding Serenity: Anti-heroes, Lost Shepherds and Space Hookers in Joss Whedon's Firefly.

ROXANNE LONGSTREET CONRAD

THEY SCANNED OUR BRAIN WAVES
FROM ORBIT . . .

Well, yes, admittedly this episode that Roxanne Longstreet Conrad analyzes um . . . how . . . do I say this . . . pushed the envelope of realism to the limits. When I first read the script, I remember thinking that scanning brain waves from outer space seemed absurd too. But in the world of Alias, *anything goes. And, hey, it's still darn entertaining! (I mean, at least we didn't "jump the shark," right?)*

LOVE *ALIAS*. I'm a first-adopter; I was an *Alias* fan from the premiere on. I hooted when I got my new HDTV and realized the show was wide-screen and psychedelically high-deffy. I love the kickboxing, the cool shoes, the bad-ass wigs, the shameless use of lingerie and frequent use of automatic weapons. Okay, like a lot of people, I started getting bogged down in the increasingly sticky mythology of Rambaldi, but heck, it was still kinda cool, because science fiction? DaVinci? Cool.

I even like Evil!Lauren. I like the sexual heat of want-Sydney-can't-have-her-because-I'm-married-to-an-evil-traitorous-bitch Vaughn. I can even kind of buy the idea of Redeemed!Sloane, though I'm still secretly waiting for him to bury the knife in someone's back.

So you can imagine my shock when I saw an episode of *Alias* that went completely off the rails, crashed, burned and exploded. *Surely*, I thought, *this cannot be the fault of my beloved writers!* Like Sydney presented with evidence of the latest betrayal by someone she trusted, well, I just couldn't accept it. So, like any good *Alias* fan, I did a little digging. It involved cool gadgets, spy planes, fake IDs, a purple wig and spandex, but I'm prepared to give my all for my fandoms.

I can now reveal that I am in possession of secret documents, retrieved at great personal risk from the vaults of SD-6's secret Los Angeles bunker, that show a *mole inside the* Alias *staff.* The episode in question was a *terrorist act.* And, thank God, I'm here to expose it, lest any of you die-hard fellow *Alias* fans actually believe that it was, ah, one big, huge, enormous screwup on the part of the *Alias* creative team.

Just remember that this episode demonstrates the sinister global reach of someone who *wants to destroy the show lest we find out just how accurate it is.*

Ahem.

Let me present the evidence of SD-6's massive involvement.

Ladies and gentlemen, I give you the third-season episode "Blood Ties."[1]

Our story begins with Vaughn and Dixon having a top-secret conversation in the CIA Shooting Range, for no apparent reason except to show off the coolness of Manly Men With Guns. We have this conversation out in the open because, you know, the CIA has *never* had any security problems.

Vaughn and Dixon recap a bunch, just to make sure you're thoroughly confused, but ultimately, they talk about using Lauren, Vaughn's hell-bitch-traitor wife, to *feed disinformation to the Covenant.*

Let me pause a moment.

Feed disinformation to the . . . First of all, we never know what the hell is going on, right? And we never know what the Covenant is doing, either. Or what the game is. Or what they want. Remind me again what disinformation we're feeding. . . ? Oh, forget it, it doesn't really matter. The important thing is, of course, that *Weiss will maintain surveillance on Lauren.* So we're going to detail *one* agent (and hey, I love Weiss, I'm down with the Weiss-love) to watch the single most dangerous double agent we've ever seen while she traipses around with all kinds of vital information, tra-la-la. Oh, and of course, she would *recognize him on sight.*

I don't know about you, but this sounds like a seriously bad plan.

---

[1] Transcript from http://www.addictedtoalias.com/BloodTies.htm

It would be a bad plan if I detailed Weiss to follow around a guy in a Goofy suit shoplifting at Wal-Mart, much less Double Agent Girl who can seemingly appear and disappear at will. And did I mention that she would *recognize him on sight?*

(SD-6 wants us to believe that the CIA would be bone-headed enough to do this. Pshaw. Pshaw, I say. It's a weak attempt to sway us.)

Meanwhile, Sydney and her dad (and Sloane) have some conversation about Sloane not being really, completely dead, and she's shocked. D'oh! Sydney, where were you during the last dozen "I thought you were dead!" scenarios? *We* knew Sloane wasn't dead. Jeez. But I admit Sloane's dialogue here is a priceless example of why SD-6's infiltration of the *Alias* staff is so insidiously horrible:

> SLOANE: Your father was kind enough to offer me a final glass of wine. It was laced with a tetrodotoxin compound. It counteracted the lethal injection while reducing my cardiac and respiratory functions.

So, so many things wrong with that speech. Forget about the CIA: what prison in the world will allow you to waltz in with a bottle of amontillado (or whatever it was they were drinking) and quaff a glass or two with the condemned prisoner? The CIA would be just a *little* more careful. Especially given the twisty cleverness of Jack Bristow and his amazing ability to subvert rules and get away with it. But no. Nobody in the warped SD-6 version of the *Alias*verse raises an eyebrow. "Sure, buddy, go on in. Party like it's 1999! Save some for us!"

Second: I felt it was necessary to do a little research on the whole tetrodotoxin issue. Tetrodotoxin—which is well-known for its tendency to poison people who insist on ordering *food that can kill you,* like puffer fish—actually *is* water-soluble. Step one: check. You can pour it into the glass of wine. Oh, and I looked it up: the pH balance of wine is 3.5, which is acid, not alkaline.[2] The tetrodotoxin will remain heat-stable and effective. So I'll give them that one.

Now, the specific *effects* of tetrodotoxin are pretty interesting. According to my medical resources,[3] "Tetrodotoxin blocks diffusion of sodium through the sodium channel, preventing depolarization and propagation of action potentials in nerve cells. All of the observed toxicity is secondary to the action potential blockade. Tetrodotoxin acts on

---

[2] http://www.aim4health.com/phind.htm
[3] http://www.emedicine.com/emerg/topic576.htm

the central and the peripheral nervous systems (*i.e.*, autonomic, motor, sensory nerves). Tetrodotoxin also stimulates the chemoreceptor trigger zone in the medulla oblongata and depresses the respiratory and vaso-motor centers in that area."

So . . . the stuff paralyzes your nervous system, slows down your respi-ration and heart and eventually kills you either by suffocation or heart attack. Right? And Sloane did say, ". . . while reducing my cardiac and respiratory functions."

Of course, he would have been showing signs of it before being walked in for lethal injection. But that's a nitpick. So, charitably, step two: green light. It does what he said.

But wait! "It counteracted the lethal injection. . . ."

Lethal injections are a combination of three drugs. The first (sodium pentothal) is a sedative that puts you out. The second chemical is usually Pavulon, which is—wait for it!—a curare derivative that locks up the heart and lungs. The third is the stuff (potassium chloride) that kills you.

Back up. *Tetrodotoxin* locks up the heart and lungs . . . *Pavulon* locks up the heart and lungs . . . and by SD-6-infected *Alias* logic, *they counter-act each other.* Of course! In much the same way that taking one brand-name barbiturate on top of another will *negate the effects!* Wow. Alert the ER! I have a whole new treatment for overdoses!

Yes. My head imploded. Because even just my cursory and shallow knowledge of how drugs interact tells me that tetrodotoxin doesn't can-cel out potassium chloride.

(Okay, fine. You Google it for proof and send me the chemical evidence if it does. But if you do, it just proves that *you're working for SD-6.*)

Damn. I'm only on page 2 of 20 of the transcript. Let me sum up.

Blah, blah, blah. Hourglass Rambaldi doohickey from a previous epi-sode. Sloane smashes it to get green goo. Lots of talk about elixirs and Passengers and Rambaldi, none of which makes a whole hell of a lot of sense. (See, at this point, SD-6 had given hallucinogenic compounds to the entire *Alias* staff and was rewriting at will. Sure, it *looked* like a giant party. But in reality it was a masterful, untraceable coup. Genius.)

Vaughn flirts with Evil!Lauren. When he's forced to kiss her, we all make vomiting sounds. Then Vaughn has a meeting with Plot Device Guy (a.k.a. Agent Brill), who delivers an expository bunch of nonsense about how Vaughn's father, who was killed by Sydney's mom, was really a double agent for the ultra-secret cult of Rambaldi. (For an ultra-secret cult nobody ever heard of, they sure are popping out of the woodwork, eh?) And Vaughn's dad died protecting "The Passenger."

Significantly, Vaughn says, "The man you're describing is not my father."

Well, hey, buddy, I'm with ya. Didn't sound like him to me, either. But then, nobody's acting in character this episode (curse that SD-6!), so why not Dearly Departed Dad as well?

Brill and Vaughn finish yakking, Vaughn leaves and is promptly—I mean *instantly*—abducted by the Covenant. Oh yeah, remember Weiss, who was following Lauren to make sure she didn't do anything bad?

Oops. Couldn't see that one coming, could we? (By this point in the script, the SD-6 agent had used a clever Rambaldi artifact to upload encoded viruses into the digital files, which were busily corrupting subplots. It's astonishing how vulnerable we are to technology.)

I'm skipping ahead again, because there's some pointless scene changes and equally pointless plot complications (the result of a Randomizer in the SD-6 rewriting virus). Oh, and Sydney and her dad have the inevitable who's-your-daddy talk. (Thankfully, the answer is Jack, not Sloane, or we'd all just give up and drink the tetrodotoxin cocktail already. Even SD-6 has its limits.)

Gratuitous Vaughn torture ensues. Sark says, "[The object I hold in my hands is] capable of delivering up to 500,000 volts—not enough to kill you, just enough to let you wish it would."

Oy. Let's review our basic knowledge of electricity. (And if you don't have one, well, neither did I, but I took a crash course.[4,5]) Ohm's law states that voltage equals current (in amps) times resistance (in ohms). Now, clearly the *voltage* is "up to 500,000 volts," so we know that part of the equation. I looked up the resistance of the human body, and it's surprisingly high and surprisingly variable, depending on things like how thick or thin and how wet or dry your skin is...anywhere from 2,000 to 50,000 ohms.

Let's take the extreme example. If we assume that Sark is switching his fearsome shock stick (oh baby) up to full power (and hey, it's *Sark*! Does he ever use the "stun" setting?), then the voltage he's delivering is 500,000 volts. Resistance is probably somewhere on the low side—Vaughn was sweating a lot, you notice—so by the equation I (current in amps) = V (500,000) / R (2,000), Vaughn is receiving a shock of about 250 amps.

I quote from the marvelous electronics whiz Dan Rutter: "If 240 amps passes through any significant amount of a human body for any signifi-

[4] http://hyperphysics.phy-astr.gsu.edu/hbase/electric/lightning2.html
[5] http://57.1911encyclopedia.org/E/EL/ELECTROCUTION.htm

cant period of time, investigators may have to employ DNA analysis to determine who that stuff they found all over the place used to be. You really don't want to make yourself part of a 240 amp circuit. Actually, only about 30 milliamps (0.03 amps) across the human heart has a good chance of stopping it."[6]

Hmmmmmmmmmmmm. I'm just sayin'....

Vaughn gets shocked a lot, showing off beautifully defined muscles. For the sake of charity, we'll pretend that Sark has his portable lightning bolt set on 0.001% of its potential, so as not to fry Vaughn like a chicken, but instead make him suffer attractively.

(I'm quite curious as to why the SD-6 agent chose to put this scene in. I suspect it's just because she—had to be a *she*—liked seeing Vaughn suffer. Well...okay...I admit it has its attractions.)

Moving on. Sloane gets magic glasses to capture retinal impressions. Sydney impersonates a geek (that's *always* so convincing; really, she looks just like every geek I know) and gets to flirt in dinosaur languages. Oddly, while she's discussing the daring theory that birds evolved from dinosaurs (fact check: um, actually, that's pretty well accepted now), she mentions Giordano Bruno getting burned at the stake. Now, I'm pretty certain that Bruno didn't have an opinion on dinosaur evolution, but this apparent non sequitur signals the curator to mention something about an artifact from Hainan, which is bizarre even by SD-6 Randomizer Virus standards, as Bruno lived in Italy, but maybe we're talking dinosaurs again. Apparently we are. And I'm still stuck on Bruno. After spending eight years in prison and being burned at the stake, he deserves better than to be a throwaway line showing how smart-ass Sydney is. Bruno is very cool.[7]

Blah, blah, blah. Sloane scans eyeballs and has odd conversations that in any normal show would instantly spark the suspicion of five rent-a-cops guarding the donut factory, much less the five guys in charge of the Secret Rambaldi Doohickey of the Week. Does anyone say, "Hey, Sloane was acting weird, and anyway, isn't he supposed to be dead, *again?* Shouldn't we be checking on the Great Rambaldi Doohickey that's our pride and joy, in case he's out to repossess it?"

No. *Because SD-6 is in possession of the plot.*

We pour green goo into said stolen Secret Rambaldi Doohickey of the Week, and this priceless conversation ensues:

---

[6] http://www.dansdata.com/gz013.htm
[7] http://www.infidels.org/library/historical/john_kessler/giordano_bruno.html

SLOANE: There it is.
SYDNEY: What is it?
JACK: It looks like brain waves.
SLOANE: We found her.

Stand back and marvel at its magnificence. In fourteen short words, we have managed to make *three* accomplished actors look like complete idiots. Okay, Sydney actually comes off the best. Her "What is it?" is actually a perfectly legitimate question.

I'm not even going to discuss how we got from "brain waves" to "we found her." Somebody call the FBI; tell them that instead of all that noisy and annoying chasing people, they should just pull up a brain scan, for Christ's sake. Works every time. It's like GPS for your head. (And by the way, those crazy people wearing the tinfoil hats? They may be on to something.)

SD-6, you *bastards!* The genius of this! The evil subtlety! I weep.

Vaughn and Lauren have a tender moment in which she totally plays him, and like an idiot he falls for it. Again. But on the bright side, Lauren gets slapped.

However dumb *that* scene is, it's a debate between Aristotle and Socrates when compared to the next one, which stands in my mind as the single worst exchange of television dialogue ever written and still delivered with straight faces. Oh, and it's a continuation of the *earlier* mega-stupid conversation, which gives it extra mega-stupid-acceleration points.

Here's where the SD-6 evil influence nakedly shows itself and cackles with dastardly enthusiasm in its attempt to destroy our love for the show.

And I admit it was a close call. (Gulp.)

Ready? Here we go. . . .

SYDNEY: I don't understand. How can a brain scan help us find her?
SLOANE: Each individual has a signature brain wave pattern as unique as a fingerprint. So to exploit this, the DoDs developed an experimental satellite network capable of remote encephalography.
SYDNEY: Reading brain waves from orbit.
SLOANE: Right.

Oh, the pain, the pain. I'm wiping tears from my eyes, writing these words. I can barely keep from banging my head on the keyboard. . . .

asdflkjasdflikj pqoqityuigygh jlasdkfj

Oops. Lost control. Better now. Though, ow. I have the "J" key stuck to my forehead.

It's *possible* that EEGs could be used as identification tools, I guess. I did locate a paper from the University of Piraeus in Greece that claims the process to be 80% to 100% effective, on a case-dependent basis.[8] (I suspect that means it's not very reliable. And they seemed to be cheating by matching against a very shallow pool of genetically related people.) However—and here's the real problem—who's got the *database of brain waves?* We don't even have a reliable national fingerprint database, and that method has been around since the demise of the Bertillon method. Bertillon favored identifying criminals by a series of body measurements. (He also apparently coined that wonderful scientific phrase "approximately exact.")[9] But I digress.

There is no database of brain scans.

Nevertheless, we're going to read brain waves *from orbit.* (Nevermind what we're matching against, son, them's details.) Soooooo...we have a satellite. It's scanning the world's population, indoors and out, in concrete bunkers, in mine shafts, scuba diving, lost in the Amazon jungle, whatever. What orbit is this satellite in? Polar? LEO? GEO? Elliptical? How the hell do you re-task a satellite to scan *every brain on Earth?* And how do you know when you're finished, anyway? Don't people, like, move around?

Okay. I'll be charitable. DARPA (Defense Advanced Research Projects Agency) actually has a project that will allow for the scanning of brain waves, using a line-of-sight laser. And now I've probably broken several laws by saying so. But DARPA's not going to swear out a warrant, because they're too busy cracking up over the idea of *scanning brain waves from orbit.*

Oh, let's face it, SD-6 has control of the script. It's all downhill from here, folks; the guards have been knocked out, the evil equivalent of Marshall has tampered with the security system and the hackers are attacking the show with gay abandon.

So, the magic satellite covers the *entire globe and every person on it* in about, oh, five minutes (you think I'm kidding? Watch the timeline on the screen!) and locates Sydney's missing sister, who's in a prison in Chechnya. Why? Because it gives us an exotic location to jet to. And people to speak foreign languages, or at least have bad foreign accents.

---

[8] http://www.ionio.gr/~mpoulos/papers/neuralfinal.pdf
[9] http://chnm.gmu.edu/courses/magic/plot/bertillon.html

Meanwhile, Vaughn escapes from Sark. Even more astonishing than that, Sydney time-travels or uses some kind of wormhole technology, no doubt also invented by Rambaldi, to arrive in Chechnya with backup in just over two hours. She looks just like Sydney, only without lipstick, wearing a prisoner outfit. Nothing suspicious about *her!* I'm reminded of Marisa Tomei in *My Cousin Vinny*, rolling her eyes and saying, "Oh, yeah. You blend."

In Chechnya, Sydney immediately manages to plant a smoke bomb. Confusion ensues. Meanwhile, back on the other side of the planet, Vaughn gets picked up by an *obviously* fake truck driver, who loans him a cell phone to call the office. Now...how many CIA operatives are going to have a conversation about top-secret intel on a *borrowed cell phone?* I could have gone for it if Vaughn had just given his agent number and location and requested retrieval. But noooooo. Anyway, Vaughn isn't too excruciatingly stupid, but he does manage to get himself caught by Sark and Lauren again. Lauren tells him, "You're smarter than I thought." Which tells you just how low her opinion of him really is.

You know, I was really bummed at this point, before the whole global conspiracy angle occurred to me. When Sydney finds her long-lost (and hitherto completely unknown) sister strapped to a gurney in a Chechen prison, I fully expected it to be Sydney playing her own double. Because that would have completed my list of clichés. But no, they couldn't even give me that satisfaction. (See, that's how I *knew*, deep in my guts, that SD-6 was behind it. No follow-through.)

Sydney says, "I don't know if you can hear me, but I'm your sister. I know that sounds crazy." Truer words were never spoken. *Everything* in this episode should have that disclaimer added.

At this point, we get Marshall. Yay, Marshall! We needed way more Marshall and way fewer other people; Marshall appears to be immune to SD-6's rewriting virus. Anyway, Marshall is tracking Vaughn. Good luck, Marshall. Meanwhile, Sark's now off the whole torture thing, and instead giving Vaughn really good drugs, which seem to do the job so much better than the whole 500,000 volts thing it makes you wonder why he bothered in the first place. Lauren cranks up the dosage when they get what they want. Vaughn is left to die.

"I expect you to die, Mr. Bond! BWAHAHAHAHA!"

Does SD-6 not watch movies? Television? I've never understood the amazing ability of villains to fail to do the obvious. I'll bet SD-6 hated *Austin Powers:*

SCOTT EVIL: Wait, aren't you even going to watch them? They could get away!

DR. EVIL: No, no, no. I'm going to leave them alone and not actually witness them dying. I'm just gonna assume it all went to plan. . . . What?

I'll bet SD-6's video collection *sucks*.

Marshall is able to identify where Vaughn is; he warns Dixon and Weiss. The rescue effort is underway, and Vaughn will doubtless survive. I'm shocked, I say. Shocked!

By the way, by my count, it took two hours and eleven minutes from the time Lauren cranked up the dosage to when Weiss finds Vaughn clinging to life in the warehouse. The Covenant *really* needs to find some better drugs.

Anyway, back in the Chechen prison, Sydney's sister says, "I feel faint." Don't we all. Oh, and we find out that she's a secret agent for—*Argentine Intelligence*. First of all, I have no earthly idea why the Argentineans were infiltrating Chechnya, but okay, it's not any more absurd than anything else at this point. (Randomization virus. See? It works.) Sydney saves her, don't ask how. There's a safe house. Sloane has mysteriously appeared there. And then he gives a speech that makes me, well, want to bang my head into the keyboard again, just for old times' sake:

SLOANE: How I found out. . . I felt totally complete joy. I just wanted to go out and find you immediately. But then it struck me. Shame. I was ashamed of the man I was. I knew I wasn't worthy of you. I wasn't worthy of your love. I wasn't worthy of your respect. From that moment on I vowed to change. I didn't want to meet my daughter face-to-face and have her despise me.

All right, that is the single most out of character speech I've ever heard Sloane make. *Ever.* (And that's saying something, because so far as I've been able to determine, Sloane's never really said a true word anyway.) But worse, it's just smarmy. It's the equivalent of the cliché of a villain being redeemed at the last minute by the love of a good woman; he's redeemed by the mere *suggestion* that he has a kid running around he's never even known. That's all it took? Sloane's deceived, betrayed and murdered with absolute disregard for anyone or anything except his own agenda. Yet the very *idea* that an affair he had twenty-whatever years ago produced an offspring he's never even met, that's enough to give him a Saul-on-the-road-to-Damascus conversion! Wow.

(I hope to heaven that SD-6 is behind this part of the script, because if it's not, I will be forced to gouge out my eyes with a teaspoon.)

Anyway, after that heartrending (and gut-wrenching) speech, Sark & Co. show up, exploding things and shooting the crap out of the safe house. (You know, just once I'd like to see them doing this and killing their target accidentally. "Whoops!") Jack and Sydney escape, of course. Sloane somehow manages to spirit his daughter off, despite the overwhelmingly bad odds of that happening. Sark decides not to thoroughly search the (very small) safe house, allowing Sydney and Jack to live to thwart him another day.

Vaughn and Sydney have a not-very-emotional reunion at the hospital, in which they exchange these head-hurting lines:

VAUGHN: The Passenger, did you find her?
SYDNEY: Yes, but she's gone, she's missing.

Well, then, Sydney, technically you didn't really *find her*, did you? Ah well. Vaughn goes on to deliver some incredibly fortuitous piece of information about how The Passenger and The Chosen One (apparently Sydney) will battle, and neither will survive. (I forget. When did Vaughn become a believer in prophecies...? Was there some Rambaldi conversion that happened when I was gagging on the Evil!Lauren kiss...?) Some googly-eyes are exchanged between our heroes, but Our Love Is Still Chaste. (Because SD-6 wants it to stay that way. *Evil plot.*)

We end with Sloane injecting his beloved, life-altering miracle daughter with Rambaldi goo, so I guess he was lying after all. Yay. I feel better knowing he's the same lying bastard he always was.

The end. And if you freeze-frame the end credits, use the correct filter and blow up the pixels in the bottom left-hand corner of the screen on the high-def presentation at 10,000 power magnification, you'll see this message:

This episode has been brought to you by SD-6, purveyors of chaos and mayhem around the world. The CIA thinks it has eradicated us. Fools! SD-6 will never be eradicated, not even with the use of classified bacteriological warfare products. SD-6 will still be here after the nuclear winter, telling the roaches what to do.

If you're a goal-oriented self-starter with the desire to inflict random chaos and mayhem on your fellow man (and woman), SD-6 may be the career opportunity you're looking for. We have attractive Minion and Spear-Carrier positions available in a visually exciting international location near you. Don't bother to call us. We know who you are. Now turn off your TV and never watch Alias *again, or we'll kill you.*

Bastards.

I still love my old *Alias*. The one where Sydney was playing a double game, wearing cool outfits, carrying out daring (and at least *slightly* convincing) plots and outwitting the bad guys, who were smart and cruel and clever on their own. The one where she had a normal life waiting at home, with her friends. (I miss Francie. I *really* miss Will. Wherefore art thou, Will?) I miss the show where our heroes didn't scan brain waves from orbit and expect us to believe it without guffawing hysterically.

So I'm buying seasons one and two on DVD. And I'm treating "Blood Ties" like the evil conspiracy it is, and deleting it from my *Alias* playlist. *It never happened.* Say it with me. . . .

And I'm working on my tinfoil hat, people.

Because SD-6 is out there, man. And it's distinctly possible that they *really are scanning our brain waves from orbit.*

You've been warned.

Roxanne Longstreet Conrad operates under a number of aliases, including Rachel Caine, Julie Fortune and Ian Hammell. She will neither confirm nor deny an association with SD-6 or the Covenant, although she has some early work that she'd like the opportunity to blame on them. She has published a total of nineteen novels since 1991, and appeared in seven anthologies for both fiction and nonfiction (sometimes confusing the two). She owns only one wig, but has been known to have a confusing array of hair care products. (The rumor that there might be password information to the Covenant's ultra-secure bank accounts encoded in the magnetic ink of this biography are as yet unproven . . . but keep looking.)

ADAM-TROY CASTRO

THE SIXTH STAGE
ON THE APPEAL OF ARVIN SLOANE

What is the appeal of Arvin Sloane? I've always thought Ron does an amazing job portraying the evil genius. Ron has made the golden decision in this situation: he justifies every choice his character makes, so Sloane seems honest and well-intentioned despite his sometimes beyond-evil deeds. It's the right choice for an actor playing a villain. We, the audience, start to empathize and comprehend that Sloane is the way he is because of it. No character should ever exist within a black and white world—there's only gray. As one of the most villainous characters ever to grace the television screen, Sloane knows how to manipulate people by living in that gray area . . . even the audience. Brilliant. Oh, and Ron smells nice too—I think it's the aftershave.

SYDNEY BRISTOW MAY BE THE STAR of *Alias*, but for some of us the most compelling character is her nemesis Arvin Sloane: a cold, ruthless betrayer who commits some of the show's most vile acts but remains tormented by a core of essential humanity.

Why is he so fascinating?

Because he's the very best kind of villain.

Stories that require villains, like (picking an example at random) fast-paced spy thrillers about pretty ladies who get sent on death-defying missions, only work to the extent that the villains make some kind of narrative sense. Few writers are talented enough to get away with villains who just skulk about, being evil and doing bad things, because they have some kind of deep, inborn personal love of sneering. Shakespeare did with Iago, whose malice toward Othello bears no explanation beyond, possibly, getting out of the wrong side of the bed every morning of his life; but come on, this was *Shakespeare*, and his refusal to provide an explanation has provided generations of academics with a form of full-time employment that consists entirely of arguing with each other about the precise species of bug Iago stored six inches up his intestinal tract.

In practice, storytellers in need of villains need to pick theirs from a very short list of basic models, which we're about to rank in order of increasing complexity. Make no mistake: all can be done well. (Iago may belong to the least promising category, but he'll be remembered the longest.) But as types, some are more complicated than others, and the more complicated they are, the more potentially interesting they can be. Warning in advance that Arvin Sloane doesn't make his own appearance until the end of the list, the categories now appear in ascending order of storytelling potential:

STAGE ONE: VILLAINS WHO ARE BAD JUST BECAUSE THEY'RE BAD. The already-mentioned Iago fits into this simplest category, but so does the villain of so many James Bond movies, who is frequently something like an unspeakably wealthy industrialist who has nothing better to do with his money than set off World War Three so he can wipe out humanity and live in a palatial underground shelter with his mistress, private army and a large collection of Persian cats. Nobody ever asks such a fellow the obvious question, which is just what he believes he would get out of such a lifestyle change, or how he thinks he's ever going to justify such a plan to his Board of Directors. He just wants to do it, that's all: probably because he woke up on the same wrong side of the bed Iago did. He's bad because he's bad, and there's no reason to even try to understand him.

STAGE TWO: VILLAINS WHO ARE BAD BECAUSE THEY'RE CRAZY. This stage introduces an explanation, if only one that reduces the bad guy's mania to a mere syndrome. An argument can be made for placing the aforementioned James Bond villain here, but I don't think so: that guy is educated, cultured, civilized and sufficiently in control of his own noodle to maintain a fake British accent and become a connoisseur of fine wines. These guys, on the other hand, are just plain out of their minds, and operating from motives that would give the rest of us head- ˌ aches to contemplate. Batman's perennial nemesis, The Joker, is one. So is the typical villain in a typical serial killer story, whether Jason, Freddy or some other guy with a one-word frat-boy name. So is the fellow who kidnaps a pretty kindergarten teacher because he's upset she didn't like the finger painting he did at age five, especially if he's actually older than her and she hadn't even been born at the time. Make no mistake. All of these guys are bad. All of them are threats. But because the only explanation for them is that they're nuts, there's no reason to even try to understand them. They're just forces of nature, wound up by wonky brain chemistry and pointed at anybody unlucky enough to stand in their way.

STAGE THREE: VILLAINS WHO ARE BAD BECAUSE THEY WANT SOMETHING. In this stage, we first encounter characters whose motivations make some kind of rational sense. The silent-movie cad who tries to burn down the orphanage because he's discovered oil on the land and doesn't want to share it with the kids, the Old West cattle baron who tries to burn out the peaceful homesteaders so his cows can graze without too much exposure to hymns and gingham, and the soap-opera hussy who tries to ruin her best friend Janet's wedding day so she can have the shirtless hunk Brad for herself. All of these people may be a tad greedy, not to mention woefully deficient in the morality department, but they also all operate with such understandable goals, which they all communicate in the clearest, most lucid terms, that they might all qualify for great careers in the U.S. Senate. They're bad, they're threats, they're not nice people, but by God it is possible to see where they're coming from. Not to mention where they're eventually going.

STAGE FOUR: VILLAINS WHO ARE BAD BECAUSE THEY'VE BEEN HURT. Now we add another element. These are people who might have been decent enough at one point in their lives, but who have been so grievously wronged that they've since cast aside all precepts of good and bad in order to indulge themselves in a huge, world-threatening snit. A typical example would be the origin once posited for Superman's nemesis Lex Luthor: he was the future Man of Steel's best friend in high school, until he lost all his hair in a chemical fire and vowed to become the enemy of all mankind. Aside from establishing that young Lex really needed to cut down on the caffeine, this model introduces tragedy into the mix in that we're supposed to weep at the premise that Luthor would have been a noble benefactor of mankind had a minor loss experienced by millions of men every day not caused him to permanently (excuse me) wig out beyond all reason. In practice, a guy that tightly wound would have sooner or later thrown that kind of life-altering tizzy over something else, like a missed parking space, but that's just him; most of the representatives of this category aren't over-reacting on the same epic scale. Becoming the Phantom of the Opera, for instance, would make anybody a little bit cranky. And it's not only possible to understand people of this ilk, it's also conceivable to feel sorry for them. Because while they may be bad, they do, by God, present their case.

STAGE FIVE: VILLAINS WHO DON'T THINK THEY'RE BAD. Stage Three introduced understandable motivation. Stage Four introduced tragic resonance. This stage introduces moral complexity. Iago aside, few people really get out of bed in the morning, look out the window and decide that they're going to be the living embodiment of evil today. Most people do try to do the right thing, even if their version of the right thing is evil by our own standards. This stage would include the despot who wants to take over the world because he believes he can do a better job running it, the sniper in an enemy army who wants to put a bullet through your heart because you're threatening his homeland, and the social worker who wants to take the children from the sympathetic family of performers because she thinks that foster parents would provide a better home. A villain of this ilk can be just as hissable as the one who twirls his moustache while threatening little Nell; after all, he does just as much damage. Some of the worst monsters in the history of the world were folks who thought they were doing the right thing. But this kind of villain gives us an opportunity denied us by most of the others we've seen: the chance to not only understand, and pity, but also to sympathize.

Finally, there's STAGE SIX: VILLAINS WHO KNOW THEY'RE BAD AND DON'T LIKE IT. This is the deepest, most complicated, most self-contradictory kind of antagonist for any storyteller to pull off, which may be one reason why so few storytellers make the effort. To reach this stage, a villain of this sort needs to have not only understandable motivation, tragic resonance and moral complexity, but the one last attribute, which makes all the difference: self-awareness. He is capable of committing acts of great evil as he pursues his concrete goals; he is driven to those extremes by reasons that may include grievous wrongs committed against him in the past; he believes that the ends justify the loathsomeness of his means; he will not stop, ever; but unlike the villains of the first five stages he also sees the damage he does, the pain he inflicts and the wreckage he leaves behind. He feels shame. Self-loathing, even. None of it stops him from continuing to commit the same sins all over again, whenever the situation warrants. None of it makes him any less dangerous or any of his crimes any more forgivable. After all, he doesn't change. But there's a reason he possesses a tragic dimension even greater than those demonstrated by villains who have been grievously wronged. He's in hell, and he knows he's sentenced himself there.

Could there possibly be a better explanation for Arvin Sloane?

Granted, Sloane's dimensions were not always obvious. In the earliest episodes of season one, when he was just Sydney's boss at SD-6, he seemed like any other sinister megalomaniac barking orders from behind a desk. He was well-played, of course, with Ron Rifkin's cold presence, oily line deliveries and stubbled cheeks instantly marking him as the voice of moral corruption, and rendering him perfect as the guy you wanted Sydney to high-kick through a plate-glass window as soon as possible. And, of course, he cemented his position as the show's premier hate-object in the very first episode when he ordered the assassination of Sydney's nice-guy fiancé, Danny. The absolute dispassion with which Sloane gave his deadly orders, with little apparent concern for the well-being of the duped patriots under his command, furthered the initial illusion that this guy was just a two-dimensional sociopath and nothing else.

Hindsight tells us differently. The very first indication of deeper currents appeared at the end of that pilot episode, when Sydney marched into his office and dropped what turned out the first of many Rambaldi artifacts on his desk. He'd already killed Sydney's fiancé and ordered her assassination for trying to quit; he could have very well said, then, that she was still too unstable to be trusted and that her execution should go ahead as planned. Instead, he smiled and told her okay. At the time, it seemed a cold command decision: no reason to waste a valuable asset like Sydney while he can still get some use out of her. But those who return to this scene after seeing subsequent developments recognize something else: that he was genuinely relieved. He would have killed her without a second thought. But he likes her, indeed loves her like a daughter, and was happy to have her back.

It's only visible in hindsight. You need to watch the man at length in order to catch it. But it's there, as messed up as Sloane himself.

The man's inner hell is visible in glimpses throughout the first season, notably in a monologue he delivered to Jack Bristow about the day he was walking along a D.C. street and caught the first glimpse of the darkness that would someday come to define his life. It was a powerful moment, offering Sloane at his most revelatory as a man who knows what he's become and cannot help but be a little horrified by it. (Rifkin is especially fine here, but there's even more subtle acting on the part of Victor Garber, whose listening Jack Bristow projects, without any notable change in facial expression, the sheer contempt he feels for Sloane at that moment.) There was another nasty development in which Sloane found himself obliged to murder a much-beloved friend who he suspected of betraying the Alliance, only to find, later on, that the friend had been innocent. Sloane was aghast at the crime he'd been manipulated into committing. One might even say he was sickened. But the path he's on is paved with such betrayals, and this vivid reminder of the price didn't change his behavior one whit.

By far, however, the most substantial measurement of Sloane's nature was his relationship to his dying wife Emily. We could see that his love for her was passionate and uncomplicated, that her illness was tearing him apart and that he had no little trouble reconciling his dread of losing her with his willingness to inflict the same kind of loss on people like Sydney. He became a warmer, more likeable person in Emily's presence, and became warmer and more likeable toward Sydney when discussing their mutual relationship with her.

At one point during what seemed to be the final stages of Emily's illness, at a moment which may have been the closest Sloane ever comes to changing his ways, he even broke down in Sydney's presence, telling her he appreciated all the friendship she'd shown his wife in this difficult time, then admitting he was sorry about what he'd had to do to Danny, and wishing he'd tried harder to find another way. Although some subsequent developments established that Sloane had been manipulating people to an unsuspected extent throughout his tenure with SD-6, this scene felt real. He did feel close to Sydney at that moment. He did love her for befriending his wife. He did regard her as a daughter. And even Sydney, who's driven by her hatred for the man, could not help but respond. She found herself feeling sorry for him. And well she should have. It was, after all, a genuine moment of contrition, from a man feeling very real grief. We should also note that it's worthless contrition, as even that moment of extreme self-awareness didn't stop Sloane from later agitating, again, for the assassination of Sydney's snoopy reporter friend Will Tippin. Sloane was sorry he broke Sydney's heart by killing Danny. He did wish he had found another way. But given another chance, he targeted another of her friends. And midway through the second season, another: Francine. Self-aware he might be, but he will keep killing, and keep shattering lives, for as long as it serves his needs to do so. Even if he then feels bad about it.

Emily's story continued well into the second season, but its moment of greatest ironic impact occurred late in the first. That's when Emily revealed to her husband that she knew all about his secret life, and SD-6 directives indicated that this meant she should die. At this point, she had mere weeks left to her, and Sloane had to beg his superiors for the right to forgo the usual assassination to keep her quiet, in favor of the right to allow her a natural death. After passionate argument and desperate intrigues, he was finally granted this boon—only to find out that Emily's disease had gone into an unexpected remission. There was no reason she couldn't live a normal life—except that the deal he'd made now dictated that she should die anyway. As she embraced him in jubilation, we were treated to a close-up of this, the complicated emotions playing across Sloane's face. Has there ever been a nastier example of a villain hoist by his own petard than at this moment when Sloane saw the impossible decision he was now condemned to make? And has there ever been a bad guy so deserving of a foul end, who so engaged our sympathies at a moment when karma repaid him with an irony even he didn't deserve?

His own choices had led him there.

But now he'd taken his wife with him.

The genius of this characterization is that, at season's end, when Sloane slipped something into her drink, there was very real doubt about what was in it. Was he pulling a fast one to save Emily's life? Or was he doing what he'd always done: the next logical thing? Even if it took him one step lower into hell? At that point, we didn't know. We may have had our suspicions, but they were based more on what the show's writers were likely to want than on any scruples Sloane might've been willing to entertain. For Sloane is capable of anything. His love for Emily is boundless. But so is his ambition.

Midway through the second season, we learned that Sloane's entire involvement with the Alliance was part of a larger ruse, aimed at obtaining the full power of the Rambaldi artifacts for himself. Part of his ruse turned out to be his hiding his knowledge of Jack and Sydney Bristow's existence as double agents. He claimed to have known all along. This may well be true. But it doesn't change the fact that, before and after that moment, he showed real concern over what they thought of him. From this point on, whenever circumstances placed him in the same room with them, he tried to justify himself, to make them see that he really cared about them. He believed it, too; he made these arguments even after he had proven himself an ongoing threat. It wasn't just chicanery; he knew them too well to believe that they would be fooled by cheap lies. He probably even knew that nothing he could say to them would excuse the crimes he had committed against them in the past. He's too smart not to know. But he had to say such things; had to justify himself. He really thinks he can.

When, in the third season, he brokered an immunity deal with the CIA and became an international philanthropist, his attempts to broker forgiveness from Jack and Sydney intensified. He talked about his charity work. He told Sydney he considered her a daughter. He showed genuine concern over what Jack thought of him. He helped them out whenever he had a chance. Some of this was self-serving, of course; he still wanted the Rambaldi artifacts, and helping Jack and Sydney was the best way of accomplishing that. But, again, the attempts at emotional reconciliation seemed real. He cared about them. He had committed crimes beyond redemption against both, and will again, but his feelings remained palpable.

The revelation, in the third season, that he secretly believed Sydney to be his daughter by Irina Derevko offers a partial explanation. Indeed, some long-time viewers, myself included, were awaiting the revelation of such a connection since the first season. He cares. He feels. Just not enough to give up whatever he believes the Rambaldi artifacts promise him. Note that when he did find his real daughter, his love for her was not enough to stop him from torturing her in the name of Rambaldi. He cried and agonized over the fear and pain he was putting her through, but he did not stop. He just apologized and explained, while taking yet another step into hell. His form of villainy is not about bad intentions. It's about always being willing to take the next step, even if it makes him feel bad.

No, there's only one point, in the entire run of the series, when he acted like a conventional supervillain, and that was in the second season, when he ordered the hit on Dixon's wife in retaliation for Dixon's role in the death of Emily. The moment was dramatic enough, but it seemed out of character for him, somehow; it didn't feel like him. This may be an odd thing to say, since Sloane had been ordering hits on the loved ones of his enemies since the very first episode. But it still seemed wrong. Examine the incident and you'll see why. For Sloane, ordering the assassinations of Danny, or Will, or Francie, or even Sydney herself, are acts of sheer expediency. In no case is there anything personal; it's just the kind of thing a man in his position has to do, that's all. And it's no more pleasant to him than murdering a friend of many years, or injecting his real daughter with Rambaldi's formula. These crimes are just necessary steps in his big picture. Ordering a hit out of mere malice, even with Emily as provocation, didn't advance his quest for the Rambaldi artifacts one iota; it was the worst possible sin, in Sloane's moral universe. It was unprofessional.

There remains one last issue: the similarities between Jack Bristow and Arvin Sloane.

Jack is also a cold, ruthless killer, willing to do whatever's necessary in order to further his goals. He's as tightly controlled as Sloane and, we perceive, as tormented as Sloane; he rarely smiles, except with grim satisfaction, and it seems clear that he's been emotionally shut down since Irina's betrayal. Were it not for his much-repressed love for Sydney, he wouldn't have an emotional inner life at all.

All that matters for him, but for Sydney, is the job. The work. And he pursues that with a zeal that extends to breaking the law whenever necessary.

Like Sloane, he always does the next thing.

Like Sloane, he seems incapable of walking away.

Like Sloane, he has paid an emotional price.

Like Sloane, he often seems to be in hell.

In all these characteristics, and more, he bears an uncanny resemblance to his daughter's greatest enemy. It's quite possible that had his path been a little different, he would have been a sixth-stage villain, too. Instead, he's what can be called a sixth-stage hero. And it's fascinating to watch him, and his opposite number, come close to meeting at the center of the graph.

When Ron Rifkin auditioned for *Alias*, he was originally trying out for Jack's part. Instead, he got Sloane's. It's not uncommon for actors seeking one part to get another. But is there any doubt, in this case, that the skills that allow an actor to do a bang-up job as one character would also allow him to nail the other? The passions are the same. The mannerisms are the same. The hard strength is the same. Even the love for Sydney is the same.

It seems clear. Sydney Bristow has two fathers. She was estranged from one. She looked up to the other. Early developments caused her attitudes toward both men to switch places.

Three seasons later, these relationships remain complicated.

Viewing the show as an ongoing drama about Sydney's feelings toward these two men, it remains more than possible that Jack Bristow will finally step over a line that Sydney will not forgive—that will, in fact, render him just as contemptible as Sloane to her eyes. (Indeed, he's come close a few times, and the beginning of the fourth season, which alleged his killing of Irina, briefly estranged the pair.)

Is it just as possible that Sloane might step over the same line, going the other way? That he might reach a point where he decides that whatever he hopes to achieve with the Rambaldi artifacts is not worth the escalating price tag? That he might, in fact, evolve from the Stage Six villain he is to join another order? Let's say Stage Seven: Bad Guys Who Aren't Bad Guys Anymore? The fourth season raised that possibility as well.

There's no way of telling for sure. Even J. J. Abrams may not know the answer yet.

But it is one of the questions that will keep us watching.

Adam-Troy Castro's short fiction has been nominated once for the Stoker Award, two times for the Hugo and five times for the Nebula. The author of four Spider-Man novels and several books of short stories, he advises readers to check out his upcoming paperback, Vossoff and Nimmitz: Just a Couple of Idiots Reupholstering Space and Time. Adam lives in Miami with his long-suffering wife Judi and a rotating collection of cats that now includes Maggie the Cat, Uma Furman and Meow Farrow. He once tried plugging in a Rambaldi device, but it blew the fuse.